"*Leadership Excellence* is an outstanding book! In fact I stayed up late because I couldn't stop reading it. The framework, Pat Williams's personal journey, and the examples from across the military, sports, and business sectors are well-done and compelling."
 —Noel Tichy, professor at the University of Michigan and co-author of *Judgment—How Winning Leaders Make Great Calls*

"Tremendous! *Leadership Excellence* is a great read from start to finish."
 —Rick Carlisle, head coach of the Dallas Mavericks

"*Leadership Excellence*'s credibility isn't driven so much by the presentation of these 'seven sides of leadership' as much as it is the experience of its author, Pat Williams, whose life has been devoted to practicing these leadership techniques. Having had to lead my state through the worst natural disaster in American history with the long renewal that followed, I recommend this book as a must-read for aspiring leaders."
 —Haley Barbour, former governor of Mississippi

"This is another gem by Pat Williams. Anyone in any walk of life can benefit from the messages in this book. No matter how old you are or what you do in life, you can take these seven qualities and grow as a person."
 —A. J. Smith, former general manager of the San Diego Chargers

"In an era when we decry the lack of leaders in our society, *Leadership Excellence* provides us with the powerful lessons of men and women leaders who have shaped our world for the better. But the best thing about *Leadership Excellence* is Pat Williams himself. He weaves his life story into the narrative in a way that makes the lessons not only tangible but personal."
 —John Baldoni, author of *Lead With Purpose* and *Lead By Example*

"*Leadership Excellence* is for everyone. It's the only life Pat Williams has lived. He's mastered and shared it freely!"
 —Nancy Lieberman, Basketball Hall-of-Famer and author of *Playbook for Success*

"Pat Williams has done it again in his newest book on what it takes to be a great leader. Pat incorporates anecdotes and principles you can apply in your everyday life to get the best out of yourself and others."
 —Lawrence Frank, Executive Vice Pr   ions for the Los Angeles Clippers

"Pat Williams offers a personal, heartfelt account of the core skills for effective leadership with character and integrity. His book's hopeful message and practical advice will inspire people not to wait to be asked but to simply get up and lead, and thereby accomplish great things."
—Rosabeth Moss Kanter, Harvard Business School professor and bestselling author of *Confidence* and *SuperCorp*

"Pat Williams has spent much of his life successfully leading others. The principles he shares on these pages are timeless examples that, when put into practice, will help us all achieve a more effective life of leadership."
    —John Mara, co-owner of the New York Giants

"An expert at producing magic both on and off the basketball court, Pat Williams shares his seven 'profoundly practical insights' of *Leadership Excellence*. Read *Leadership Excellence* and you'll get quite an education, with a dose of heartwarming personal stories to boot."
    —Marshall Goldsmith, *New York Times* bestselling author of *MOJO* and *What Got You Here Won't Get You There*

"*Leadership Excellence* captures the essence of leadership in clear, concise language that will impact leaders for years to come. I greatly enjoyed all of Pat Williams' stories and anecdotes. This is Pat's most important contribution to the world of leadership development."
    —Kevin Johnson, former NBA All-Star and former mayor of
    Sacramento, California

"*Leadership Excellence* is a crystallized presentation of seven vital leadership principles every leader needs to master. Each page of this book is bursting with valuable and interesting stories that make for very entertaining and practical reading."
    —Tim Pawlenty, former Governor of Minnesota

"Pat Williams is a survivor, an innovator, a motivator. . .and, above all, a *leader*. He has written the new manual for Leadership 2.0—*Leadership Excellence* transcends sports and should be required reading for anyone looking to inspire and motivate others."
    —Erik Spoelstra, head coach of the Miami Heat

Leadership Excellence

PAT WILLIAMS

WITH JIM DENNEY

Advantage.

I dedicate this book to
my oldest grandchild, Laila Kindy.
May it inspire and challenge her
to become a seven-sided leader
for the 21st century.

Published by Advantage, Charleston, South Carolina.
Member of Advantage Media Group.

ADVANTAGE is a registered trademark, and the Advantage colophon is a trademark of Advantage Media Group, Inc.

Printed in the United States of America.

10 9 8 7 6 5 4 3 2

ISBN: 978-1-64225-011-4
LCCN: 2018932267

This publication is designed to provide accurate and authoritative information in regard to the subject matter covered. It is sold with the understanding that the publisher is not engaged in rendering legal, accounting, or other professional services. If legal advice or other expert assistance is required, the services of a competent professional person should be sought.

Advantage Media Group is proud to be a part of the Tree Neutral® program. Tree Neutral offsets the number of trees consumed in the production and printing of this book by taking proactive steps such as planting trees in direct proportion to the number of trees used to print books. To learn more about Tree Neutral, please visit **www.treeneutral.com**.

Advantage Media Group is a publisher of business, self-improvement, and professional development books and online learning. We help entrepreneurs, business leaders, and professionals share their Stories, Passion, and Knowledge to help others Learn & Grow. Do you have a manuscript or book idea that you would like us to consider for publishing? Please visit **advantagefamily.com** or call **1.866.775.1696**.

CONTENTS

FOREWORD

Leadership Lessons That Ring True

Bobby Bowden coached the Florida State Seminoles football team from 1976 through 2009. He led FSU to an AP and Coaches Poll National Title in 1993, the BCS National Championship in 1999, and twelve Atlantic Coast Conference championships. Bobby announced his retirement from coaching on December 1, 2009, shortly after his eightieth birthday. He ended his career second in career Division I wins with 389. Three of his sons—Tommy, Terry, and Jeff—have followed him into successful coaching careers.

I love coaching. I've always taken great pleasure in devising strategies and plays, studying game film, getting to know the strengths and character traits of my players, enjoying the camaraderie in the locker room, delivering speeches and pep talks, feeling the adrenaline rush of the game, experiencing the post-game celebrations—I have loved it all.

But what I'll miss most about coaching is the daily influence I had on the lives of young leaders. Teaching them the game of football was in reality training them for life and leadership. I loved taking a bunch of young men in late summer, then molding and motivating them into a cohesive, high-performance team through the fall. It's not just the game of football that I miss—it's the day-to-day contact with the players, the opportunities to teach and mentor these young men, as well as the opportunity to learn from them.

One of my most memorable experiences with Florida State happened during a 1992 game against Georgia Tech. Our talented quarterback, Charlie Ward, was having a bad night. He threw two interceptions that put us behind the eight ball, so I pulled him out of the game to settle him down, to give him a chance to stand back from the game and think. Charlie's self-confidence was shaken—but my confidence in Charlie stood firm. The whole coaching staff knew he could win for us—and we knew we had to get him back under center for the sake of his self-confidence.

In the fourth quarter, I sent Charlie back onto the field. A lot of fans let me know they disagreed with that call. Well, that's okay—fans are free to express their opinion. But my job as a leader went beyond winning football games. My job was to make a difference in the lives of my players. And I knew that the best thing for our team and for Charlie was to re-energize his self-confidence.

When he took the field, we were down by two touchdowns. But I had made some changes to the offense that worked well with Charlie's skills. The quarterback I'd removed from the game looked frustrated and defeated; the quarterback I sent back into the game showed confidence and control.

The long and the short of it is that Charlie Ward led us to three touchdowns in the final quarter—and a stunning 29–24 victory. That win gave us the ACC championship.

I didn't know sending Charlie back into the game would turn out that well. But it was one of those moments when you just know the decision you make as a leader is going to have a big impact—both on the game and on the life of one of your players. I knew, win or lose, Charlie needed to take charge of the team when things were going against us. It was the only way he could grow as a leader, and his teammates could grow together through adversity. Charlie Ward's ability to step up and win that game was essential to his leadership growth and the future success of the team.

The following season, Charlie won the Heisman Trophy and led our team to its first-ever national championship. He later told a reporter that my decision to send him back into that Georgia Tech game was a pivotal moment in his life. He said that having the chance to redeem himself against Tech boosted his confidence, changed his life, and shaped his entire future.

Making that kind of impact on the lives of my players was one of my biggest reasons for getting up every morning. Even now, in retirement, I look forward to having that same impact through the friendships and mentoring relationships I have with my former players through phone calls, e-mails, and letters. That's the thrill of being a leader.

My fascination with leadership goes back to 1943. I was thirteen years old and completely obsessed with sports—but when I came down with rheumatic fever, I had to spend more than a year confined at home, including six months of bed rest. Listening to the radio constantly, I heard news from the European and Pacific theaters of World War II—and I was enthralled. I imagined the battlefield terrain, the movements of the soldiers and tanks, the strategy sessions of the generals. And I began to read books about great military leaders of the past, such as Napoleon and Stonewall Jackson. I wanted to learn everything I could about strategic planning, discipline, motivation, and preparation.

That boyhood study of great generals and their deeds in wartime fired my interest in leadership. Over the years, I've found that many of the decisions made by a Patton or an Eisenhower involved strategic principles that can be applied to coaching.

In this book, *Leadership Excellence*, Pat Williams shows that the principles of leadership hold true in *every* arena, whether sports or military or business or religion. No matter where you are or what you do, you are a leader if people look up to you. If they choose to follow you, it will be because they believe in you. In this book, Pat shows you how to become the complete, seven-sided leader that people admire and follow.

What are the seven sides of leadership? Pat Williams lists vision, communication, people skills, character, competence, boldness, and a serving heart. Pat understands that leadership isn't just about winning—it's about influencing the lives of others. As I've examined this presentation, packed with stories of these seven traits in action, the one thought I've had again and again is, *Pat, you nailed it. That's exactly what I've seen again and again in my own leadership experience.*

Then Pat tops off these stories with a set of practical steps to help you apply them immediately to your own circumstances. If you live up to this book's principles daily, it will transform you as a leader.

Read *Leadership Excellence* and step up to a new level of leadership, a whole new way of transforming the lives of the people you lead and serve.

BOBBY BOWDEN
OCTOBER 2011

FOREWORD

Here's Your Assignment

Retired U.S. Army General Tommy Franks served as Commander-in-Chief, United States Central Command, leading U.S. and Coalition forces in Operation Enduring Freedom (Afghanistan) and Operation Iraqi Freedom (Iraq). Though his troops called him "a soldier's general," General Franks simply calls himself "a soldier." He travels the world, speaking on leadership, character, and freedom. His auto-biography, American Soldier, *is a* New York Times *bestseller.*

In war, you don't *manage* soldiers up a hill under fire. You *lead* them.

Although the stakes are higher in war than in any other leadership arena, the challenges a general experiences on the battlefield are essentially the same as a coach faces on the football field or a CEO in the competitive marketplace. You must have a strategic vision, and you must communicate that to your people. You must inspire and motivate the troops, display exemplary character and rock-solid competence under fire, and be tactically aggressive. And you must love your troops.

Pat Williams has spent a lifetime studying and applying the principles of leadership in the sports world. In fact, the very existence of the Orlando Magic, a team he cofounded in 1986, is a tribute to his leadership skills—and the seven leadership principles he teaches in this book. They are vision, communication, people skills, character, competence, boldness, and a serving heart.

The components of leadership excellence that Pat Williams writes about are the same principles I've seen proven under battle conditions from the rice paddies of Vietnam to the sands of Iraq. Unfortunately, these traits seem to be in short supply in the upper echelons of our political and business worlds today. We have to ask ourselves:

- What kind of leadership plunges the United States of America more than fourteen *trillion* dollars in debt—with far worse to come?
- What kind of leadership allows a catastrophic banking crisis to occur despite repeated warnings of the danger of subprime mortgages and "liar loans"?
- What kind of leadership allows America to lag behind the rest of the developed world in education, reading and math proficiency, and graduation rates?
- What kind of leadership permits America to become a debtor nation to China?
- What kind of leadership allows America to outsource jobs and manufacturing capability (including critical defense-related manufacturing) to nations that are openly hostile to our interests?
- What kind of leadership permits America to take a back seat to Russia, China, and other nations in the exploration of space?
- And what kind of leadership allows the United States to remain dependent for its energy on imports from the most volatile and unpredictable region of the world?

America desperately needs leadership. We need people

of vision. We need people who can communicate and implement that vision. We need people who will boldly take on the challenges of the future, and who will serve as role models of character and competence. Above all, we need people who are committed to serving others, not just their own egos and selfish interests.

Today, more than ever before, we need *leaders*.

Some think of leadership as taking charge, bossing people around, intimidating others to get things done. Well, it's true that leadership involves giving orders and holding people accountable. But there's a lot more to leadership than being "the boss."

I learned one of the most important leadership lessons of my career when I was stationed in West Germany in the early 1970s, a captain in charge of the First Squadron Howitzer Battery of the Second Armored Cavalry Regiment. We had a young trooper—I'll call him Garcia—who had suddenly, unaccountably gone from being one of our best soldiers to one of our worst. Garcia's platoon leader told me he was chronically late to formation, showed up unshaven in a disheveled uniform, and had even cussed out a superior officer. The platoon leader wanted Garcia court-martialed.

I looked at Garcia's paperwork. He'd been an excellent soldier, had reenlisted just six months earlier, passed the GED tests for his high school diploma, and was nominated for Soldier of the Quarter. Then, without explanation, his soldiering had taken an unexplained nosedive. It made no sense. So I called him into my office for a talk.

Garcia arrived looking sullen and insolent. He gave me a sloppy salute, then glared at me with open hostility. "Wanted to see me?" The omission of the title "Sir" was clearly deliberate.

"What's wrong with you, Garcia?" I said. "You used to be a sharp trooper. All of a sudden, your platoon leader is recommending we court-martial you right out of the Army. What's your story?"

He looked at me for several seconds, studying me closely, as if trying to decide whether or not to trust me. "You really want to know?"

"Let's hear it."

So he told me his story. Four months earlier, the Red Cross had informed him his grandmother had died. "She raised me and my little brother," he said, starting to cry. "I put in for emergency leave, but they said I couldn't be spared. The team needed me. Request denied."

He told me that the authorities back home in Brooklyn had placed his little brother in a group foster home. Garcia worried about his brother in that environment, but there was nothing he could do. Then, after his brother was placed in the group home, the Red Cross told him that some thug had raped his younger brother and cut his throat. Through tears, Garcia told me, "I wanted to go home and bury him—but the lieutenant told me the organization was more important. Request denied."

I was stunned. Garcia was my trooper, one of 180 soldiers under my command. How could this have happened without word reaching me? Garcia glared at me with open hatred, and he told me exactly what I could do with "the organization"—the Battery, the Squadron, the Army, the entire country.

And when he said that, I began to cry for this good soldier, and for all the needless hurt that had been inflicted on him by the leaders of his outfit—*for no reason at all*. And I came out from behind my desk and put an arm around him. "This is my fault," I said. "I know it's too late to help you, but I'm giving you that leave. Go home and take as much time as you need. When you get back, if you still want out of the Army, I'll make sure you receive an honorable discharge."

The following morning, I assembled the officers and senior NCOs, and I told them that soldiers are human beings, and human beings will do almost anything you ask of them if they know you care about them. I told them about Garcia, and I didn't blame anyone but myself. I said, "I've learned that being in charge doesn't automatically mean you know what's going on. That's going to change."

Then I had the clerk bring in all the personnel folders for the Battery. I gave those officers and NCOs—those *leaders* under my command—an assignment. But first I gave myself the same assignment. I said, "I'm going to read at least twenty of these folders every day. By the time I've read them all, I'll know every soldier's first name. I'll know his hometown. I'll know something about his family. And I expect each of you to do the same. And any time a trooper comes to you with a problem, just remember that it's *your* problem and it's *my* problem, too." That leadership lesson has stuck with me and guided me throughout my military career and to this very day.

And you'll find leadership lessons like that one on every page of this book. Pat Williams understands leadership inside and out, backwards and forwards, from taking charge to taking risks to taking care of your troops. *Leadership Excellence* is a fascinating, readable book, filled with stories that teach—and stories that simply grab your heart and won't let go. It's a practical book, filled with bullet-point principles that will impact your leadership life from the very first chapter.

So let me give you an assignment: *Read this book*—and really lead.

GENERAL TOMMY FRANKS
OCTOBER 2011

INTRODUCTION
They Just Led

Let me tell you an unlikely story about leadership.

February 15, 1947, was a snowy day in Wilmington, Delaware. I remember standing outside the hospital with my sisters, Carol and Ruthie. Somewhere inside, my mother was giving birth. We had to wait outside in the cold because children weren't allowed in the hospital in those days.

In the pre-ultrasound era, we didn't know whether Mom was having a boy or a girl. I already had two sisters, one older, one younger. I *desperately* wanted a little brother to play ball with.

Finally, the word came down that Mom had given birth... *to a baby girl.* I wept inconsolably into my baseball glove.

At my sister Ruthie's suggestion, we named the baby Mary Ellen—though we soon shortened it to Mimi. Sometime after we brought Mimi home, Mom and Dad realized something was wrong with her. Looking back, I think the doctors knew the moment Mimi was born that there was a problem, but they didn't have the heart to tell my parents.

I recently talked to Ruthie about those days. Though she's three years younger than I, she remembers many details—especially emotional details—better than I do.

"Mom noticed that Mimi was slow to develop," Ruthie told me. "She had difficulty eating. She was sluggish. She couldn't sit up when babies were supposed to. She didn't start to walk at the appropriate age, so we had to carry her a lot. Over the first couple years of her life, I think the pediatrician tried to break it gently to Mom that Mimi had significant developmental problems. He had a hard time telling her the brutal truth that Mimi wasn't just 'slow,' she had a severe disability. Back then, they would call her 'retarded.' Mimi had Down syndrome.

"In those days, there was no support system for families with children like Mimi—no educational resources, no community programs, no quality care facilities. Unless you were very wealthy, it was unlikely you could afford to hire specialized nurses to keep such a child at home. Down syndrome kids need a lot of care. In fact, it was not uncommon for such kids to be whisked away the moment they were born. A friend of mine had a baby sister she had never met because the sister was institutionalized immediately after birth.

"When Mimi was two and a half, it became obvious we couldn't keep her at home. The only place she could go was a facility in downstate Delaware, a place with an absolutely medieval-sounding name: The Delaware Colony for the Feeble Minded at Stockley—'the Colony' for short. The Colony was a state-run facility located in the middle of nowhere. It took a good two hours to drive there from Wilmington. It was the only place our parents could afford."

I don't remember that time as clearly as Ruthie does, but I do remember Dad and Mom sitting us down and explaining the decision to us. They knew they didn't have the resources and ability to care for a Down syndrome child while raising three other children. Caring for a child with Mimi's needs was a full-time occupation that would take away from their ability to adequately raise my sisters and me. So my parents came to the agonizing decision that Mary Ellen would have to be institutionalized.

Ruthie reminded me that Dad and Mom had Mary Ellen baptized in the living room of our home before she left for the Colony—an event I had forgotten all about. I was nine and Ruthie was six, yet she has a vivid memory of Mimi's baptism. She told me, "A young associate minister from our church came to our house and did the ceremony. It was summertime, and it was terribly hot. At one point in the ceremony, Mom began to cry. She had to go to the little den next to the living room and hide her tears. I saw her leave, and I knew she was crying. I remember being terribly upset, because I had never seen Mom cry—she was not the type of person who cried.

"So that baptism was frightening and painful for me, because I knew something terrible was happening to our family, and I didn't understand what it meant. Sometime after the ceremony, they took Mimi away to the Colony. She was two and a half, and she never came home after that, except for visits at Christmastime.

"It was difficult to explain to my friends what had happened to Mimi. She was part of our family for a couple of years—and then she was just gone. I had a standard explanation I recited to my friends to explain why my little sister didn't live in our home anymore.

"Back then, people with Down syndrome usually didn't live long because of heart conditions, infections, and other problems. As time went on, antibiotics and medical technology improved and life expectancies increased. Mary Ellen lived to be thirty-seven, and she spent thirty-five of those years in the Colony. Mom drove down to visit her at least once a month. She'd take a whole day, in all kinds of weather, year round. I often went with her, especially when I was too young to stay home alone.

"So I was exposed to the conditions in the Colony, and I had a lot of difficulty dealing with it. The place was scary and horrible, and I didn't cope with it very well. There were a lot of people with various mental disabilities all grouped together in one institution. The place had a terrible smell that they tried to cover up with a very strong disinfectant. The things I saw there scared me as a child. There were babies with hydrocephalus—a condition in which cerebrospinal fluid gathers in the brain and swells the entire head. In those days, they didn't use shunts to drain the fluid. The sight of those babies with enlarged heads would frighten any child.

"I call that place 'the snake pit,' because it reminds me of the Olivia de Havilland movie that depicts horrifying conditions in a state mental hospital. The Colony was just like that, a place where the conditions were simply grotesque. Mimi was housed in an old cinder block building, probably built around the end of the nineteenth century. It was dark and depressing, and the moment I walked in, I would shudder.

"Mom always called the Colony before she went down to visit Mimi so they'd know she was coming. But once, when I was sixteen, my best friend and I drove down to Rehoboth Beach, and we impulsively went to see Mimi at the Colony without calling ahead. It was a shocking experience for me—and, I'm sure, for my friend.

"Mimi was down in the basement. It was a hot summer day, and there was no air conditioning. She was barely clothed. Mom used to buy nice clothes for her and take them down to the Colony when she visited; but when I came unannounced, Mimi didn't have any of the clothes that Mom had given her. They had simply disappeared. It didn't even cross Mom's mind that anyone would steal the clothes she had brought for Mimi—and because we lived ninety miles away, she couldn't check to see how Mimi was being treated.

"So there was my little sister, half naked in the snake pit, with all the heat and darkness and horrible smells. It was unbearable. Even today I try not to think about it, because the memories are so painful."

CHANGING THE WORLD THROUGH LEADERSHIP

It's painful for me to hear Ruthie's memories of those days. I wasn't aware of a lot of the things Ruthie recalls, because I was off in my own world of sports dreams and sports heroes. I sometimes went down with the family to visit Mimi, but not as often as Ruthie did. I remember going a few times with Mom when we picked up Mimi and took her to the beach at Rehoboth. I remember going inside the Colony and really hating that place—and then trying to forget it as soon as we left.

In those days, Down syndrome was known by a different name, and there was a stigma of shame and tragedy attached to parents of "retarded" children. Some people even viewed the birth of a disabled child as a punishment from God. Today we know that Down syndrome is a genetic abnormality caused by an irregular number of chromosomes. It's not a punishment or a personal failure on the part of the parents. It's simply an error in the genetic makeup. Back then, however, there was little research being conducted and very little help or understanding for families like ours.

Why is Down syndrome viewed so differently today than it was then? What caused the change in hearts and minds from the dark era of the 1940s to the enlightened era of today? Certainly, many people and factors contributed to today's more open-minded attitude toward people with disabilities, but a large share of the credit goes to two people—my mother and father, Jim and Ellen Williams, whose contribution can be summarized in two important words: *leadership excellence.*

My parents were leaders. Even though they were financially unable to care for Mimi at home, they refused to treat her condition as a shameful secret to be locked in a closet. Instead, they saw this tragedy as an *opportunity* to make a difference in the way so-called mental retardation was treated in our society.

Mom and Dad adopted Mary Ellen's health issue as their number one cause. They networked with other parents of Down syndrome kids, and they recruited politicians, journalists, health-care professionals, and even the governor of Delaware to their crusade. They hosted strategy meetings and brainstorming sessions. They were frequently on the phone, running up huge long-distance bills, drumming up support for reform of mental health care in the state. They spoke at community meetings. They gave interviews on radio and TV. This cause gave them a sense of mission. They knew they were doing something on behalf of Mary Ellen and thousands like her.

This kind of organizing and activism came naturally

to Jim and Ellen Williams. Though they were not wealthy industrialists like the DuPonts or famous politicians like Joe Biden, they were well-known grassroots leaders in the state of Delaware. They were deeply involved in Democratic Party politics in the state, and I remember many times during my boyhood when people gathered in our living room and talked about important grown-up issues that were way over my head. Activist leadership was a way of life for Dad and Mom.

My parents never *talked* about leadership. (I doubt I heard the word *leadership* even once when I was growing up.) They didn't *teach* leadership. They didn't *preach* leadership. They just *led*—and they changed a bit of the world for the better. By simply living a leadership lifestyle, they became role models of what a leader looks, sounds, and acts like. That's how I first learned about leadership excellence.

My parents never told me, "Pat, when you grow up, you have a duty to be a leader." They never had to say a word. They modeled it, and I knew—it was simply understood—that a life of leadership excellence was *expected* of me. I caught it more than they taught it.

My best friend in those days was Ruly Carpenter, son of Bob Carpenter, owner of the Philadelphia Phillies. One hot afternoon in June 1955, while Ruly and I were playing baseball—I was catching, Ruly was pitching—my dad and Mr. Carpenter were behind the backstop, talking excitedly about something. My family and the Carpenters had something in common: we both had mentally disabled kids. Ruly's brother Kemble had a disability similar to Mimi's. Ruly and I didn't know it at the time, but our dads were making big plans for an event to be called the Delaware All-Star High School Football Game—more commonly known as the Blue-Gold Game.

The purpose of the game was to benefit children with special needs, and the funds raised by the game were administered by the Delaware Foundation for Retarded Children (now called the Delaware Foundation Reaching Citizens with Cognitive Disabilities). The first Blue-Gold All-Star

Game was played on August 25, 1956, before a crowd of ten thousand fans. Two years later, I helped quarterback the North team (Ruly played tight end) and we beat the South, 27–0. More than a half century later, the game is still an annual event, having raised millions of dollars to benefit research and assistance programs for people like my sister and Ruly's brother. Equally important, the Blue-Gold Game has also been emulated by communities around the country.

The motto of the game is "We Play So That They May Learn." Players and cheerleaders are each assigned a "buddy," a mentally disabled child. Many participants have kept in touch with their buddies down through the years.

One such participant is famed author and cardiothoracic surgeon Dr. Mehmet Oz, host of the syndicated TV program *The Dr. Oz Show*. Dr. Oz grew up in Wilmington and attended Tower Hill School, where Ruly and I attended years earlier. I have a pair of photos: one of a young Mehmet Oz holding the hand of his buddy, both smiling at the camera, and the other taken thirty years later, of Dr. Oz and his buddy—both adults, same pose, same smiles. This is just one of the many heartwarming connections that have been made between players, cheerleaders, and people with disabilities over the decades that the Blue-Gold Game has been played.

My father died just a few years after this tradition began, so he never saw the full fruit of his labor. But I know he would have been thrilled to see the Blue-Gold Game serving the needs of countless people with disabilities right up to this very day.

Though the games didn't directly benefit Mimi or Kemble, our families knew that millions of people like them would be helped by new treatments and a new awareness of Down syndrome and similar disabilities. I think my parents found it easier to accept Mimi's disability knowing that the lives of other people would be blessed.

Dad also helped start the Opportunity Center, a day program and job training program for people with disabilities, including Down syndrome, cerebral palsy, autism, and similar challenges. The Center is still thriving more than fifty years later.

Most important of all, my parents threw themselves into the crusade to improve conditions for the patients at the Colony. They campaigned for better treatment and improved facilities. Largely because of their efforts, it's no longer called "the Colony." It's now the Stockley Center, administered by the Delaware Division of Developmental Disabilities Services. Patients at the Stockley Center are treated with respect and quality health care, and the conditions are clean and comfortable. As a testament to my parents' efforts, you can find a cottage on the grounds at Stockley named in memory of my father, Jim Williams.

The world has changed enormously since Mary Ellen was born. The ignorance and stigma that once surrounded Down syndrome and similar disabilities have largely been replaced by understanding and acceptance. There are many programs to help special-needs kids and their families—programs that didn't exist when my little sister was born. Many of these changes can be traced directly to the leadership example of Jim and Ellen Williams.

With that as my background, is it any wonder I have such a passion for leadership excellence?

STEP UP AND LEAD!

"Everyone hungers for leadership," writes former presidential speechwriter Peggy Noonan. She adds that people "want so much to be able to respect and feel trust in their political leaders. Everyone hungers for someone strong, honest and capable—as big as the moment."[1] It's absolutely true. We live in momentous—and yes, *dangerous*—times. We sense that there is a vacuum of true leadership in our government, our business and financial community, and in our own communities. We hunger for leaders to match the challenges of this critical moment in history. We hunger for leadership excellence.

In the fall of 2009, I toured Fort Monroe at Old Point Comfort on the southern tip of the Virginia Peninsula. The six-sided, stone-walled fort guards the Chesapeake navigational channel and is the only fort in the nation that is still an active US Army post. Fort Monroe was a key military fortification during the Civil War. President Lincoln visited there in the spring of 1862, and Confederate president Jefferson Davis was imprisoned there for two years after the Civil War. (I have visited his cell.) Fort Monroe is a fascinating monument to our history.

Near the end of my tour, I noticed a building with a sign reading LEADERSHIP EXCELLENCE over the door. When I asked my tour guide what went on in that building, he said, "Sir, there we train young men and women to be leaders of excellence—leaders who are the very best they can be."

As I looked around at Fort Monroe, I saw young soldiers—young *leaders*—carrying out their duties, taking on responsibilities, training and preparing themselves for leadership roles in our nation's future.

I've been thinking a great deal about leadership excellence ever since. I've been thinking about how my father and mother modeled leadership during my early years, and how they led in the fight to improve conditions for people with mental disabilities. I've been thinking how, just by growing up in the Williams household, I absorbed by osmosis the notion of leadership.

There were no leadership books, leadership conferences, or leadership retreats in those days. There was no leadership training in the corporate or academic world. "Leadership" was not a concept that people studied or emphasized or talked about.

Yet, when I was a young athlete at Tower Hill School in Wilmington, I seemed to naturally gravitate toward the leadership positions. I was the quarterback in football, the catcher in baseball, the point guard in basketball. I just took on those leadership roles as if it were expected of me. Nobody appointed me. Nobody said to me, "Williams, you're the leader." It was just the area that seemed natural for me, and I knew that leadership would be expected from me when I played those positions.

The turning point in my leadership journey came after I enrolled at Wake Forest University, near Winston-Salem, North Carolina. I was a catcher on the baseball team and active in the Monogram Club, the letterman's association on campus. Every year, prior to the basketball season, the Monogram Club staged a freshman versus varsity basketball game. Less than a week before the date for the game, Jerry Steele, president of the Monogram Club, came to me, stuck his finger in my chest, and said, "Williams, you're in charge of the freshman-varsity game."

I wasn't about to argue. Jerry Steele stood six feet eight inches tall and weighed about 240 pounds. (He went on to have a long career as a college basketball coach at High Point University in North Carolina.) I asked him what had been done so far to organize and promote the game.

"Nothing," he said. "So you'd better get busy."

I had less than a week to get tickets printed, organize a halftime show, get a national anthem singer and pep band lined up, and arrange for a promotional blitz. So I quickly contacted my fellow Monogram Clubbers and told them, "You're in charge of this! You're in charge of that! And you've got to get this done! Hey, you—the one ducking behind that post! You're overseeing this, that, and the other thing! Come on, people, let's *move!*"

Within hours, I had my team assembled. The game came together far more quickly than any of us thought possible—and it was a wonderful success. We had a huge crowd in the Coliseum, and all the little sideshows and halftime events came off perfectly. It was a night of glittering entertainment—and we got rave reviews. I'll never forget the exhilaration I felt that night when I went to bed.

I woke up the next morning, and my first thought was, *You know, I might like to do that for a career!*

And guess what? Fifty years later, looking back over my long career in professional sports, that's exactly what I have been doing. I've been building teams, trying to win championships, putting on shows, selling tickets, and promoting my brains out. And it was all triggered that night when Jerry Steele shoved his finger in my chest and informed me that, like it or not, I was going to be a leader.

That event changed my life. It gave me a career path I had not considered. What if Jerry hadn't thrust me into that leadership role? Would I be doing what I'm doing today? I don't know. I definitely wanted a career in sports, but I envisioned myself as a leader on the playing field, not in the front office. By pushing me into a leadership role, Jerry gave me the confidence that I could assemble an organization, delegate responsibility and give people their assignments, check back with them, create an atmosphere of fun and entertainment, and put on a show.

And that has been my life for the past five exciting, electrifying decades.

When Jerry Steele showed confidence in me—indicating he thought I could pull off a difficult leadership feat in a very short time frame—he opened my eyes to a whole new self-image. I actually began to look at myself differently. "Hey!" I said to myself, "here's a whole new arena where I can be a leader. In fact, I *like* this kind of challenge, and I'm *good* at it."

I graduated from college a year and a half later, did my graduate work and my military duty, then went to Miami and pursued a minor league baseball career for two years. When my playing career ended at age twenty-three, I got to do some front-office work for the team before moving to Spartanburg, South Carolina, where I became the youngest baseball general manager in America. There I did everything that Jerry Steele had roped me into doing at Wake Forest. And those leadership skills stuck with me and served me well throughout my adult career.

One thing I've learned through the years is that leadership

is like a three-legged stool. The first leg is viewing yourself as a leader. The second leg is preparing yourself as a leader. The third leg is stepping up and taking a leadership role when the opportunity presents itself.

When I say you should take on a leadership role "when the opportunity presents itself," I'm not suggesting you should simply stand by passively, waiting for your opportunity to come along like an old-fashioned streetcar. No, a leader goes out and *makes opportunities happen.*

Don't wait to be noticed. Don't wait for someone to come up to you, jab his finger in your chest, and say, "You're the leader." Instead, raise your hand. Raise your voice. Volunteer. Take the bull by the tail and face the situation.

Step up and lead.

HOW TO USE THIS BOOK

Though I absorbed an excellent leadership example from my parents, and though I was in leadership roles throughout my playing days and on into my sports management career, I never made a focused study of leadership until I arrived in Orlando in 1986. That's when I was questing to bring an NBA expansion team to central Florida. As I shouldered the overwhelming responsibility of building a professional sports team from the ground up, I began studying the lives of great leaders. As I studied, I began to learn how much *more* I had to learn about leadership.

Once the Orlando Magic became a reality, our young team became very good very quickly. After drafting Shaquille O'Neal in 1992 and acquiring Penny Hardaway in 1993, we became a hot ticket. At the same time, the city of Orlando was exploding as a convention destination. Thousands of meetings and conventions are held in Orlando every year—and they are all in need of speakers. I began to get opportunities for speaking in the corporate world. Prior to each speech, I talked to the event planners and corporate leaders who had booked me for that gig, and I asked, "What message would you like me to bring to your organization?" Again and again, the answer was the same: "Please speak on leadership. Our organization desperately needs to develop leaders."

So I was forced to come up with a cohesive, challenging, and practical message about leadership. And I had plenty of experiences and observations to draw on. I observed the leadership dynamics within our own Magic organization— and I had many opportunities to observe and learn from the magical leadership traditions in the Disney organization, which is a huge corporate presence in central Florida.

At the same time, I began building my leadership library at home. That library now contains more than seven hundred leadership books, and I've read them all. I've extracted all the great insights, stories, and practical advice those books contain. In the course of my intensive leadership research, I've become convinced that the fundamental principles of leadership excellence can be distilled into seven basic ingredients, seven profoundly practical insights into what it takes to be an outstanding leader:

1. Vision
2. Communication
3. People skills
4. Character
5. Competence
6. Boldness
7. A serving heart

These seven sides of leadership are truly timeless. It doesn't matter whether you are a biblical king like Solomon, a Revolutionary War general like Washington, a Civil War president like Lincoln, a legendary coach like John Wooden, an inspirational religious leader like Billy Graham, a corporate strategist like Jack Welch, or a successful entrepreneur like Steve Jobs—the essential principles of leadership are always the same. They are true in every era, in every field of endeavor, and in every successful leader.

These seven principles produce magical results every time they are tried. In these pages, I'm going to prove to you the power of these seven principles to produce leadership excellence in your life. I will prove it from the lives of great leaders I have known, great leaders I have studied, great leaders of the past, and great leaders of today.

Even more important, I'm going to give you practical, bullet-point instructions for how to build these seven principles into your own leadership. You undoubtedly have at least a few of these qualities already. You can build on that foundation and improve those skills exponentially. And you can acquire the leadership dimensions you are lacking. Every one of these seven sides of leadership is a learnable skill. You *can* achieve leadership excellence. In this book, I'll show you how.

Let's face it: There are a lot of leadership books on the market. I know, because I've read them all. When a book comes out called *Leadership Excellence*, you're apt to be a bit skeptical. Maybe you're thinking, *I've heard it all before. I've read books on great leaders, but how do I translate their leadership style to my leadership challenges? How do I translate their leadership secrets to my business, my team, my church, my organization, my military unit, my club, my school?*

I'm glad you asked. I've distilled the leadership secrets of the great leaders from every era and field of endeavor, and I've reduced those secrets to a set of step-by-step principles that you can apply to every leadership opportunity and challenge you face. You may think you've heard it all before. But after you read this book, I hope you'll drop me a line and tell me what you think. My contact information is at the end of the book.

In these pages, you and I are going to take a journey together through the seven-sided foundation of leadership excellence. Take out your pen, pencil, or highlighter, and feel free to scribble notes in the margin. Dog-ear the pages, or tab them with Post-it notes. Have a conversation with me as you read. Wrestle with these concepts. When you're ready, turn the page and let's begin our journey of a lifetime.

A lifetime of *leadership excellence.*

1

THE FIRST SIDE OF LEADERSHIP: VISION

On Sunday, January 9, 2011, I took part in the eighteenth running of the Walt Disney World Marathon—the fifty-eighth marathon of my fifteen-year marathon career. Two days earlier, at my yearly physical, my doctor had given me a clean bill of health, and I felt fine throughout the run. Afterward, I experienced the usual post-marathon soreness in my limbs—nothing out of the ordinary.

Monday and Tuesday, I felt fine. But Wednesday morning, I woke up with my back screaming in pain. Something was horribly wrong—and the pain seemed to radiate from my spine.

Soon I was back in my doctor's office. After running a few tests, Dr. Vince Wilson sat me down for a serious talk. "We have a problem," he said.

"Well, I knew I had a problem the moment I felt that pain," I chuckled. "But how bad could it be? A ruptured disk? A compression fracture? Arthritis?"

Dr. Wilson frowned. "Pat," he said, "look at my face and listen to what I'm telling you. *We have a problem.* We found an abnormal protein in your blood work."

I didn't have a clue what "an abnormal protein" meant, but he suddenly had my full attention. I listened and he proceeded to tell me about something called multiple myeloma, a cancer of the plasma cells in my bone marrow. "We aren't certain yet," he said, "but we think that's what your blood tests are telling us. I'm going to refer you to one of the top oncologists and hematologists in the nation, Dr. Robert B. Reynolds."

A few days later, I went to see Dr. Reynolds. He confirmed the diagnosis and explained to me that while multiple myeloma is not curable, it is treatable. The goal is remission. I later found out that Mel Stottlemyre, the longtime Yankees pitcher, and Don Baylor, the former American League power hitter, are both in remission with this same disease. With chemotherapy, Dr. Reynolds said, I had a 70 to 75 percent chance of remission.

"Well, Doc," I said, "I like those odds." Then an inspiration hit me. "Hey, I've got a great motivational slogan for my treatment: 'The Mission is Remission!'"

"I like it," Dr. Reynolds said. "You've got a number of factors in your favor. Number one, your optimism and positive attitude—that's important. Number two, your good fitness level. Number three, your strong faith in God. Number four, the love of your family. Number five, the support of your team and the entire Magic organization."

"What's our next move?"

"We'll start chemo and move as fast as we can."

"I like an aggressive doctor. Let's get going!"

So I began chemotherapy—two treatments a week for two weeks, then a week off. The worst side effect was fatigue, but I could tolerate that. I continued my regular work, travel, speaking, and writing schedule, as well as my daily stint on the exercise bike, but I had to discontinue my heavy workouts—no more weight lifting or marathon training. It was a huge blessing that I could keep working, because work is therapeutic. If I couldn't have kept that up, I would have been sitting around thinking about cancer and chemo, and that's no way to live.

Over the next few days, I wondered: Whom should I tell? What should I say to my nineteen children? (Yes, nineteen children—four biological, fourteen adopted, and one by remarriage.) Should I keep my diagnosis private or make a public announcement? I knew if the news somehow leaked out, the information would not be under my control and would probably become distorted.

My doctor agreed that I should tell my family first, and then the public. "My counsel," he said, "is that you gather the media and tell them all at once."

I conferred with Joel Glass, the Orlando Magic's media director, and we scheduled a press conference for February. Dr. Reynolds was at my side throughout the briefing, and he gave the reporters a clear, concise explanation of what this illness is, how it is treated, and what the treatment goals would be.

"It's a very treatable disease," he told the reporters, "but it's not yet a curable disease. That's what we're striving for."

At the conclusion of the press conference, I removed my blazer and revealed a Magic-blue T-shirt. Lettered across the front was my motivational slogan: "The Mission Is Remission."

THE VISION POWERS THE MISSION

Immediately after the press conference, I was flooded with e-mails, letters, cards, and phone calls from friends and well-wishers. I heard from people I had known from my school days, playing days, and throughout my NBA career. I heard from people who had read my books or heard me speak. Every note and card was touching and life-affirming. I read each one, and I was overwhelmed by the good wishes and prayers.

For most of my life, I've tried to live by faith. Well, now it was time to put my faith into action. I can talk about faith in God all I want, but it takes a crisis like multiple myeloma to find out if my faith is real or not. In times like these, you can either get mad at God and withdraw into a shell of self-pity, or you can run to God and cling to him for all you're worth. Well, ever since I heard the words *multiple myeloma* from my doctor, I've been sitting in God's lap and seeking His will.

I've always felt that there was going to be another chapter in my life—an encore, a grand finale to all my years in baseball, basketball, team-building, promoting, speaking, and writing. I didn't know how it would play out, but I had a sense that something was coming. I think this is it.

Soon after I was diagnosed, I came across a great quote by an unknown author: "What may seem upside down to us is right-side up to God." I believe that's true. I don't want to have cancer, and I wish it were possible to make it go away. But at the same time, I think God has a new adventure for me—even a new leadership role—at this stage in my life.

For years, I've delivered motivational speeches to teams, corporations, organizations, church groups, and youth groups. One of my recurring themes has been, "Don't give up! Be bold! Be courageous! Have faith! Persevere!" Now, I get to live out all the great truths I always talk about, and that is a great privilege.

As I write these words, I'm only half a year into this journey. Yet I can already see so many good things coming out of this experience. I'm thankful that God has allowed this to happen. It's going to change my life. In fact, it has already changed my life. I've told God that I want him to use me, and I will do whatever he wants. I'll be bolder in speaking out for what truly matters in life. I'll become a spokesman for cancer research and for men's health. And none of this would have happened if not for this thing called multiple myeloma.

One of my pastors said, "Pat, God could have stopped this from happening, but he let it take place. He's got a plan to use this cancer and bring some good out of it." I don't want to miss the good things to come. I'm going to stay on the path he puts me on, and no matter where this path leads, I know I'll look back and be grateful.

I recently heard about a woman who received the same diagnosis I have. She has decided she doesn't want to battle the disease. She doesn't want to go through chemo. She's chosen to surrender to the cancer. When I heard her story, I asked, "Why is she giving up? Why doesn't she fight it?" The answer: "Pat, she doesn't have all the things to live for that you have. She doesn't have a mission in life. She doesn't have a vision for the future. She's tired, and she wants to let go."

And you know what? She has that right. I won't criticize her choice. Everyone has to choose his or her own path.

But I'm so grateful to have this mission before me—and *the mission is remission*! You might even say that the *vision* is remission, too. It doesn't rhyme quite as well, but it's just as true. My vision for the future is remission, and that vision powers my mission.

What's more, I believe that this vision is also powering my remission. When the day comes that Dr. Reynolds tells me, "Pat, your cancer is in remission," I'll give the credit to God, to my doctors, and to my vision of a new life—a life with an exciting new cause to live for, a life with a whole new dimension of leadership excellence to shout about to the world.

This vision of remission has captured my heart and soul, and I'm pursuing it for all I'm worth.

FOCUSED AND FUELED TO FINISH

Leadership is about the future, so all true leadership begins with *vision*.

Men and women of vision are people who have trained themselves to look over the horizon, to see what doesn't yet exist, to see things others can't see. Visionary leaders see earlier than others, farther than others, and more than others. Then they assemble teams of followers who catch that vision and hammer those dreams into reality.

A visionary leader can look at a plot of bare land and see a building already built. A visionary leader can look at an empty street and envision a victory parade. A visionary leader can look up at the night sky and see human habitats planted on the soil of distant planets. A leader starts with a vision and then works backward from that vision, figuring out each step it will take to turn that vision into a reality.

Vision has always been a prime ingredient of leadership excellence, and it always will be. General Colin Powell put it this way: "I don't know that leadership in the twenty-first century will be essentially different from the leadership shown by Thomas Jefferson, George Washington, and their colleagues two hundred years ago. Leadership will always require people who have a vision of where they wish to take 'the led.' Leadership will always require people who are able to organize the effort of others to accomplish the objectives that flow from the vision."[1]

One of the greatest leaders of the ancient world was the Persian emperor Cyrus the Great, who lived almost six hundred years before Christ. He founded the first Persian Empire. Under Cyrus, Persian rule extended from the Mediterranean in the west to the Indus River in the East—the largest empire in history up to that time. Unlike most empire builders of the ancient world, Cyrus was not primarily a military conqueror. He was a genuine leader—a visionary, not a tyrant. In their book *Power Ambition Glory*, Steve Forbes and John Prevas explain the secret of Cyrus's greatness:

> What set [Cyrus the Great] apart from other leaders of his time were his extraordinary vision and his willingness to build an empire based on tolerance and inclusion of other cultures. With Cyrus, leadership was more than just conquest; it included vision. Even in his early years as a nomadic tribal chief, he was able to see beyond the parched deserts of Iran and recognize the potential of an empire situated at the crossroads of the lucrative trade

routes that ran between China and the West. Then he went out and built it.[2]

The moment I read about Cyrus the Great and his vision for an empire situated around lucrative trade routes, I thought of Sam Walton and his Walmart empire. Walton was truly the Cyrus the Great of retailing. In the 1950s, he bought a shiny little Ercoupe 415-C two-passenger airplane and flew it around the country to scout locations for new discount stores. Sam's brother Bud, a former navy pilot who had taken off from carrier decks during World War II, said he was afraid to fly in Sam's little airplane. "It had a washing machine motor in it," Bud recalled, "and it would putt-putt, and then miss a lick, then putt-putt again."

But that little airplane was indispensable to Sam Walton's vision for his Walmart empire. Like Cyrus the Great, he recognized the potential of situating his empire at the crossroads of lucrative trade routes. From the air, Walton could scout out the vacant properties at the intersections of busy roadways, and he could envision his stores rising up from the ground to become retail meccas, attracting vast crowds of bargain-hungry shoppers. Sam later wrote in his autobiography, *Made in America*:

> From up in the air we could check out traffic flows, see which way cities and towns were growing, and evaluate the location of competition— if there was any.
>
> I'd get down low, turn my plane up on its side, and fly right over a town. . . . Until we had 500 stores, or at least 400 or so, I kept up with every real estate deal we made and got to view most locations [from the air] before we signed any kind of commitment.[3]

The *vision* principle of leadership is exactly the same today as it was in the ancient world, centuries before Christ.

No matter what kind of empire you wish to build, you must begin with a vision.

Vision produces three vital effects in the life of a leader:

First, *vision keeps you focused*. It wards off distractions. It keeps you from wandering down rabbit trails. Your vision of the future keeps you on the main highway to your goals. Leadership guru John Maxwell puts it this way: "Vision leads the leader. It paints the target. It sparks and fuels the fire within, and draws [the leader] forward."[4]

The Wright brothers had a vision for humanity's future in air travel. Their vision kept them intensely focused on all the different problems that had to be overcome in order to build the first airplane. Biographer Mark Eppler describes how Orville Wright's vision kept him focused on solving the problems of heavier-than-air flight:

> One morning, while working on their flyer in Kitty Hawk, Orville announced that during the night he had solved a problem regarding the control of their machine. "I was lying awake last night," Orville said, "and I studied out a new vertical, movable rudder to replace the fixed rudder we have used." Orville's ability to visualize a solution would be a key component of the brothers' eventual success. . . . Many experts on the Wright brothers feel that their ability to "see" things in their heads before they tangibly existed was one of their greatest assets.[5]

That ability Orville Wright described is called *vision*.

Sometimes the future is clouded by today's turbulent events. But even when we cannot see very far ahead, our vision keeps us focused on the way we should go. Novelist E. L. Doctorow puts it this way: "It's like driving a car at night. You never see farther than your headlights, but you can make the whole trip that way."[6]

Tom Landry, the late, great Dallas Cowboys coach, was

known for using the "vision of the headlights" approach to the game of football. He always had a vision for winning that kept him focused on the path to victory. When his team was playing in the first quarter, he wasn't thinking about the fourth quarter. He kept his focus on what he wanted to accomplish in the next few plays. He once said: "I don't see the game the way the fans do. I'm one play ahead all the time. While the team is running one play, I'm looking ahead, planning the next one. I suppose that's why I don't react to a play the way the fans do."[7]

Leaders of excellence are leaders of vision. Their vision keeps them focused on what they must do to succeed.

Second, *vision keeps you fueled*. It gives you energy, passion, and enthusiasm for the challenges you face. Energy, passion, and enthusiasm are the most contagious of all human qualities. If you want to measure the temperature of an organization, just stick a thermometer in the mouth of the leader. If he's on fire, the organization will be on fire. If he's a cold fish, the organization is a dead duck.

Andy Stanley, founding pastor of Atlanta's North Point Community Church and author of *Visioneering*, explains it this way:

> Vision evokes emotion. There is no such thing as an emotionless vision. Think about your daydreams. The thing that makes daydreaming so enjoyable is the emotion that piggybacks on those mind's eye images. When we allow our thoughts to wander outside the walls of reality, our feelings are quick to follow.
>
> A clear, focused vision actually allows us to experience ahead of time the emotions associated with our anticipated future. These emotions serve to reinforce our commitment to the vision. They provide a sneak preview of things to come. Even the most lifeless, meaningless task or routine can begin to "feel" good when

it is attached to a vision. Through the avenue of vision, the feelings reserved for tomorrow are channeled back into our present reality. . . .

Vision is always accompanied by strong emotion. And the clearer the vision, the stronger the emotion.[8]

A leader's excitement, fervor, and passion radiate throughout the organization. In *The Presentation Secrets of Steve Jobs*, Carmine Gallo writes:

Passion stirs the emotions of your listeners when you use it to paint a picture of a more meaningful world, a world that your customers or employees can play a part in creating.

Marcus Buckingham interviewed thousands of employees who excelled at their jobs during his seventeen years at the Gallup organization. After interviewing thousands of peak performers, he arrived at what he considers the single best definition of leadership: "Great leaders rally people to a better future."[9]

When Steve Jobs stepped down as CEO of Apple, a few weeks before his death, *The New York Times* wrote, "Steven P. Jobs, one of the most successful chief executives in corporate history, once said he never thought of himself as a manager, but as a leader."[10] *USA Today* compared Jobs's impact on our culture to that of Henry Ford and Walt Disney. Jay Samit, CEO of the digital advertising company SocialVibe, said that Jobs was one of the few executives who possessed "the vision to look farther down the road than the competition while micromanaging the present."[11] And Peter Sealey, former chief marketing officer of Columbia Pictures, said, "You'd have to go back to the 1940s and Walt Disney to find a CEO who's had as big an impact on culture as Jobs. Maybe it's a stretch to compare him with [Leonardo] Da Vinci, but he was just that good."[12]

Steve Jobs himself once described the passion-charged vision that drove him and his colleagues from the earliest days of Apple Computer:

> Apple was this incredible journey. I mean, we did some amazing things there. The thing that bound us together at Apple was the ability to make things that were going to change the world. That was very important. We were all pretty young. The average age in the company was mid- to late twenties. Hardly anybody had families at the beginning, and we all worked like maniacs, and the greatest joy was that we felt we were fashioning collective works of art much like twentieth-century physics. Something important that would last.[13]

Building amazing things. Taking an incredible, joy-filled journey. Changing the world. That's the stuff of passion, and the power of that passion is why vision keeps a leader fueled.

Sir Richard Branson is the founder and chairman of the Virgin Group (which includes Virgin Atlantic Airways), and he is listed on the *Forbes* list of billionaires. He got his start in business at age sixteen when he founded a successful youth-culture magazine. At twenty-two, he founded a chain of record stores called Virgin Records, which he later expanded into a highly successful recording label. In 2004 Branson founded his most visionary company of all—Virgin Galactic, a company that will soon take paying passengers on suborbital spaceflights. (He has offered a window seat on the first flight to actor William Shatner, *Star Trek*'s Captain Kirk.)

Branson once told *Entrepreneur* magazine, "A successful business isn't the product or service it sells, its supply chain or its corporate culture: It is a group of people bound together by a common purpose and vision."[14] Richard Branson's leadership vision is taking his company to the stars because vision keeps a leader fueled.

Third, *vision helps you finish*. Leadership isn't easy. The road is hard, and there are deserts to cross, valleys to traverse, and mountains to climb or tunnel through. Your vision keeps you going through the tough times.

Every great leader, from Washington to Lincoln to Churchill to Disney to Jobs, has experienced discouraging failures and setbacks. Every one of these leaders would certainly have quit somewhere along the line *if not for a vision*. Because these leaders could see what others could not see, they refused to let any opponent or obstacle stand in their way. Their vision kept them focused and fueled—and their vision kept them moving toward their destination. As Steve Jobs once said, "If you are working on something exciting that you really care about, you don't have to be pushed. The vision pulls you."[15]

Stay focused, stay fueled, so you can finish strong. Be a leader of vision.

IT'S THE VISION THING

In her groundbreaking novel *The Fountainhead*, Ayn Rand's heroic protagonist, architect Howard Roark, talks about the power of a leader's vision:

> Throughout the centuries, there were men who took first steps down new roads, armed with nothing but their own vision. Their goals differed, but they all had this in common: that the step was first, the road new, the vision unborrowed, and the response they received—hatred. . . . Every great new thought was opposed. Every great new invention was denounced. . . . But the men of unborrowed vision went ahead. They fought, they suffered and they paid. But they won.[16]

Historic change often comes about because of the courage and perseverance of one leader with a vision. Great leaders understand the importance of a big, bold, breathtaking vision—what I call an *extreme dream*. A vision is much more than a mere goal. Never mistake a sales quota, a productivity target, or a set of performance expectations for a vision. Numbers don't excite anyone. Pie charts don't inspire anyone. Bar graphs don't motivate anyone to reach for the stars. If your vision doesn't cause your pulse to quicken, if your vision isn't so huge and awe-inspiring that it seems almost beyond your reach, then it's not truly a vision.

Question: What sets the great American presidents apart from the merely good or mediocre?

Answer: Vision.

Let me give you a few examples.

On April 12, 1961, the Soviets launched cosmonaut Yuri Gagarin into orbit, making him the first human being in space. A few weeks later, on May 5, 1961, the United States launched the first American astronaut, Alan Shepard, into space. His fifteen-minute flight lasted only a fraction of Gagarin's 108-minute orbital journey. In fact, Shepard's flight was so short that, had he gone in the opposite direction, he might have landed in Tallahassee and never left the state of Florida.

Yet, just twenty days after Shepard's flight, President John F. Kennedy stood before Congress and proclaimed an astonishing, audacious vision for America's future. Though America lagged far behind the Soviets in its development of a space program, President Kennedy boldly announced, "I believe that this nation should commit itself to achieving the goal, before this decade is out, of landing a man on the moon and returning him safely to the earth. No single space project. . . will be more exciting, or more impressive to mankind, or more important. . .and none will be so difficult or expensive to accomplish."[17]

It seemed like a wildly improbable dream, and no one knew if America could pull it off. Yet Kennedy's dream captured the imagination of the American people.

The day before an assassin's bullet took his life in Dallas,

President Kennedy went to San Antonio to dedicate NASA's new Aerospace Medical Health Center. In his dedication speech, he said, "This nation has tossed its cap over the wall of space, and we have no choice but to follow it. Whatever the difficulties, they will be overcome. . . . With the help of all those who labor in the space endeavor, with the help and support of all Americans, we will climb this wall with safety and with speed—and we shall then explore the wonders on the other side."[18]

President Kennedy didn't live to see his vision fulfilled, but his bold purpose was so compelling, so inspiring that it created a momentum that drove NASA toward its lofty goal. Bullets could take President Kennedy's life but not his dream.

On July 20, 1969, at 4:18 p.m. Eastern Daylight Time, the lunar landing module settled onto the ashen surface of the moon. From the command seat, astronaut Neil Armstrong radioed: "Houston, Tranquility Base here. The Eagle has landed."

Back on earth, an unknown visitor stepped up to President Kennedy's grave at Arlington National Cemetery and left a note that read, "Mr. President, the Eagle has landed." Mission accomplished. Vision fulfilled.

Great visions outlive us. Great dreams are bigger than any one individual and can propel a team, an organization, or a nation anywhere—even to the moon.

Another visionary president of the twentieth century was Ronald Reagan. He came into office with a bold vision for transforming America—a few grand ideas, stated so simply that everyone could understand them. The three main features of Reagan's vision were (1) revitalizing the economy through lower taxes, (2) revitalizing American society through smaller, less intrusive government, and (3) restoring America's leadership in the world through a strong defense.

On October 8, 1976, more than four years before he was elected president, Reagan had outlined his economic vision in a syndicated newspaper column called "Tax Cuts and Increased Revenue." In that column, he reminded the nation that presidents Warren Harding and John F. Kennedy had cut the tax rates—and the result was that federal revenues went up instead of down, because the tax cuts had caused the economy to expand. "Since the idea worked under both Democratic and Republican administrations before," Reagan wrote, "who's to say it couldn't work again?"[19] When Reagan was elected, he cut the tax rates, and just as he predicted, his 25 percent across-the-board tax cuts drove economic expansion, causing federal revenue to nearly double by the time he left office.[20] His vision was proven true.

President Reagan's elder son, Michael, once described his father's dream of an end to the Cold War and the tyranny of Communism. In *The New Reagan Revolution*, he observes that his father "set an example of visionary leadership."

> Long before he was elected president, my father had a vision for dismantling the Berlin Wall and bringing down the Iron Curtain. No one else, not even his closest advisers, believed it was possible. Yet Ronald Reagan remained true to his vision—and now the Berlin Wall is nothing but a bad memory. . . .
>
> We need leaders with the vision to imagine a world beyond terrorism, a world beyond poverty and hunger, a world beyond energy shortages and energy dependence, a world beyond cancer and heart disease and Alzheimer's and AIDS. We need leaders with the bold, optimistic vision to believe that nothing is impossible, that every problem has a solution.
>
> Visionary leaders refuse to accept limits on what is possible. They are constantly asking, "What if. . . ?" And when others tell them, "That'll never happen," they become more determined to make their dreams come true.[21]

After the release of Michael Reagan's book, I had him as a

guest on my local Orlando radio show. He told me that his father had always been a visionary, and that he possessed an amazing ability to envision the world as it could be. In 1969, shortly after Neil Armstrong and Buzz Aldrin walked on the moon, the nation's leading airline at the time, Pan Am, declared that it was accepting reservations for the first passenger flight to the moon, scheduled for the year 2000. One of the first people to book a seat, said Michael, was his father, Ronald Reagan.

Michael Reagan says that the Strategic Defense Initiative— a technological shield designed to render nuclear missiles and nuclear warfare obsolete—was not suggested to him by an adviser. The nuclear defense shield was Ronald Reagan's own vision, which he first conceived sometime in the 1960s. Michael Reagan writes:

> In 1967, [then-governor of California Ronald Reagan] was invited by the Hungarian-American physicist Edward Teller—known as "the Father of the Hydrogen Bomb"—to attend a briefing on defensive technologies at the Lawrence Livermore National Laboratory in California. Teller later recalled that Ronald Reagan asked "good and fundamental questions" about the possibilities for an antimissile defense. Clearly, the seeds of SDI were planted long before Ronald Reagan went to the White House. . . .
>
> In his defense policy speech of March 23, 1983, he revealed his dream for SDI to the nation: . . . "Let me share with you a vision of the future which offers hope. . . . I call upon the scientific community in our country. . .to give us the means of rendering these nuclear weapons impotent and obsolete."[22]

Dinesh D'Souza, president of The King's College in New York City, agrees with Michael Reagan that the key to President

Reagan's greatness lay in his visionary ability to imagine a brighter future, and then to organize the effort to turn that vision into a reality. D'Souza writes:

> Reagan's greatness derives in large part from the fact that he was a visionary—a conceptualizer who was able to see the world differently from the way it was. While others were obsessed and bewildered by the problems of the present, Reagan was focused on the future. This orientation gave Reagan an otherworldly quality that is often characteristic of great men.
>
> The source of Reagan's vision was his possession of what Edmund Burke termed moral imagination. He saw the world through the clear lens of right and wrong. This kind of knowledge came not from books but from within himself. Moreover, Reagan firmly believed that however prolonged the struggle, good eventually would prevail over evil. . . . He understood the moral power of the American ideal and saw how it could be realized most effectively in his time.[23]

Ronald Reagan came into office in 1981 with a vision for where he wanted to take the country. He wanted to restore prosperity. He wanted to topple the Berlin Wall. (In a 1978 visit to Berlin, he told aides Peter Hannaford and Richard Allen, "This wall has got to come down.")[24] He wanted to begin work on the Strategic Defense Initiative, a missile shield that he hoped would make nuclear war obsolete. And he accomplished *all* of those goals.

During Reagan's eight years in office, his vice president was George H. W. Bush. Standing at Reagan's side, Mr. Bush was able to see President Reagan's vision come to pass—yet Mr. Bush himself never seemed to grasp the power of a vision. He never understood that vision is the essence of great leadership. While Ronald Reagan had the visionary mind-set of a great leader, George H. W. Bush had the mind-set of a manager. There's nothing wrong with being a manager—but managers do not make great presidents. Management is about the present. Leadership is about the future.

The January 26, 1987, issue of *Time* appeared on newsstands as Vice President Bush was beginning his run to succeed Reagan as president. In the feature article entitled "Where Is the Real George Bush?" *Time* reporter Robert Ajemian writes:

> Ideas and ideologies do not move Bush. . . . Colleagues say that while Bush understands thoroughly the complexities of issues, he does not easily fit them into larger themes.
>
> This has led to the charge that he lacks vision. It rankles him. Recently he asked a friend to help him identify some cutting issues for next year's campaign. Instead, the friend suggested that Bush go alone to Camp David for a few days to figure out where he wanted to take the country. "Oh," said Bush in clear exasperation, "the vision thing." The friend's advice did not impress him.[25]

"The vision thing." Not only did Vice President Bush seem incapable of clearly articulating a vision for America's future, he didn't even seem to grasp the importance of vision as a dimension of leadership. The suggestion that he ought to have a leadership vision seemed only to annoy and irritate him.

Mr. Bush's lack of a leadership vision for America undoubtedly helped make him a one-term president. In the spring of 2000, Catherine L. Langford, professor of communication at Texas Tech University, asked Mr. Bush about the role of vision and leadership. His response showed that he still didn't understand "the vision thing." He said:

My problem, very frankly, was that I wasn't articulate. I didn't feel comfortable with some of the speech writers' phrases, so I would cross them out. I didn't quote Shelley and Kant. . . . Not feeling those things, I would ex them out.... I think it was maybe a mistake—because part of being seen as a visionary is being able to have flowing rhetoric, and. . .you know, coming out of the clouds and being quoted all the time. My vision was for a kinder and gentler nation, my vision was for more freedom, more democracy around the world. . . . [I] wasn't particularly good at. . .flowing rhetoric that can rally people along the way. And so maybe that's part of why I was hit on the vision thing.[26]

George H. W. Bush never came to grips with "the vision thing." Vision is not about rhetorical flourishes. It's not about quoting Shelley and Kant, or "coming out of the clouds and being quoted all the time." Vision means having a clear, inspiring, challenging sense of where you want to take your team, your organization, or your nation. Mr. Bush is a good man and was a good president, but he was not a great president. The gap between being good and great was something he was never able to grasp—this concept he called "the vision thing."

It's important to be able to communicate your vision in a compelling way, and we will explore the leadership dimension of communication in the next chapter. But before you can communicate a vision, you must be able to *envision* a vision. You must be able to look into the future and see what no one else sees. That vision must challenge and thrill you to the marrow.

Retired aerospace executive Harry Stonecipher (widely viewed as the visionary force behind the resurgence of

Boeing) tells a story about one of America's greatest, most visionary presidents: "The story is about Abraham Lincoln at an important turning point in the Civil War. Union General George Meade had just won a great victory over Robert E. Lee at the Battle of Gettysburg. But as Lee was beating a retreat, Meade was slow in his pursuit. As a result, Lee escaped, back to Virginia, with much of his army intact."

General Meade boasted that he had successfully chased "every vestige of the invader from our soil." When Lincoln heard of Meade's remarks, he was furious. "Drive the invader from our soil!" the president shouted. "Is that all? Will our generals never get the idea? The *whole country* is our soil!"

Stonecipher concludes, "Lincoln had a vision. To him, it was a mighty compass—guiding his action through every crisis and through every twist and turn in the war. At the center of his vision was the idea of one country—whole and indivisible. . . . Even in the darkest days of the war, Lincoln would not contemplate a compromise solution that would end the bloodshed at the cost of giving up the ideal of union." If America had broken into two countries, Stonecipher adds, world history would have been very different—and it's unlikely that America would have been a beacon of freedom during two world wars and assorted other conflicts.[27] In short, Stonecipher suggests, if Lincoln hadn't had a vision for America as one indivisible nation, we might be living in a world in which Hitler had won World War II. It's sobering to realize how different the world might be had Lincoln failed to grasp "the vision thing."

Our earliest presidents, our founding fathers—men like Washington, Adams, Jefferson, and Monroe—all understood "the vision thing." They all looked into the future and saw a shining image of an America that was yet to be—and they fought and sacrificed to make that vision a reality. One of those visionary leaders was John Adams of Massachusetts, who served two terms as vice president before succeeding George Washington and becoming the second president of the United States.

In 1776, the day after the Second Continental Congress declared the thirteen colonies of America to be free and independent states (and twenty years before Adams was elected president), he wrote his wife and expressed his vision for Independence Day celebrations to come:

> I am apt to believe that it will be celebrated by succeeding Generations as the great anniversary Festival. It ought to be commemorated as the Day of Deliverance by solemn Acts of Devotion to God Almighty. It ought to be solemnized with Pomp and Parade, with [Shows], Games, Sports, Guns, Bells, Bonfires and Illuminations from one End of this Continent to the other from this Time forward forever more. You will think me transported with Enthusiasm but I am not. I am well aware of the Toil and Blood and Treasure that it will cost Us to maintain this Declaration, and support and defend these States. Yet through all the Gloom I can see the Rays of ravishing Light and Glory.[28]

John Adams knew that the Revolutionary War would be harsh, costly, and bloody—yet he had a vision of an America at peace, celebrating liberty with Independence Day parades and fireworks displays, from sea to shining sea. The next time you watch a July Fourth fireworks display or sing "The Star Spangled Banner," remember John Adams and his vision for America.

HOW TO BECOME A VISIONARY

The Cathedral of Seville is the largest Gothic cathedral in the world. Its domes, spires, towers, and stone statuary inspire a sense of awe and wonder. Its central nave is twelve stories high, lavishly accented with gold. Construction of the cathedral began in 1402 and was completed more than a century later, in 1506. The altarpiece—the massive and intricately carved panel behind the communion table—was the work of one craftsman who spent his entire adult lifetime carving it. The cathedral is the burial place of explorer Christopher Columbus and a number of Castilian monarchs, including Fernando III, Elisabeth of Hohenstaufen, and Alfonso X.

According to oral tradition, the Cathedral of Seville exists today because a religious leader—a dignitary of the cathedral chapter whose name has been lost to history—stood in a meeting and shared his vision with the other members of the chapter. He said, "Let us build a church so great that those who come after us may think us mad to have attempted it!" Now, *that* is a vision.

A vision should make the people around you question your sanity. It should make your heart race and your palms sweat. It should seem well-nigh impossible. If your organization's goal can be achieved with relative ease, if it can be achieved without risk, without courage, without persistence, then what does the organization need *you* for? Why would your organization need a leader?

The purpose of leadership is to organize and motivate people to do the impossible and the unthinkable. As Walt Disney once observed, "It's kind of fun to do the impossible." He deliberately and continually challenged himself to achieve the impossible on a daily basis. If a vision wasn't nearly impossible to achieve, he wasn't interested.

Disney once explained, "If management likes my projects, I seriously question proceeding. If they disdain them totally, I proceed immediately."[29] This may sound like sheer orneriness, but in reality it was Walt Disney's way of forcing himself to dream big, audacious dreams. He believed that if his brother Roy (Disney's chief financial officer), his board members, and the rest of his organization instantly approved of his ideas, then he must not be dreaming big enough dreams. Only when people fought his ideas and told him he was crazy was he convinced that he had dreamed up a vision worthy of his mettle.

So how do you become a leader like Cyrus the Great, Sam

Walton, Steve Jobs, or Richard Branson? How do you develop the far-seeing vision of a JFK, a Ronald Reagan, or a Walt Disney? Here's where we get down to brass tacks. Here's where we take these inspiring examples and distill from them the practical insights and bullet-point principles that will enable you to acquire the skill of visionary leadership. Here we go:

Vision Skill No. 1: Uncork Your Imagination. Most of our limitations are ones we impose on ourselves. The moment you limit your imagination, creativity shuts down and you restrict your horizons. Walt Disney once said, "I resent the limitations of my own imagination." So should we! Discard your assumptions. Toss out the rules. Don't just "think outside the box"; tell yourself, *"There is no box!"*

Force yourself to dream up the wildest, most impossible ideas—then sit down with your team and brainstorm ways to turn those impossibilities into realities. Set logic aside. Allow intuition to run free.

Vision Skill No. 2: Silence Your Inner Critic. We get an idea—and in the very next moment we say, "That will never work. That's too wild, too crazy, too impractical." We worry about what people will think. We worry about the "proper" way of doing things. We worry about falling on our faces and looking foolish. And many wonderful ideas are strangled in the cradle because our inner critic says, "You can't do that."

The inner critic is that little voice inside us that nags at us and warns us not to take a risk or color outside the lines. Little children are naturally creative because they don't have an inner critic. They see the world with childlike eyes. Everything around them is fascinating—flowers, blades of grass, bugs, puppies, rain puddles. Nothing is impossible to a child. Little children look up in the sky and see castles, faces, and dinosaurs. Grown-ups look at the sky and see only clouds. You've got to regain the ability to see the wonder and endless possibilities of the world around you.

Vision Skill No. 3: Consider Every Possible Solution. People of vision are not content with one solution. They want hundreds to choose from. There is rarely just one right way to solve a problem. Gather your team and brainstorm a dozen solutions, two dozen, a hundred. Uncork the imagination of every person in the room, and unleash their collective vision.

Vision Skill No. 4: Ask Yourself, "What If—?" Visionary leaders are never satisfied with the status quo. They don't say, "Do it the way we've always done it." They are constantly asking, "What if we could find a better way?"

In 1983 General Electric CEO Jack Welch shocked the business world by selling GE's housewares division to Black & Decker for $300 million. That division was one of the oldest divisions in the company, and its products had always been viewed as a staple of the GE brand. Writing in *Industrial Management*, Stephen C. Harper explains Welch's decision:

> Quite a few observers thought Welch was selling out the company's heritage. Welch, however, recognized that GE's resources should be redeployed and invested in emerging industries rather than trying to squeeze a profit out of a highly saturated and mature market. Welch believes GE must strive to be the leader in each industry it is in. To be the leader, GE must be number one or number two in everything the company does. According to Welch, companies that refuse to think likewise, who hang on to losing or stagnant operations, won't survive the decade.[30]

In short, Jack Welch is a "What if—?" thinker. He refused to allow GE's "heritage" to limit his thinking. For Welch, all options were on the table. That's why he became one of the most visionary leaders in the history of American business.

Visionary leaders also ask themselves, "What if the world

changes this way or that way? How should we respond?" Visionaries continually lift their eyes from the known present to search the far horizon. They have shed the blinders worn by their stodgier colleagues. Visionary leaders ask, "What if the economy tanks? What if the economy soars? How will changing demographics, consumer demands, or technological breakthroughs affect my business? How can I best take advantage of those changes? How can I keep my organization agile and responsive to our fast-changing marketplace and the global economy?"

To find a better way, continually ask, "What if—?"

Vision Skill No. 5: Train Yourself to Notice What Others Miss. In their book *Launching a Leadership Revolution*, Chris Brady and Orrin Woodward write, "Leaders have watchful eyes. They scan their world for emerging opportunities all the time. It is the job of the leader to identify, analyze, and decide which opportunities to exploit and which to ignore, all the while casting and recasting the vision so the organization accepts the new challenges with wholeheartedness."[31]

Longtime Walmart executive Don Soderquist became known as "Keeper of the Culture" after the death of Sam Walton in 1992. Soderquist recalls how he often accompanied Sam Walton on trips to visit the stores of competitors just to see if other retail chains had products or ideas that could benefit Wal-Mart. On one occasion, Walton and Soderquist drove to Huntsville, Alabama, and visited a run-down store. As they entered, Soderquist looked around and saw nothing but cluttered aisles, unkempt merchandise racks, unfriendly clerks—and no customers. Walton went one way, and Soderquist went the other. After strolling the aisles, Soderquist quickly concluded that this was the worst store he had ever seen—there was nothing to be learned from it. But when he rejoined Sam Walton on the sidewalk in front of the store, Sam was bursting with excitement. "Don, did you see the pantyhose rack? That's the best merchandise rack I've ever seen! I pulled it out and got the name of the manufacturer. When we get back, I want you to call them up and have them meet with our fixture people. I want that rack in all of our stores! And did you see the ethnic cosmetics? This store shelves three times more ethnic cosmetics than we do. We're missing the boat! I got the name of the distributor, and I want our cosmetics buyer to talk to them."[32]

Don Soderquist learned a big lesson that day: Great leaders of vision always make an effort to notice what others miss.

Vision Skill No. 6: Think "Tomorrow." Become a futurist. Absorb all the information you can about the future. Look for books, magazine articles, and TV shows with phrases like "The Future" or "Tomorrow" in the title. Take time to imagine where today's trends will lead us in the future.

The Kingdom of Tonga comprises 176 mostly uninhabited islands in the South Pacific, between New Zealand and Hawaii. From 1965 to 2006, Tonga was ruled by King Taufa'ahau Tupou IV (and no, I won't tell you how to pronounce his name). The population of the Kingdom of Tonga is just over 100,000 people, and one of its chief exports is space. That's right, *space*—as in outer space, orbital space, blue sky.

It seems that in the late 1970s and early 1980s, as various nations and communications companies began to recognize the importance of orbital positions for communications satellites, the king of Tonga also took notice. Orbital satellites are vital to many industries, including television and telephone communications. There are only a limited number of orbital positions available for use by satellites, because if the space lanes become too crowded, the satellites start to interfere with each other. These limited orbital slots are administered by the International Telecommunication Union, a United Nations agency.

The king of Tonga realized something that other leaders had missed: The fixed number of orbital slots would make each of those slots increasingly valuable as technology advanced and more and more satellites crowded the skies. So the king applied for twenty orbital slots. Other nations cried foul—but only because they hadn't thought of it themselves. As it turned out, the

ITU had no rules limiting the number of slots a single nation could apply for—but it quickly plugged up that loophole before any other nations could get in on the game. In the end, the ITU granted Tonga six orbital slots, which the tiny island nation now leases at exorbitant rates to the highest bidder. Tonga reaps a significant percentage of its gross national product by renting out empty space to communications companies.[33]

Now, that's what I call vision! To be successful today and in the future, think *tomorrow*.

Vision Skill No. 7: Make Your Vision Clear and Simple. A complicated vision is not a vision. A well-articulated vision communicates instantly, with power and emotion, and needs no explanation. Former GE head Jack Welch put it this way: "Every idea you present must be something you could get across easily at a cocktail party with strangers."[34] Welch echoes the ancient wisdom of the Bible: "Write a vision, and make it plain upon a tablet so that a runner can read it" (Habakkuk 2:2 CEB).

Vision Skill No. 8: Learn to Think Backwards. As you plan your leadership journey, begin with the destination in mind, not the starting point. In his book *On Becoming a Leader*, Warren Bennis writes:

> Mountain climbers don't start climbing from the bottom of the mountain. They look at where they want to go, and work backward to where they're starting from. Like a mountain climber, once you have the summit in view, you figure out all the ways you might get there. Then you play with those—altering, connecting, comparing, reversing, and imagining—finally choosing one or two routes.
>
> Second, you flesh out those routes, elaborate them, revise them, make kind of a map of them, complete with possible pitfalls and

traps as well as rewards.

Third, you examine this map objectively, as if you were not its maker, locate all its soft spots, and eliminate them or change them.

Finally, when you have finished all that, you set out to climb your mountain.[35]

If you plan your journey from where you stand right now, you'll feel hemmed in by circumstances and limitations. But if you start with your destination in view and work backwards, you replace limitations with possibilities. When John F. Kennedy announced his vision of putting a man on the moon, all we had done so far was dunk one astronaut in the Atlantic Ocean. But JFK didn't allow himself to be limited by NASA's 1961 capabilities. He started with the destination, with a vision of landing a man on the moon, confident that NASA would work out all the steps between here and there. To be a leader of vision, start with the destination in mind, then think backwards.

Vision Skill No. 9: Tap into the Imagination of the Entire Team. Call your team together and conduct regular brainstorming sessions. Invite ideas to improve and transform your organization. Make sure your team members feel comfortable tossing out wild, improbable ideas. Tell them, "There are no bad ideas. The more outrageous the idea, the better. We are shooting for the moon."

Motivate your people to submit ideas to your suggestion box. In the 1940s, Walt Disney tacked cartoon storyboards on the studio walls and offered a five-dollar bonus for comedy gags that would make his cartoons even funnier. He found that some of the best gag ideas came not just from his "creative" staff—his writers and artists—but also from receptionists, secretaries, and messenger boys.

Why not offer a hundred-dollar bounty for ideas that you implement to improve products, services, production, supply chain, or other aspects of your business? An idea that costs you a C-note might end up making or saving you thousands or millions of dollars. So tap into the vision and imagination of your entire organization. You'll find brilliant, visionary ideas arising from the most surprising places—and you and your organization will benefit in a big way.

Vision Skill No. 10: Get Your Entire Team to Buy In. "My vision" must become "*our* vision," and not just in name only. The entire team or organization must share the vision and take ownership of it. If your team thinks of your vision as "the boss's vision," it will never come to pass. Peter Senge, author of *The Fifth Discipline*, explains:

> At its simplest level, a shared vision is the answer to the question, "What do we want to create?" Just as personal visions are pictures or images people carry in their heads and hearts, so too are shared visions pictures that people throughout an organization carry. They create a sense of commonality that permeates the organization and gives coherence to diverse activities. . . . When people truly share a vision, they are connected, bound together by a common aspiration. . . .
>
> Today, "vision" is a familiar concept in corporate leadership. But when you look carefully, you find that most "visions" are one person's (or one group's) vision imposed on an organization. Such visions, at best, command compliance—not commitment. A shared vision is a vision that many people are truly committed to, because it reflects their own personal vision.[36]

A shared vision takes place when people throughout the organization buy into that vision with enthusiasm, intensity, and a sense of personal commitment. How, then, do you persuade people to buy into your vision?

First, *share credit.* If ideas and components of the vision were contributed or suggested by members of your team, applaud them and have them take a bow. People are eager to own what they have had a hand in creating.

Second, *make sure that the vision pays big benefits for everyone in the organization, not just the leader.* Make sure there are built-in incentives to motivate the entire team to work toward the vision. Make sure everyone in the organization is a stakeholder in the vision and will gain prestige, recognition, income, stock options, career advancement, and other tangible benefits when the vision becomes a reality.

You can't force your vision on the team with threats or penalties. You must *sell* your vision through inspiration and persuasion. Sell it every day through a leadership style of walking around and greeting your team members and reminding them of the vision they are pursuing.

Don't be stingy with incentives. Money is a great motivator. Adman David Ogilvy put it this way: "Pay peanuts, and you get monkeys." The Bible expresses the same idea with a different animal in mind: "Do not muzzle an ox while it is treading out the grain" (Deuteronomy 25:4). Those who do the work are entitled to a reward. If you share the wealth that comes from the fulfillment of your vision, you'll find that your team will be motivated to go above and beyond to make that vision happen.

Third, *build relationships with the team.* Build a bond of trust with your people. Leadership guru John C. Maxwell puts it this way: "One of the laws of leadership is the law of buy-in. People buy into the leader before they buy into the vision. All visions begin with relationships. My relationship with God is where I receive the vision; my relationship with my people is where I give the vision."[37] As you build relationships with your people, remember to talk about the vision as "our vision."

Fourth, *keep the vision constantly before your team.* Use banners, signs, buttons, ceremonies, prizes, e-mails, and every other means available to remind your people of "our vision."

When Walt Disney was building Disneyland, his architects and construction managers told him that the most efficient and cost-effective way to build the park was to construct the outlying sections first and build the Sleeping Beauty Castle last. This would allow construction crews to make use of existing roads, water lines, and other infrastructure when they began work on the castle at the center of the park. Building the castle last would eliminate weeks of construction time and save tons of money. Disney listened to the experts and replied, "Build the castle first." Why did Walt Disney reject the advice of his experts? He wanted the construction crews to see the castle at all times—to have the vision of Disneyland always before their eyes. He wanted them never to lose sight of what the Disneyland dream was all about. He wanted every carpenter, mason, and heavy equipment operator to buy into his vision. To this day, the Sleeping Beauty Castle at Disneyland is the visual symbol of the Walt Disney Company.

Vision Skill No. 11: Give People an Elevated Vision of Themselves. Help people to see themselves as winners and achievers—people who are capable of turning your vision into a reality. Viktor Frankl, the Austrian psychiatrist and Holocaust survivor, once said, "If you treat people to a vision of themselves, if you apparently overrate them, you make them become what they are capable of becoming. If you take them as they *should* be, you help them become what they *can* be."[38]

John William Gardner was secretary of Health, Education, and Welfare under President Lyndon Johnson and was responsible for implementing LBJ's Great Society agenda. Gardner also founded Common Cause and presided over the creation of the Corporation for Public Broadcasting. And he was a friend of Dr. Martin Luther King Jr.

In his book *On Leadership*, Gardner observes, "The future is shaped by people who believe in the future—and in themselves. . . . Leaders must help people believe that they can be effective, that their goals are possible of accomplishment, that there is a better future that they can move toward through their own efforts."[39] Gardner recounts a conversation he had in 1967 with Dr. Martin Luther King, Jr., at a seminar on education: "The black woman leading the seminar had entitled her talk 'First, Teach Them to Read.' King leaned over to me and said, 'First, teach them to believe in themselves.'"[40]

As you give people an exalted vision of themselves, make sure you also help them see themselves as leaders and visionaries in their own right. A leader's most important task is not to recruit followers, but to build leaders. As someone once observed, there is no success without successors. The task of building leaders begins with giving people a vision of themselves as leaders.

Scott Cook is a former Procter & Gamble executive who founded the highly successful software company Intuit in 1983. He is also a billionaire, listed on the Forbes 400. Interviewed by *Business 2.0*, he said, "Everybody at Intuit has two jobs: One is to do their job as it is today. The other is to figure out how to revolutionize it so they can do it dramatically better in the future."[41]

That is what great leaders do. They don't simply stick people in a job and tell them to do as they're told. Great leaders want to develop *more* leaders. They say, "I believe in you; now believe in yourself. Be a visionary. Be a revolutionary. Be a leader in your own right."

Vision Skill No. 12: Prepare People for a Celebration. Let the people on your team know that when your vision comes to pass, there will be a huge celebration. There will be bands playing, fireworks popping, and glasses raised. There will be recognition. There will be bonuses. There will be rewards. Remind them continually of the celebration to come, and create a sense of anticipation and expectation.

THE HEART AND SOUL OF LEADERSHIP
I was introduced to the concept of vision in February 1965,

long before I knew what the word really meant. I was twenty-four years old.

The Philadelphia Phillies had named me general manager of a minor league baseball team in Spartanburg, South Carolina. I'll never forget that cold February day when I arrived in Spartanburg to get ready for the 1965 season. I was shaking with excitement—and a good bit of fear. I had never taken on a challenge of this size before—and I wasn't sure if I was up to it.

When I got my first look at the team's field, Duncan Park, I *knew* I wasn't up to it. It was old and run-down, and everywhere I looked I saw peeling paint and weeds. The place needed fresh paint (lots of it!) plus some serious remodeling of the ladies' lounge, some landscaping and flower planting—tons and tons of work. For a few moments, I just stood and stared, asking, "What have I gotten myself into?"

But then I began to let my imagination roam free. I looked around the ballpark on that wintry day and imagined it was summer. The playing field was green and manicured, the stands and walls were beautifully painted and trimmed. The bleachers were packed with fans, all having the time of their lives as they cheered their hometown Phillies to victory.

That was my vision. It seized me. And for the next few weeks, as I worked sixteen-hour days to transform that ballpark, the vision sustained me. I hired out as much of the work as I could, but I also spent many hours mowing grass, hammering nails, and painting trim with my own ten thumbs. I had never worked so hard in all my life, and my vision drove me on, day after day.

On opening day, five thousand people streamed into our field of dreams, proving that if you refurbish it, they will come. We drew record crowds throughout the season, and our ball club received national attention and acclaim.

After three more seasons in Spartanburg, I was ready to move on to bigger venues and bigger dreams. I moved from minor league baseball to the NBA and served as general manager of the Chicago Bulls, the Atlanta Hawks, and the Philadelphia 76ers. Finally, in the summer of 1986, our family moved from Philadelphia—where I had been general manager of the 76ers for a dozen years—and we settled in Orlando, Florida.

I had come to chase the biggest, most audacious, most improbable vision of my career—to build an NBA expansion team out of nothing but dreams and pixie dust. We had no money to speak of. We had no fan base. We had no arena. We had no commitment from the NBA. The city of Orlando didn't even have a history or tradition of professional sports.

But we did have one thing. We had a vision.

My partners in getting this vision off the ground were two brothers, Orlando businessmen Jimmy and Bobby Hewitt. We rented a little hole-in-the-wall office, hired a secretary, and went to work. For ten months, I crisscrossed central Florida, speaking to business leaders, political leaders, civic groups, and on and on, selling the vision, working sixteen-hour days, trying to persuade the people and institutions of greater Orlando to buy into this dream. I was selling season tickets wherever I could—even in the checkout line at the health food store.

Again and again, I created word pictures, planting images in my listeners' minds—images of a clean, sparkling arena, images of pulse-pounding excitement on the court. I used words to paint a vision of opening night, an evening of dazzling entertainment and exciting basketball. I showed them a vision of the wealth that would flow into this community—wealth that would build schools, civic centers, and libraries, improving the lives of all the people in the community.

Even though Orlando had a Magic Kingdom right at the edge of town, the city was not yet the convention and vacation destination it is today. Few of the citizens of Orlando had ever been to an NBA game. In 1986 Orlando was a rather modest-size town in central Florida, but the Hewitt brothers and I were convinced that Orlando had the makings of an NBA city. And a *great* one.

The people of Orlando bought into the vision. They owned it. They purchased *14,046 season tickets* for a team that had no name, no arena, and might never exist. Those season ticket sales were absolutely crucial, because without those tangible commitments, we would never have been able to convince the NBA that Orlando would be a strong basketball market.

Why did the city of Orlando buy into this vision? I believe it's because the vision became so real, so vibrant, so drenched in color and passion and excitement in my own heart and soul that I was able to make it come alive in the minds of my hearers. I was able to transplant that electrifying vision from my heart to theirs. It was so real to me that I could make believers out of the people of central Florida.

And that is one of the key reasons why the Orlando Magic exist today. It's not because I am such a brilliant promoter or administrator or speaker. It's because that vision was so powerful and persuasive. When a leader is absolutely captivated and possessed by a vision, that vision simply *must* become a reality.

Your vision is the fountainhead of leadership, and everything else flows from that. That's why vision is the first side, the foundational dimension, of everything else you do as a leader.

Vision is the heart and soul of leadership.

2

THE SECOND SIDE OF LEADERSHIP: COMMUNICATION

When my career as a minor-league baseball player came to an end in the summer of 1963, I packed my belongings and prepared to leave Miami to trek north to Bloomington, Indiana. My goal was to complete my master's in physical education at Indiana University. Before leaving Miami, I called my mother and told her I planned to visit her in Wilmington before going on to Indiana.

"Pat, I've got a better idea," she said. "Let's meet in Washington DC. I'm going to the March on Washington to hear Dr. Martin Luther King Jr. He's giving a speech at the Lincoln Memorial on August 28." I wasn't surprised. Mom had been active in social causes for as long as I could remember—and she'd been a huge fan of Dr. King, ever since the 1955 bus boycott in Montgomery, Alabama. I was only vaguely aware of Dr. King at that time, because my entire life to that point had been consumed with sports. But I agreed to meet my mom and sister Carol in DC.

I'll always be grateful to my mother, because she enabled me to become a witness to history. Mom, Carol, and I were part of that vast crowd of 250,000 in front of the Lincoln Memorial who heard Dr. King's famous "I Have a Dream" speech. It was a hot, humid day—but no one seemed to mind.

I saw actors Sidney Poitier, Charlton Heston, and Marlon Brando give speeches about justice. Gospel singer Mahalia Jackson sang "How I Got Over," Bob Dylan sang "Only a Pawn in Their Game," and Peter, Paul, and Mary performed Dylan's "Blowin' in the Wind." But all of these stars were just the warm-up to the main event—Dr. King himself.

Though I didn't understand the historic importance of his speech at the time, my emotions were stirred as Dr. King's words swept over that crowd like a wave of the sea. It was not a long speech—only seventeen minutes total—yet it became the pivot point that turned our entire nation in a new direction.

"I still have a dream," I heard him say. "It is a dream deeply rooted in the American Dream. I have a dream that one day this nation will rise up and live out the true meaning of its creed: 'We hold these truths to be self-evident, that all men are created equal.'"

Less than five years after he spoke those words, Dr. King was gone, felled by an assassin's bullet. But even after his death, his words and his dream continued to change the trajectory of American history. And his dream still lives today.

Great leaders are great communicators. That's why the second side of leadership is communication.

COMMUNICATE THE VISION

In the previous chapter, we saw that vision is the heart and soul of leadership. But what good is a vision if no one knows about it? Vision alone is not enough. As a leader, you must *communicate* your vision to your followers.

So the question is: How can I become a more effective communicator and leader? What are the ingredients of effective communication?

In *How to Win Friends and Influence People*, Dale Carnegie writes, "Leadership gravitates to the man who can talk."[1] The ability to speak effectively and persuasively is an indispensable component of leadership. Every four years, we elect a president—and we almost always elect someone who can electrify us with powerful words and powerful ideas. I can't think of a single great leader who was not also an effective speaker. You cannot command, inspire, and motivate your team or organization unless you can communicate effectively.

Dave Kraft, a pastor at Mars Hill Church in Seattle, puts it this way in *Leaders Who Last*:

> One of the primary roles of an effective leader for the twenty-first century is that of vision caster. This would include crafting and birthing a vision, then cultivating and clarifying the vision through creative communication. The leader doesn't do it alone, but should be the primary point person for this communication. I have yet to see any success when the leader delegates the responsibility for the caretaking of the vision to a board or committee. It is the leader's responsibility to ensure the vision is kept before the people.[2]

Daniel Harkavy, CEO and head coach of Building Champions, points out a common danger among organizations and teams: a leader who mistakenly assumes that, having communicated the vision once, he has communicated it for all time. Harkavy writes:

> As a leader, it is your duty (and your pleasure!) to keep a clear vision in front of your team at all times. Continued focus on the vision makes the difference between excellence and mediocrity. It promotes discipline in the trenches, where battles are won and lost. A team well focused on the vision is better equipped to deal with daily wins and losses than a team merely headed in the general direction of some ideal place.[3]

Effective leaders communicate the vision again and again and again. By the tenth or twentieth time you have pitched the vision to your team, you are definitely getting sick of talking about it—*but your people are just beginning to grasp it.* Don't let up. Keep communicating your vision.

In my decades-long study of leadership, I have come to the conclusion that there are six keys to effective leadership communication. Let's look at each of those six principles in turn:

1. Believe in the power of communication.

To be an effective leader, you must *believe* it's important to be an effective communicator. You must *believe* in the power of communication—and *you must become a talker.*

This may seem so obvious that it goes without saying—but many leaders do not truly believe in the power of communication, especially spoken communication. They sit in their ivory towers, issuing edicts and orders through underlings, or firing off memos, e-mails, and text messages. But they don't communicate the vision, they don't fire up the troops, they don't see the point of spoken communication—which is really one of the most essential tasks of genuine leadership.

Any functionary or bureaucrat can issue orders and demand compliance. But only a genuine leader can inspire a team and motivate people to go above and beyond mere compliance. Leaders believe in communicating eye to eye, face-to-face. Every team and organization, from a family unit to a Fortune 500 company, needs to plug into the power of communication.

When a leader doesn't believe in communication, the organization lacks passion and enthusiasm. Such organizations tend to bottle up both emotion and information. They are frequently stagnant and dysfunctional. You can't energize people with e-mails. If you want an organization of drones who put in their time—no more, no less—then you don't need to communicate. But if you want to excel, to achieve extreme dreams, to shoot for the moon, then you must become a communicator.

When late Massachusetts congressman Tip O'Neill was

getting his start in politics (long before he rose to become a formidable Speaker of the House), he met an elderly constituent on the sidewalk of his North Cambridge district. "I hope I can count on your vote," the young O'Neill said.

"Nope," the oldster replied. "I'm voting for the other fella."

O'Neill was shocked. "Haven't you known me and my family all my life?"

"Yes, I have."

"Didn't I cut your grass in the summer and shovel your walk in the winter?"

"Yes, you did."

"Don't you agree with all of my policies and positions?"

"I certainly do."

"Then why won't you vote for me?"

"Because you didn't ask me to."[4]

So many leaders neglect the power and importance of communication—then wonder why their organizations go nowhere, and why their vision never becomes a reality. They wonder why their people seem to wander off in random directions instead of flying in formation toward the goal. They wonder why nothing seems to get accomplished. The answer is usually as simple as the fact that the leader neglected to communicate.

I see dysfunctional communication all the time in the sports world. It's a world of big egos, big ambitions, and major league secrets. Much of the communication that does take place in this business is in the form of rumors, which tend to fill information vacuums. Therefore, the best way to scotch a rumor is to provide high-quality information and high-quality communication throughout the team or organization.

Over the years, with the various teams I've worked with, I have seen many young sports executives vent their frustration because they can't get through to the boss. They have important information that affects the team, but the boss can't be bothered. Either he doesn't return calls, or there are so many layers of bureaucracy that the word never gets through. I know top executives are busy, but no leader should ever be so busy that he or she has no time for communication—especially face-to-face communication. Any leader who becomes insulated and isolated from the people he serves is headed for catastrophe.

When I had Michael Reagan as a guest on my Orlando radio show, I asked him, "What was your dad's greatest strength as a leader?" Without hesitation, he replied, "They called him the Great Communicator, and it was absolutely true. Not only was my father the commander in chief, but he truly saw himself as the communicator in chief."

It's interesting to compare and contrast the Great Communicator with another president from the same party, who had many similar views and values, but whose presidency ended on a very different note than Ronald Reagan's—George W. Bush.

Early in his presidency, Mr. Bush seemed to demonstrate the makings of another great communicator. On the evening of the 9/11 attacks, he addressed the nation from the Oval Office. In his touching, stirring speech, he announced, "A great people has been moved to defend a great nation. Terrorist attacks can shake the foundations of our biggest buildings, but they cannot touch the foundation of America. These acts shatter steel, but they cannot dent the steel of American resolve."

I once had General Richard B. Myers, chairman of the Joint Chiefs of Staff under Bush, as a guest on my Orlando radio show. He told me about a meeting of the National Security Council in the Situation Room of the White House the morning after 9/11. General Myers told me that everyone in that room was struck by the force of Mr. Bush's personality as he opened the meeting on a somber but resolute note. General Myers recalled: "The president said, 'The terrorists started this war, but we're going to finish it. We'll do whatever it takes to win. We'll probably have to do a lot of things that will be criticized. We'll have to make a lot of unpopular decisions. If that means that this will be a one-term administration, so be it. We're going to do what's right.'"

In those early moments of the crisis, President Bush was the "communicator in chief". He communicated in a powerful way to the American people and to his national security team. A few days later, on Friday, September 14, he grabbed a bullhorn, climbed atop the rubble of the World Trade Center, put his arm around a firefighter, and shouted to the rescue workers, "The nation stands with the good people of New York City and New Jersey and Connecticut as we mourn the loss of thousands of our citizens—"

One rescue worker shouted, "I can't hear you!"

"I can hear you!" Mr. Bush replied. "I can hear you! The rest of the world hears you! And the people who knocked these buildings down will hear all of us soon! . . . Thank you for your hard work. Thank you for making the nation proud, and may God bless America."

In those unrehearsed moments, speaking without prepared remarks, President Bush rallied the nation. He comforted, inspired, and motivated us all. He was a leader.

Near the end of George W. Bush's first year in office, Ronald Reagan's former speechwriter, Peggy Noonan, offered this assessment of Mr. Bush's leadership in the wake of 9/11:

> He has become, as everyone has pointed out, a leader. Our leader, the American president. . . .
>
> Mr. Bush continues to prove that he is not eloquent, and that he does not have to be. People need a plain speaker who'll tell them what he thinks and why. Mr. Bush does this. He does it with the words of the average American, simple flat words. I like the way he talks because I understand it.[5]

I agree that no president, no leader of any kind, needs to be "eloquent" if we define eloquence as the ability to speak in lofty phrases and rhetorical flourishes. But I would define eloquence differently. To me, eloquence is merely the art of using fluent and appropriate language to communicate with your audience. When George W. Bush was at his best as a communicator, he had a plainspoken eloquence that stirred the emotions. His "simple flat words" were precisely the right words (and the eloquent words) for communicating with the American people. The eloquence of Abraham Lincoln and Ronald Reagan was similarly plainspoken, delivered in simple flat words.

George W. Bush was a great communicator in the days immediately following 9/11. But somewhere along the line, he ceased to view himself as the communicator in chief. He became well-known for his verbal flubs and gaffes, such as his statement during the 2000 campaign that his opponents "misunderestimated" him, and his persistent mispronunciation of *nuclear* as "nucular." The news media and late-night comedians delighted in highlighting what came to be known as "Bushisms." Here are a few examples:

> Our enemies are innovative and resourceful, and so are we. They never stop thinking about new ways to harm our country and our people, and neither do we.[6]

> Too many good docs are getting out of the business. Too many OB-GYNs aren't able to practice their love with women all across this country.[7]

> In my line of work you've got to keep repeating things over and over and over again for the truth to sink in, to kind of catapult the propaganda.[8]

> As yesterday's positive report card shows, childrens do learn when standards are high and results are measured.[9]

I'm not criticizing Mr. Bush and his verbal flubs. I've made enough of my own, and so has anyone who has given a lot of speeches. A few gaffes and flubs won't do you any harm as long as you can laugh them off.

Jacob Weisberg, a journalist who cataloged the president's Bushisms, agrees—and he puts Mr. Bush's verbal stumbles into perspective. "I don't think it does him any harm, because people who are appalled by the way he speaks tend not to like him for other reasons." In fact, Weisberg added, the president's verbal flubs seemed to actually help him connect with average people. "People identify with his problem. You know, it's hard to speak in public—one makes mistakes, it can be embarrassing. And this bonds him to people."[10]

It may be, however, that Mr. Bush didn't see it that way. Though he was a strong communicator in the days immediately following 9/11, he seemed to retreat into the Oval Office very soon afterward. I suspect he avoided public communication in an effort to reduce the likelihood of making public gaffes and inviting public ridicule. As the following table shows, Mr. Bush held far fewer solo press conferences and granted far fewer interviews than his predecessors and his successor, Barack Obama:

President	Solo Press Conferences in First Two Years	Solo Interviews in First Two Years
George H. W. Bush	56	87
Bill Clinton	29	136
George W. Bush	7	83
Barack Obama	21	269

Radio talk show host Scott Hennen, in his book *Grass Roots*, tells a story of an August 2007 visit he made to the White House, along with a number of his colleagues in the talk show business. In the Oval Office, Hennen and the others received a briefing from Mr. Bush himself about the success of the surge strategy in Iraq. As the president explained the reports he received from Iraq and showed how the American forces were dismantling and destroying Al Qaeda in that country, Scott Hennen spoke up and asked, "Mr. President, isn't there some way that you could go before the American people and express what you have just told us—from the statistics to the anecdotal evidence—so that the people could see the success of this mission?"

President Bush replied that he felt it best that he not be seen touting the successes of the war, lest it be interpreted as politically motivated. As Hennen put it, the president said, in effect, "I'm fighting to win the war on terror, not a popularity contest."

At this point, talk show host Glenn Beck spoke up and said, "Mr. President, with all respect, I urge you to reconsider your position. The war on terror is too important, and you need to engage the American people and regain their support for the war. Tell them what you've just told us. Address the nation from the Oval Office with a bank of flat-screen TVs behind you, so you can get out from your desk and point and say, 'Look at what we did in Baghdad and in Al Anbar.' You need an MTV kind of presentation!"

"Glenn," the president replied, "I'm more of a CMT [Country Music Television] guy than an MTV guy."[11]

In other words, the president was not going to personally communicate his case to the American people. He was going to leave that to the talk show hosts. In my view, Mr. Bush made a huge mistake. He rejected the role of communicator in chief and tried to lead the country from behind his desk in the Oval Office. He tried to be a wartime president without communicating with the American people.

President Bush left office with a dismal 34 percent approval rating, one of the lowest of any modern president. No doubt, these low marks can be traced to a number of factors, including Hurricane Katrina and the financial collapse of 2008. But I'm convinced that one of the most important factors in that low approval rating was that Mr. Bush did not believe in the importance of communication.

Mr. Bush insisted on remaining mum about the surge successes, claiming that speaking personally on the subject would politicize the war effort. That, frankly, is absurd. As Franklin D. Roosevelt and Winston Churchill have proven, it's absolutely *vital* for wartime leaders to communicate with the people about the war effort. It's one of the most important responsibilities of wartime leadership.

Roosevelt began his radio conversations with the American people, known as "fireside chats," during the depths of the Great Depression, and he continued those talks all the way through the war years. He gave a fireside chat about the declaration of war against Japan in December 1941. He delivered chats on the progress of the war, on the war effort on the home front, on the importance of buying war bonds, and on plans for postwar peace.

Churchill, too, understood the importance of leading by speaking. On April 9, 1963, President Kennedy welcomed Churchill to the White House for a ceremony conferring honorary US citizenship on him. In his remarks, Kennedy said of Sir Winston, "In the dark days and darker nights when Britain stood alone—and most men save Englishmen despaired of England's life—he mobilized the English language and sent it into battle. The incandescent quality of his words illuminated the courage of his countrymen."[12]

This principle is true at all times and in all situations, whether in wartime or in peace, whether you are president of the United States or president of the PTA: *you must believe in the power of communication.* You must speak to the people in order to lead them. You cannot lead from behind a desk.

2. Communicate so that people understand.
Over the years, I've walked out of many meetings and whispered to my seatmate, "What was that meeting all about? Did we decide anything in there? Could you translate it for me? What did we resolve? Were they speaking English?" To be an effective leader, you must communicate in terms people understand.

A few years ago, my wife, Ruth, and I wrote a book called *Turn Boring Orations into Standing Ovations.* I interviewed nearly 250 speakers and speech coaches, including the legendary Bob Sheppard, longtime public address announcer for the New York Yankees. From 1951 until 2007, Sheppard's distinctive intonations were the unforgettable voice of Yankee Stadium. Reggie Jackson nicknamed Bob "The Voice of God," and to this day, Derek Jeter is still introduced with the recorded voice of Bob Sheppard, who passed away in July 2010, three months shy of his hundredth birthday. Apart from his work with the Yankees, Bob was a college speech instructor. I reached him by phone and interviewed him about the keys to being an effective public speaker. In his rich, resonant voice, he replied, "Pat, the keys to being a great public speaker are the same three keys I have lived by throughout my years at Yankee Stadium: be clear, be concise, be correct."

I once heard Peggy Noonan, the Great Communicator's speechwriter, deliver a talk to leaders. She had one line that truly said it all: "Speak clearly, simply, and sparingly, and it should stick." Those are Bob Sheppard's three keys of effective communicating stated in different words. Those who know effective communication give you the same clear, concise, correct advice every time.

Super Bowl–winning NFL coach Jon Gruden learned the importance of clear, concise, correct coaching from his mentor, Mike Holmgren. In his book *Do You Love Football?!* Gruden observes that Holmgren's high school teaching background prepared him to be a clear and concise communicator with his players. Holmgren always broke down the most complicated plays and assignments into a set of simple, step-by-step instructions. "He had a knack for conveying his thoughts in twenty-five words or less," writes Gruden. "He didn't start rambling and talking about things that were irrelevant to the question that you had just asked. He was always to the point." As a result, every player knew exactly where he was supposed to be and what he was supposed to do. Gruden continues:

When [Coach Holmgren] installs a game plan, showing each play and its corresponding number on the overhead projector, he always exudes confidence.

"Picture Number 73 is going to be a touchdown Sunday," he'd say matter-of-factly, about a pass play designed to have Joe [Montana] throw to Jerry Rice, who would just blow past some poor DB trying to cover him one-on-one over the middle. "Pay attention, men. It's 76 X Shallow Cross. Roger [Craig]'s going in motion to the weak side. The free safety is going to jump the tight end on the hook route, and Jerry Rice is going to be there for a touchdown. It's going to happen, man. Circle it now. Star it. It's a touchdown."

I would sit there and go, "Man, it's seven to nothing already. What's the next picture?"

But that's how you install plays. Confident. Concise. Crystal-clear. No one does it better than Mike Holmgren.[13]

To lead, you must communicate so that your people understand. Never communicate merely to impress others. Avoid big words, jargon, and bureaucratese, which are intended merely to give you an air of expertise. Don't say "diminutive" when you mean "small," "procure" when you mean "get," or "substantiate" when you mean "prove." Don't say, "I suffered a bilateral periorbital hematoma" when you mean "I got two black eyes." Don't say, "We're experiencing an unrequested fission surplus" when you mean "We're having a nuclear meltdown."

President Jimmy Carter once proposed a new urban policy that was designed, in his words, "to strengthen linkages among macroeconomic sectoral place-oriented economies." He meant that his policies would enable cities to cooperate together for their mutual economic benefit.[14] Why didn't he just say so?

Always say exactly what you mean. Say it as clearly and

concisely as you can. Never assume that, just because you've said it, others understand. Invite your listeners to repeat your meaning back to you in their own words. Encourage discussion and questions. Above all, keep it simple. If you really want to impress people with how smart you are and what a great communicator you are, be clear, be concise, and be correct. Communicate so that people can understand.

3. Communicate optimism

Every day as a leader, you must make a decision: "Am I going to be a leader of *optimism* or a leader of *pessimism* to my people?" Optimism trumps pessimism every time. In 1960, near the end of his second term as president, Dwight D. Eisenhower reflected on his experience in both military and political campaigns: "I've been through a number of these campaigns and there comes a time toward the end when the opposition looks fourteen feet tall and everyone takes alarm. But pessimism never won a battle."[15]

I'm not saying that leaders should wear rose-colored glasses. It's a dangerous and difficult world out there, and we have to be realistic. But as leaders, we choose whether to frame difficulties as challenges and opportunities or as trials and tribulations. An optimistic leader knows how to fire up the troops to tackle obstacles and overcome them. A pessimistic leader will lead people into hopelessness and fear.

Colin Powell rightly said, "Perpetual optimism is a force multiplier."[16] Optimism takes the energy and resources you have and multiplies them exponentially, increasing your advantage over the opposition. As you infuse optimism throughout your organization, you magnify the abilities of your entire team and empower them to achieve your shared vision.

Ronald Reagan reached the White House largely on the strength of his optimistic character. "In 1980," wrote Kati Marton in *Hidden Power*, "Reagan had the perfect foil in Jimmy Carter. In politics, optimists always trump pessimists .... Reagan had a winning temperament."[17]

Jimmy Carter, by contrast, had become identified with a July 15, 1979, speech he gave from the Oval Office—which became known as the "malaise" speech (though he never actually used that word in the day's comments). In that speech, President Carter spoke of "a crisis of confidence" in the nation:

> The erosion of our confidence in the future is threatening to destroy the social and the political fabric of America. . . .
>
> The symptoms of this crisis of the American spirit are all around us. For the first time in the history of our country, a majority of our people believe that the next five years will be worse than the past five years. Two-thirds of our people do not even vote. The productivity of American workers is actually dropping, and the willingness of Americans to save for the future has fallen below that of all other people in the Western world.
>
> This is not a message of happiness or reassurance, but it is the truth and it is a warning. . . .
>
> We believed that our Nation's resources were limitless until 1973, when we had to face a growing dependence on foreign oil. . . .
>
> I'm asking you, for your good and for your Nation's security, to take no unnecessary trips, to use carpools or public transportation whenever you can, to park your car one extra day per week, to obey the speed limit, and to set your thermostats to save fuel.[18]

When you boil it all down, President Carter was telling his fellow Americans, in effect, "The fabric of our nation is unraveling and the American people are to blame. Face it, our resources are dwindling, and we need to tighten our belts, park our cars, and lower our thermostats." It was a dark and pessimistic message. Reagan, with his irrepressible charm and sunny optimism, couldn't have asked for a more perfect opponent.

Warren Bennis, in his book *On Becoming a Leader*, offers this commentary on the Carter/Reagan contrast:

> Optimism and hope provide choices. The opposite of hope is despair, and when we despair, it is because we feel there are no choices. President Carter was done in by his "malaise" speech. He thought he was getting real, but we thought he was leaving us with no choice but despair. The leader's world view is always contagious. Carter depressed us; Reagan, whatever his other flaws, gave us hope.[19]

A person's level of optimism is one of the most potent predictors of future achievement. Every great accomplishment in this world was achieved by optimists. If you look at the lives of great achievers—from Christopher Columbus to Henry Ford to Thomas Edison to Walt Disney to Ronald Reagan—you'll find that the most notable common denominator was an attitude of optimism. After all, have you ever seen a statue in honor of a pessimist? Harry Truman put it this way: "I have never seen pessimists make anything work, or contribute anything of lasting value. It takes idealists to make the world work."[20]

There are logical, cause-and-effect reasons why optimists are more likely to achieve their vision and goals:

- Optimists are more decisive because they believe their decisions will likely turn out right.
- Optimists are more determined and persistent because they believe problems are temporary and setbacks can be overcome.
- Optimists don't waste time on bitterness and resentment because they don't take rejection personally.

- Optimists set higher goals because they believe in themselves.
- Optimists are resilient and bounce back from adversity.
- Optimists adjust to change by welcoming new challenges and experiences.
- Optimists have confidence in their ability to influence their circumstances, so they are motivated to work longer and try harder.
- Optimists are healthier (an optimistic mind-set is good for the heart, digestion, and immune system), so they take fewer days off from work.
- Optimists love their work.

We all come into this world with different personalities, different DNA, different upbringing, different experiences, different advantages and disadvantages; but to become effective leaders, we must all become communicators of optimism. Where others see obstacles, we must train ourselves to see opportunities.

Rich DeVos is a co-owner of the Orlando Magic, and he's my mentor, coach, and friend. After his heart transplant in 1997, Rich wrote a book called *Hope from My Heart: 10 Lessons for Life*, in which he observes:

> If you expect something to turn out badly, it probably will. Pessimism is seldom disappointed. But the same principle also works in reverse. If you expect good things to happen, they usually do! There seems to be a natural cause-and-effect relationship between optimism and success. . . .
>
> We can choose to laugh or cry, bless or curse. It's our decision: From which perspective do we want to view life? Will we look up in hope or down in despair?

> I believe in the upward look. . . . I am an
> optimist by choice as much as by nature.[21]

Optimism is a choice. It's a learnable skill, a habit of thought that we build over a lifetime. If you are not naturally optimistic, you can change the way you think. Here's my challenge to you:

Take one year of your life to study and practice becoming an optimist. Read books of positive, motivational, optimistic quotations and principles. Study the lives of great optimistic leaders. Memorize positive sayings by posting them near your bathroom mirror, your refrigerator, or on your car's dashboard. Carry optimistic quotations in your wallet.

Ask one or two trusted friends or family members to observe your behavior and call you on it every time you demonstrate a pessimistic attitude. Practice finding the optimistic perspective. Instead of grousing about problems, say, "Here's my chance to prove how resourceful I am." Instead of saying, "I can't," practice telling yourself, "I will!" Learn to see the upside where you used to see only the downside.

As a leader, focus on inspiring your troops and giving them an upbeat vision to pursue. Lift them up; don't beat them down.

One of the greatest optimists in history was Dr. Martin Luther King Jr. In May 1967, he drove to Louisville, Kentucky, with his brother Alfred and Ralph Abernathy. Arriving in Louisville, they were met by a group of white segregationists. The driver stopped the car at a corner by the white protestors, and Dr. King called out, "We've got to learn to live together as brothers."

One teenage segregationist yelled back, "I'm not your brother!" Another spat at the civil rights leader. Another hurled a rock through the open window, hitting Dr. King in the neck. The driver gunned the engine and sped off.

Dr. King wasn't seriously hurt and didn't even seem disturbed. At his next speech, he held up the rock that had struck him and told the audience what had happened. He used the rock as an object lesson in why people need to love one another, forgive one another, and live together as brothers. Dr. King added, "I am optimistic," and promised that "with bruised hands" God's people would refashion an ugly status quo into a new brotherhood of peace. A few days later, on NBC's *Meet the Press*, he insisted simply, "I think we can do it. I think we can do it."[22]

As a leader, choose optimism. Make optimism your habit, your worldview. Then communicate optimism every day of your leadership life.

4. Communicate hope.

Hope for the future is the glue that binds people together as a team, a community, or an organization. Without hope, the people perish and teams disintegrate. Whether you lead a family, a sports team, a business, a church, or a military organization, you must communicate hope. You must keep hope alive.

Ernest Shackleton had a vision of reaching the South Pole. He made five Antarctic expeditions; the most famous was his third, begun in 1914—the Imperial Trans-Antarctic Expedition aboard the *Endurance*. When Shackleton recruited his team, he said the requirements were simple: All expedition members should have good teeth, good circulation, a good temperament, and the ability to sing—or as he put it, the ability to "shout a bit with the boys."[23] Why did Shackleton want his crew to be able to carry a tune? He knew a time might come when the ability to "shout a bit with the boys" might be all they had to keep hope alive.

Endurance left London on August 1, 1914, crossed the Antarctic Circle on December 30, and headed for the Weddell Sea. Shackleton planned to put six men ashore on the Antarctic coast, and they would reach the Pole by dogsled then continue on to the opposite coast on the Ross Sea, to be picked up for the return voyage. On January 18, 1915, however, the ship was trapped by ice and couldn't be freed. The Shackleton expedition was stranded a thousand miles from inhabited land.

For months, the men survived on meager rations aboard

the icebound ship. Shackleton knew that survival was largely a matter of morale. So he had the crew keep a regular work schedule—and he made sure there was plenty of singing. They had entertainment nights aboard *Endurance*, complete with music and comedy skits. The men kept fit by playing soccer and racing dogsleds. Shackleton's lighthearted demeanor gave confidence to his crew that everything would turn out all right.

On May 1, the sun disappeared below the horizon; the night would last until September. Day after day, the ice tightened its grip on the hull of *Endurance*. From time to time, a plank would snap with a sound like a gunshot. On October 24, the ice broke through the hull and water poured through. The men removed all provisions, equipment, and lifeboats, setting them on the ice. On November 21, the ship sank from sight.

Even without a ship the crew had hope. Shackleton had a plan. Just before Christmas, he and his men set off across the ice shelf, carrying food, survival gear, and three lifeboats. They hoped to reach Paulet Island, 250 miles away. After a few weeks, however, it was clear that, at this pace, it would take more than a year to reach the island. Then set up a base called Patience Camp and, with food running low, they killed and ate the sled dogs.

On April 8, with the ice shelf becoming unstable, they launched out in the lifeboats. Threading their way between the ice floes, they made their way to rocky, uninhabited Elephant Island, arriving on April 14. The nearest human habitation was eight hundred miles away, at South Georgia Island. Shackleton chose five men, and they outfitted one boat to make the long journey. On April 24, Shackleton promised the twenty-two men he was leaving behind that he'd return with help. He gave them hope—then he and his five companions launched out to sea.

For seventeen days, the six men in their twenty-two-foot boat braved storms and fifty-foot waves. The sky was so cloudy that the navigator could take only four star readings during the journey. Several times, waves swamped the boat, and the men bailed ice water, thinking they were about to drown.

Finally, on May 18, Shackleton and his crew reached the west coast of South Georgia Island. They dismantled the lifeboats and used the heavy screws as makeshift cleats for their boots. Then they climbed the rocky spine of the island, crossing to the eastern side in thirty-six hours without sleep. They reached the Stromness whaling station on May 20.

Shackleton and his five companions were picked up by a whaling ship, the *Southern Sky*, and the whaler took them back to Elephant Island to attempt a rescue of the other twenty-two men—but a dangerous ice shelf forced *Southern Sky* to abandon the attempt. Shackleton went to South America, and launched three more attempts to rescue his men—first aboard the Uruguayan trawler *Instituto de Pesca No. 1*, then aboard the British schooner *Emma*, and finally aboard the Chilean steamer *Yelcho*.

The *Yelcho* reached Elephant Island on August 30, 1916—*sixteen months* after Shackleton had left the remaining twenty-two men on the island. As the *Yelcho* neared the coast, Shackleton counted the thin, malnourished men who waved from the shore. With tears freezing on his cheeks, he counted twenty-two gaunt figures—all alive!

From the day the Shackleton crew left England until the day of the Elephant Island rescue, almost two years and a month had passed.[24] Shackleton didn't reach the South Pole—but he kept hope alive. And he kept every man of his crew alive. He saved them with courage and ingenuity, with songs and skits, with "shouting a bit with the boys," and with words of encouragement and hope.

When everything seems hopeless, great leaders communicate hope.

Philip Yancey, one of my favorite authors, writes, "Hope gives us the power to look beyond circumstances that otherwise appear hopeless. Hope keeps hostages alive when they have no rational proof that anyone cares about their plight; it entices farmers to plant seeds in spring after three straight years of drought." Hope, he adds, is "the fuel that keeps a person going."[25]

On the night of April 4, 1968, Dr. Martin Luther King Jr., was assassinated as he stood on the balcony of a Memphis motel. At that same time, Robert F. Kennedy was flying into Indianapolis for a presidential campaign appearance in a mostly black neighborhood. Local officials told RFK about the assassination of Dr. King and advised him to cancel his appearance, saying it would be dangerous for a white man to appear before a black crowd at that moment. But Kennedy insisted on making the appearance.

He went to the neighborhood by car, stood up on the platform in the glare of the camera lights, and looked out across the crowd. The mood was upbeat and celebratory. Kennedy knew that no one in the crowd knew of the death of Dr. King. So he gave an impromptu speech—a speech that many observers consider one of the best speeches of his career:

> I have some very sad news for all of you, and I think sad news for all of our fellow citizens, and people who love peace all over the world. . . . Martin Luther King was shot and killed tonight in Memphis, Tennessee.
>
> Martin Luther King dedicated his life to love and to justice between fellow human beings. . . . In this difficult day, in this difficult time for the United States, it's perhaps well to ask what kind of a nation we are and what direction we want to move in. . . . [We] can be filled with bitterness, and with hatred, and a desire for revenge.
>
> We can move in that direction as a country, in greater polarization—black people amongst blacks, and white amongst whites, filled with hatred toward one another. Or we can make an effort, as Martin Luther King did, to understand and to comprehend, and replace that violence,

that stain of bloodshed that has spread across our land, with an effort to understand, [and with] compassion and love.

For those of you who are black and are tempted to be filled with hatred and mistrust of the injustice of such an act, against all white people, I would only say that I can also feel in my own heart the same kind of feeling. I had a member of my family killed, but he was killed by a white man.

But we have to make an effort in the United States, we have to make an effort to understand. ... What we need in the United States is not hatred; what we need in the United States is not violence and lawlessness, but is love and wisdom, and compassion toward one another, and a feeling of justice toward those who still suffer within our country, whether they be white or whether they be black.[26]

Robert Kennedy said much more that night, but the important thing to hear was the note of hope in his voice. Dr. King's life had been extinguished, but his vision had to go on. In the face of injustice, we must have hope. In the face of violence and lawlessness, we must have hope. In the face of polarization and hatred, we must love one another—and we must have hope.

Though Dr. King was gunned down, hope prevailed over despair. Two months later, Robert Kennedy himself was gunned down. Still, hope prevails. His words still ring true. Great leaders are communicators of hope.

5. Communicate to motivate and inspire.
I have been in the professional basketball business for four and a half decades, and I have never seen a team in which every player was self-motivated and self-inspired. How

refreshing it would be to have just one team, for just one season, in which everybody came fired up, full of passion, motivated to the hilt, ready to do whatever it takes to bring home a championship. But it's exceedingly rare when that happens—and that's why we need leaders who communicate motivation and inspiration.

The key to being a motivational leader is seen in the root word: *motive*. You must understand people's motives—you must understand what *moves* them—in order to motivate and inspire them. There's no shortcut, no one-size-fits-all way to motivate and inspire. Some people are motivated by a pat on the back, others by a kick in the behind. Some are inspired by having lunch with the boss, others are inspired by awards and public recognition, and others by a private word of praise or a handwritten note. Don't assume that the only thing that motivates people is money—but at the same time, be aware that money *is* a potent motivator.

When you break the issue of motivation down to its essence, you find that people are motivated and inspired by six major drives. By being aware of these six drives, you can find tangible, practical ways to motivate and inspire every individual under your leadership influence:

1. *The drive for financial security.* Everyone wants to provide for his or her family and wants to feel fairly compensated for the contribution they make to the team.
2. *The drive for acceptance and emotional security.* People want to feel accepted by their peers. They want to know they are part of a team. No one who feels like an outsider truly feels motivated and inspired.
3. *The drive for recognition and affirmation.* Everyone hungers for affirmation. When you recognize and appreciate hard work and a commitment to excellence, your people will be inspired to work even

harder to attain more recognition and affirmation.

4. *The drive for self-respect.* Everyone wants to be treated courteously and to have his or her rights respected. Many workplaces create an atmosphere that is corrosive to self-respect; by simply creating a courteous and respectful culture in your organization, you can do a lot to increase the motivation level of your people.

5. *The drive for self-expression.* Many people in your organization are creative or self-starters or simply like to be able to communicate their ideas and opinions, knowing they will be listened to. When you allow people to express themselves, you increase their level of motivation, and they will be inspired to work all the harder to turn your vision into a reality.

6. *The drive to identify with a cause greater than ourselves.* People long to be part of a great cause. They want to know they have helped make their organization, their community, or their world a little bit better. Identifying with a great cause gives meaning to life. Great causes are great motivators.

Find out which motivator (or combination of motivators) works best for each of the people on your team—then custom-design the right approach for each one. Get to know your people as individuals, and learn how to inspire them.

Former NBA coach Phil Jackson is a master motivator. He would often use statements to the media to motivate his top players. He once told the press that Shaquille O'Neal was the "focal point" of the Lakers offense. "I'm convinced," Phil later explained, "it motivates him to compete with a sense of invincibility; to be, as he likes to call himself, the MDE (Most Dominant Ever)." Of course, giving kudos to Shaq meant that Phil would also have to send a motivational message to his temperamental shooting guard, Kobe Bryant. So, days later, he made sure the sports media quoted him as saying that Kobe had reclaimed his status as "top player in the game."[27] Years earlier, shortly after he became head coach of the Chicago Bulls, Phil saw that his power forward, Horace Grant, was making a lot of mistakes on the court, and he figured out a way to motivate Grant to tighten up his game. Phil recalls, "I asked him if he minded being criticized in front of the group, and he said no. So I rode him hard in practice—thinking that my words would not only motivate Horace, but also galvanize the other players. If I was particularly harsh in my criticism, the rest of the team would rally around to give him support."[28]

At other times, Phil motivated and inspired Grant to step up his game by taking him aside and giving him a few affirming words. This was particularly important when Horace faced a tough matchup against a powerful opponent. "This is going to be a real test of your manhood, Horace," Phil would say before the game. "You're going to have to be the door that doesn't open." And that was frequently just the motivational boost Grant needed to take his game up a notch.[29]

Phil Jackson also discovered that compassion—"trying to empathize with the player and look at the situation from his point of view"—can be a powerful motivator for individuals and the entire team. Compassion not only enables individual players to feel cared for and understood, Phil observed, but "it also inspires the other players to respond in kind and be more conscious of each other's needs."[30]

He cites an example from 1990, early in his coaching career in Chicago. During a grueling playoff series against the Philadelphia 76ers, Scottie Pippen, the Bulls' starting small forward, suffered the loss of his father. He missed Game 4 to attend his dad's funeral, and was still grieving when he returned for Game 5. Jackson recalls:

> I thought it was important for the team to acknowledge what was going on with Scottie and give him support. I asked the players to form a circle around him in the locker room and recite the Lord's Prayer, as we often do on Sundays.

> "We may not be Scottie's family," I said, "but we're as close to him as anyone in his life. . . . We should tell him how much we love him and show compassion for his loss." . . . Scottie was visibly moved. That night, buoyed by his teammates, he went on a 29-point romp, as we finished off the 76ers to take the series."[31]

You can't get to know people as individuals without taking the time to talk to them one-on-one. Leaders are often so focused on leading the *group* that they fail to see their people as *individuals*. Phil Jackson made a priority of strengthening one-on-one connections with his players.

During the 1995 playoffs, Bulls small forward Toni Kukoč was troubled by reports from the battlefront in his homeland of Croatia. He had heard of artillery attacks in his hometown and worried about his parents when he couldn't reach them by phone. Phil Jackson took Toni aside and helped him work through his anxieties. His genuine concern for Kukoč enabled the two men to relate on a deeper level than a mere player-coach relationship. "Meeting with players privately," Jackson concludes, "helps me stay in touch with who they are out of uniform."[32]

I've known Phil Jackson for many years, and a number of the players he coached later wore Magic jerseys, so I got to hear from his players exactly how much they appreciated his ability to motivate and inspire. Players told me how, at Christmas and other times of the year, he'd buy books and other gifts for the players. Phil would never get fifteen copies of the same book and pass them out en masse. Instead, he'd carefully select fifteen individual books, each targeted to an individual player's personality and needs. Each gift was selected for the inspirational impact it would have on that player.

Phil always asked himself, "How can I motivate and inspire each of these players to step up to a higher level?" His eleven NBA championship rings prove he was doing something right.

Boston Celtics legend Bill Russell tells the story of being in the 1968 playoffs against the Celtics' bitterest rivals, the Philadelphia 76ers. On the brink of elimination, the Celtics were clinging to a two-point lead with twelve seconds remaining when Russell was fouled. All he had to do was make one of his two free throws and the Celtics would put the game out of reach of the 76ers. (This was in the days before three-point shots.) If Russell missed both shots, however, the 76ers would have a chance to tie and take the game to overtime.

Russell stepped to the line, launched his first attempt—and missed.

At that point, Celtics guard and team leader Sam Jones walked over to Russell, leaned close to his ear, and said something no one else could hear.

Russell launched his second shot—and made it. When time expired, the Celtics had won and escaped elimination. They went on to beat the 76ers in the Eastern Division finals, and then beat the Los Angeles Lakers in the NBA Finals, four games to two.

What did Sam Jones say that inspired Russell to make that all-important second free throw? That's what the sportswriters asked Russell after the game.

Russell grinned and explained, "Sam said, 'Flex your knees, Bill.'"

That's it? Those were Jones's words of wisdom? Flex your knees? In his book *Russell's Rules*, Bill explains what happened:

> When I shot fouls successfully, I always flexed my knees. When I missed, I was most often stiff-legged. "Flex your knees, Bill," was the inspirational word I got from him at that last, crucial moment. It was about as inspiring as a car manual, but it was the only thing I needed to hear at that moment for us to win.[33]

Effective leaders like Sam Jones communicate to motivate and inspire, saying exactly what needs to be said to achieve their goals.

6. Become a storyteller.

The greatest leaders are usually storytellers. Jesus taught the masses and mentored his disciples through stories with a purpose, called parables. Abraham Lincoln called his stories "yarns" or "tall tales." John F. Kennedy and his brother Robert were both great storytellers. So were political adversaries Ronald Reagan and Tip O'Neill. Some of our greatest business leaders, including Jack Welch and Lee Iacocca, are spellbinders with a story, as is former football coach Lou Holtz.

We are hardwired to retain stories, not PowerPoint presentations. I don't use PowerPoint myself, but I love to tell stories. I'm sure that when people walk away from my presentations, they may forget most of my bullet points and principles, but they'll remember my stories for years—and those stories pack much of the teaching wallop that I'm trying to convey. Stories reach deeper and live longer in the memory than any other form of spoken message.

Back in the 1990s, when I was working on my books *Go for the Magic* and *The Magic of Teamwork*, my editor, Janet Thoma, told me, "Save your stories, Pat. Write them down as soon as they happen and file them away by category so that you don't forget them. Then, when you need a good story for a book or a speech, you'll have them written down and ready to use." That advice changed my career as a communicator. I began saving stories from my own life, my family life, and my career. I saved stories of the many famous people I came in contact with. I saved stories I found in books and magazines. I saved stories other people told me. Today I have all of those stories at my fingertips.

Why are stories so powerful? Because they reach the emotions. Information and statistics are aimed at the logic centers of the brain, but stories go right to the human heart.

As Dale Carnegie advises, "When dealing with people, remember you are not dealing with creatures of logic, but with creatures of emotion."[34]

Philip Yancey observes that the parables of Jesus were a powerful leadership tool because they expressed profound truth in the form of everyday stories:

> A scolding woman wears down the patience of a judge. A king plunges into an ill-planned war. A group of children quarrel in the street. A man is mugged and left for dead by robbers. A single woman who loses a penny acts as if she has lost everything. There are no fanciful creatures and sinuous plots in Jesus' parables; he simply describes the life around him.
>
> The parables served Jesus' purposes perfectly. Everyone likes a good story, and Jesus' knack for storytelling held the interest of a mostly illiterate society of farmers and fishermen. Since stories are easier to remember than concepts or outlines, the parables also helped preserve his message: years later, as people reflected on what Jesus had taught, his parables came to mind in vivid detail. It is one thing to talk in abstract terms about the infinite, boundless love of God. It is quite another to tell of a man who lays down his life for friends, or of a heartsick father who scans the horizon every night for some sign of a wayward son.[35]

Jesus did most of his teaching and preaching through stories. In fact, the New Testament tells us, "Jesus spoke all these things to the crowd in parables; he did not say anything to them without using a parable."[36]

Abraham Lincoln was our "storyteller in chief" when he was in the White House. Management expert Diana McLain

Smith records, "Throughout his life, Lincoln relied on stories to make lighter sense of painful experience. An old friend from Springfield, Illinois, once said that when Lincoln told funny stories, 'he emerged from his cave of gloom and came back, like one awakened from sleep, to the world in which he lived again.'"[37]

Speaking coach Christopher Witt observes that Lincoln used stories to help him connect with audiences that were frequently hostile to his views. "Lincoln told stories not just to give his audience hope," Witt writes, "but also to amuse them and to deflate their hostility. To those who criticized him for telling so many stories, he said, 'People are more easily influenced and informed through a story than in any other way.'"[38]

Historian Doris Kearns Goodwin reveals that Lincoln's love of public speaking and storytelling goes back to his earliest years. She explains, "He would climb onto a tree stump or log that served as an impromptu stage and mesmerize his own circle of young listeners. . . . This great storytelling talent and oratorical skill would eventually constitute his stock-in-trade throughout both his legal and political careers. The passion for rendering experience into powerful language remained with Lincoln throughout his life."[39]

Lincoln's storytelling skills served him well as a lawyer, political candidate, and president. "No one could equal his never-ending stream of stories," Goodwin writes, "nor his ability to reproduce them with such contagious mirth. . . . But Lincoln's stories provided more than mere amusement. Drawn from his own experiences and the curiosities reported by others, they frequently provided maxims and proverbs that usefully connected to the lives of his listeners. Lincoln possessed an extraordinary ability to convey practical wisdom in the form of humorous tales his listeners could remember and repeat."[40]

Ronald Reagan was another excellent storyteller as president. When his son Michael appeared on my radio show, he told me, "William Clark was one of my father's closest friends and advisers throughout his career. Judge Clark once explained something about my father that I had never understood before. 'Michael,' he said, 'your dad was not just a storyteller. He spoke in parables. Even his jokes were parables. Whenever he wanted to teach an important truth, he would put it in the form of a story.'

"What an insight! I had lived with my father all those years and had never seen that before. Dad's stories were always funny and entertaining—but if you really thought about what he was saying, you could always find a deeper truth to apply to your life.

"During the Cold War, Dad liked to joke about life in the Soviet Union. One of his favorites went like this: In the Soviet Union, there was a ten-year wait to buy a car, and only one out of seven Soviet families could afford a car. They had to go through a long process and a lot of paperwork, and they had to pay the entire amount in advance. One Soviet citizen saved up his money and went to the government showroom and plunked down the cash. The official in charge said, 'Come back in ten years, comrade, and you can pick up your car.' The citizen said, 'Morning or afternoon?' And the government man said, 'Ten years from now, what difference does it make?' The citizen said, 'The plumber's coming in the morning.'

"Now, that's a funny story with a serious point. My father was giving us an insight into life in the Soviet Union. It's about the harshness of the Communist system, and how people have to put up with shortages, long waits, and red tape—but he said it in a subtle way, without hitting you over the head with it. If you just laughed at his joke, that's fine. But if you listened closely, Dad always gave you plenty to think about."

Let me share with you a few tips on storytelling I've learned over the years:

1. *Be brief.* Avoid "shaggy dog" stories. Long stories can cause attention to wander, and people may miss important details—and miss your point.

2. *Be vivid.* Use descriptive language, gestures, and facial expressions, and vary your tone of voice to make the story come alive. Lowering your voice can have even more dramatic power than shouting. As you speak more softly, you'll see your audience lean in and listen more intently.

3. *Use action.* Move around the stage or platform as you tell your story. Use your hands, use your arms. Make big, over-the-top gestures to enliven your tale.

4. *Talk—never read.* Reading a story is deadly. Instead, *become* your story. Act it out! Tell it with passion and enthusiasm.

5. *Personalize your stories.* Let your audience into your life. They will feel closer to you if you treat them as insiders and confidantes.

6. *Get to the point.* Every story you tell should have a clear point, a message, a principle to illustrate. Don't just toss in a story because you like it; make sure the story supports your message.

7. *Identify with your audience.* Tell stories about "Everyman," stories that resonate with the lives of your listeners.

In John Steinbeck's most ambitious novel, *East of Eden,* one of his characters, Lee the cook, offers this pearl of storytelling wisdom: "If a story is not about the hearer, he will not listen. And I here make a rule—a great and interesting story is about everyone or it will not last. The strange and foreign is not interesting—only the deeply personal and familiar."[41]

Stories entertain, instruct, provoke thought, and make us remember great insights long after the speech is forgotten. That's the power of storytelling. Whenever you get up to give a speech, you can never go wrong by saying, "Let me tell you a story. . . ."

A QUICK-START GUIDE TO EFFECTIVE PUBLIC SPEAKING

I'm convinced that practically anyone can become a public speaker. Why? Because of my own personal experience. Today I give at least 150 speeches a year, plus I host three weekly radio talk shows and give an untold number of TV and radio interviews every year. But when I look back to the beginning of my "speaking career," back in Miss Barbara Bullard's ninth-grade English class, I'm astounded to realize that I actually talk to audiences for a living.

Miss Bullard permitted each of us to use one three-by-five note card for a three-minute speech. I wrote out my entire speech word for word on both sides of my three-by-five card in letters so small a bug would need reading glasses to decipher it. When Miss Bullard called my name, I shuffled to the front of the class, sweating from every pore, my knees knocking like castanets. My voice was a post-pubescent yodel as I began to speak.

About a minute into my talk, the tiny handwriting on the card seemed to blur, and I lost my place. Petrified, I stopped and stood in front of my classmates, defeated and humiliated. Finally, I shuffled back to my desk and promised myself I would never speak in public again.

After class, Miss Bullard called me to her desk and gave me a pep talk. "Patrick," she said, "you can master this skill. Let me show you a better note system." I eventually made it through her class with a charitable C-minus.

I went through high school and half of my college career feeling terrified of public speaking. Then, during my junior year at Wake Forest University, something happened to me. To this day, I'm not sure what finally yanked me out of my turtle shell of shyness. I think it had something to do with my admiration for sports announcers. As a boy, I had daydreamed of a career in announcing. So I went to the campus radio station and asked Dr. Julian Burroughs, the station manager, for a chance to sit behind the microphone. He let me broadcast freshman basketball games and host a sports talk show.

I conducted interviews, lugging a big Ampex reel-to-reel tape recorder around the campus. I talked to baseball greats Ted Williams, Roger Maris, Jim Gentile, and Harmon Killebrew, golf legend Arnold Palmer, Bill Sharman of the Boston Celtics, and chapel speaker and evangelist Billy Graham (who is a big sports fan and gave me a great interview about baseball). In the process, my confidence soared—and I discovered that it's *fun* to be a public speaker. I continued taking speech classes at Wake Forest and often thought, *If Miss Bullard could see me now!*

In *The Book of Lists*, David Wallechinsky and Amy Wallace claim that the worst fear that afflicts most people is not the fear of death but the fear of public speaking. That's why comedian Jerry Seinfeld once remarked, "If you go to a funeral, you're better off in the casket than doing the eulogy." But I'm living proof that *anyone* can overcome the fear of public speaking. You can become confident, poised, and fully in charge as a public speaker. Here's my quick-start guide to effective communicating:

1. Get rid of your notes.
You may be thinking, "How can I give a talk without notes? Do you expect me to memorize my speech word for word?" No way! Audiences don't want to hear a recitation by rote. They want to hear your ideas, your convictions, and your insights expressed with passion and energy. Every time you speak, it should feel spontaneous, as if you are speaking those words for the very first time.

Passion and spontaneity don't come from memorization. Enthusiasm doesn't come from a stack of three-by-five cards. When you deliver your message to the audience, you have to feel it from the heart. And the key to delivering a powerful, heartfelt speech is to have what I call a "signature speech," a speech that you have handcrafted and rehearsed a dozen or a hundred times, a speech that expresses the core passion of your life.

Your signature speech should be long enough to fill forty to fifty minutes but flexible enough that you can edit on the fly and deliver the essence of the speech in fifteen or twenty minutes. It should be filled with fresh, compelling ideas and stories that are unique to you. Hone it, refine it, nail it to the wall, make it 100 percent yours. Practice it until you could deliver it in your sleep—or until you could deliver it *without notes* at a moment's notice.

Then go out and deliver it at every opportunity. Volunteer to speak at civic clubs, at houses of worship, at supermarket openings. Practice condensing it or stretching it out, depending on the time you are allotted. Make sure this is a message that burns within you so you can deliver it with passion and enthusiasm every time.

You'll find it won't take long before you gain the confidence to leave the "security blanket" of your notes and your lectern. You'll feel capable of launching out and talking for thirty, forty, or even sixty minutes without notes and *without fear*.

2. Study the art of public speaking.
In almost every community, you'll find a local chapter of Toastmasters or the National Speakers Association. Join a speakers club or hire a speech coach. Take a speaking class at your local community college.

The two most important courses I took when I was at Wake Forest were a pair of electives outside of my major. They were Introduction to Speech and Oral Interpretation of Literature, both taught by Professor James Walton. Professor Walton was a drama instructor, and he showed us a lot of exercises from the acting world that helped us overcome our fears and inhibitions. Those two courses changed the direction of my leadership career.

There are many good books available on public speaking—and may I humbly add that I've written two of them: *Turn Boring Orations into Standing Ovations* (Advantage Inspirational, 2005), cowritten with my wife, Ruth, and

The Ultimate Handbook of Effective, Persuasive Speaking for Coaches and Leaders (Coaches Choice, 2011). So do what I did: Study the craft of public speaking. Take every opportunity to improve your skills and gain speaking experience.

3. Organize and prepare your speech with care.

Craft a speech that is well-structured and clearly organized so that your audience can take good notes. Ask yourself, "What is my reason for speaking? What is my message? Why should people want to hear my talk?" Create a message that expresses your core values and your passion. Practice that speech again and again. Learn it, own it, and deliver it at every opportunity.

Always start your speech with a "grand opening," an attention getter. From the moment you open your mouth to speak, you have about fifteen seconds to capture your audience. If you haven't won them over in a quarter of a minute, you're in for a difficult speech. Never open a speech with meaningless chatter—"Thanks for inviting me. So good to be here. How is everybody today?" Instead, jump right into your speech with an opening that electrifies your audience.

Then keep gripping their emotions, keep riveting their attention, keep telling powerful stories. Organize your speech so that it gives your audience a white-knuckle ride from start to finish.

4. Learn to communicate with passion and emotion.

Leaders don't *dump* information on an audience. They fire them up with enthusiasm. They persuade people to a cause. Every time you speak, you should speak to convince, to excite, to motivate, to persuade—and that means you must communicate with both passion and emotion.

A few years ago, I attended a dinner held before the annual NBA lottery drawing. I sat at a table with Jay Bilas, the ESPN college broadcaster who had been in Mike Krzyzewski's first recruiting class at Duke in the early 1980s. As we talked,

I asked Jay, "What's your most vivid memory of Coach K?"

"During my freshman year," Jay said, "we finished practice. We had a big game the next night, so Coach K was talking to us before we went to the locker room. He was there in his blue Duke coaching shorts and golf shirt. As he talked to us about the upcoming game, he was all pumped up and excited. And as I looked at him, I noticed there were goose bumps all over his legs and arms and neck, everywhere I looked. He was just a mass of goose bumps!"

Understand, Jay was recalling a practice he had witnessed twenty-five years earlier—and the image was so vivid, so drenched in emotion, that it stuck with him through those years. His most vivid memory of Mike Krzyzewski: goose bumps! That's an image of a coach who communicates passion to his team.

Michael Dell, founder of Dell Computers and the youngest person ever to lead a Fortune 500 company, once told *Entrepreneur* magazine that, even after a company has a good business strategy in place, "the real challenge is to get people excited about what you're doing. A lot of businesses get off track because they don't communicate an excitement about being part of a winning team that can achieve big goals."[42]

5. Remember that the greatest impact we make as communicators comes from our nonverbal communication.

Landmark studies conducted by UCLA psychology professor Albert Mehrabian found that 38 percent of the impact and impression a speaker makes on an audience comes from tone of voice, 55 percent comes from nonverbal communication (facial expression, gestures, body language), and only 7 percent from the words that are spoken. Mehrabian refers to these findings as the "7–38–55 Rule."[43] Words, of course, are profoundly important to us as leaders and communicators. Our words carry the weight of the message we want our followers to understand and internalize. But if we want our words to make an impression on our audience, we must be aware of the nonverbal aspects of our communication.

If I stand in front of an audience and say, "I'm pumped up and excited about my vision for this team," those words amount to 7 percent of the impression I make. If my tone of voice is flat and listless, if my face is expressionless, if my eyes are lackluster, if my arms hang limp at my sides, if my feet are rooted to the floor, then the other 93 percent of my speech (38 percent auditory and 55 percent visual) will totally cancel out my words.

My tone of voice and my face and body all have to work together with my words to make a powerful impression on the audience. The nonverbal cues must reinforce the words I speak—or those nonverbal cues will undermine my message.

One of the most important forms of nonverbal communication is eye contact—looking people in the eye when you talk to them. Good eye contact is important whether you are communicating one-on-one or to an audience of thousands. When you speak before an audience, don't just sweep the room with your eyes. Find specific faces in the crowd and focus on each of those faces for three to five seconds as you speak. You'll see that those people will respond, smile, nod, and give you feedback through their eyes. Good eye communication will help you make a real emotional connection with your audience.

Dr. Jack Ramsay is a retired basketball coach and sports broadcaster. He coached the Portland Trail Blazers to an NBA championship in 1976–77. In *Dr. Jack's Leadership Lessons*, he writes:

> Eye-to-eye contact is the first and strongest bond that establishes good communication between two people. If the eyes are "the windows of the soul," as someone once wrote, then eye contact enables two people to look into the very depths of each other's being.
>
> To that end, I made it a practice to speak to every player on my team each day that we met,

which was almost every day during the season. I tried to make eye contact with them as well.[44]

He goes on to tell the story of when Moses Malone joined the Trail Blazers at training camp before the 1976–77 season. Dr. Jack greeted Moses and told him he believed Moses would make an enormous contribution to the team. Moses listened and nodded—but he wouldn't look Dr. Jack in the eye.

"Moses," Ramsay said, "when I talk to someone, I always look him in the eye. I'd like it if you'd do the same with me."

Still looking away, Moses replied, "I can't look nobody in the eye. I've never been able to do that."

"Let's try each day to do it, all right?"

Moses tried to look Dr. Jack in the eye, but he couldn't hold it. "I'll try," he said.

In the end, Moses Malone left the Trail Blazers because of salary issues, but in the years since then, Dr. Jack has often crossed paths with him. "Whenever I see him," Jack says, "I always go up to him, greet him with a handshake, and look him in the eye. We still laugh about it, but he looks back now—right into my eyes."[45]

6. Speak with authority.

A leader must inspire confidence. Great leaders speak with authority. This is not to say a leader should be pompous, arrogant, or conceited. You should never treat followers or players with disrespect or abuse. To speak with authority is to speak with boldness and conviction. To speak with timidity or uncertainty is to undermine your own leadership position. As the Bible tells us, "If the trumpet does not sound a clear call, who will get ready for battle?"[46]

General George S. Patton was one of America's great military leaders during World Wars I and II. As commander of the US Third Army in 1944, Patton led his troops farther, liberated more territory in less time, and captured more enemy prisoners than any other military leader in history. His advice to leaders: *Speak with authority.*

"I can tell a commander by the way he speaks," he once said. "He does not have to swear as much as I do, but he has to speak so that no one will refuse to follow his order. Certain words will make you sound like a staff officer and not a commander. A good commander will never express an opinion! A commander knows! No one cares what your opinion is! Never use the words, 'In my opinion, I believe, I think, or I guess,' and never say, 'I don't think!' Every man who hears you speak must know what you want. You can be wrong, but never be in doubt when you speak! Any doubt or fear in your voice and the troops can feel it. Another thing: Never give a command in a sitting position unless you are on a horse or on top of a tank!"[47]

That's good advice for any leader in any field of endeavor.

7. Practice active listening.

Don't just say what you intend to say. Make sure that people hear your message and understand it. Watch for nonverbal cues that indicate people are confused or not buying into your message. After you speak, ask questions. Ask people to repeat your message back to you in their own words. If there are miscommunications or misunderstandings, correct them.

8. Connect with listeners through stories and humor.

Audiences love a good story, they love to laugh—and yes, sometimes they even love to cry. So tug at your listeners' emotions—get them laughing, get them crying, and keep them emotionally engaged from start to finish.

9. Finish strong!

A weak ending can ruin an otherwise great speech. Your speech should motivate your audience to action, so always make it clear what action you expect from your audience. Always ask for a response—and be specific.

Close your speech with a powerful story or statement

that grabs your hearers' emotions. Make sure your ending brings them to their feet for a standing ovation.

10. Be original.
As William Safire once quipped, "Avoid clichés like the plague." Find new and inventive ways of saying things. Make an effort to expunge tired clichés from your communication. Here are a few examples of phrases that have overstayed their welcome in the English language: Kicking the can down the road. At the end of the day. Thinking outside the box. Giving 110 percent. Low-hanging fruit. Going forward. Pushing the envelope. Take it to the next level. Let's bring our A game. Scalable. Twenty-four/seven. It is what it is. The bottom line. The eight hundred pound gorilla. Circle back. Putting lipstick on a pig. Let's effort this. The elephant in the room. The perfect storm. Throwing him under the bus. Upsell. Herding cats. No-brainer. Under the radar. Move the needle. Just my two cents' worth.

Here's my challenge to you: Find an original way to express each of those thoughts. Work those new phrases into your conversations and speeches, and see if they catch on. You might become one of the great phrasemakers of the twenty-first century!

11. Promote the free flow of information.
Be honest and candid. When you give your team the facts, you help to eliminate fear and uncertainty. If there's bad news, make sure your people hear it from you first—not through an e-mail or a "tweet" or the office grapevine, but from your own lips. Bad news does not improve with age. As a leader, be a truth teller. Your people will appreciate it when you level with them, and they'll respect you and work all the harder to turn your vision into reality.

12. Practice, practice, practice.
Practice delivering your signature speech. Practice eliminating

fillers like "uh" and "you know" from your speaking vocabulary. As you rehearse, take note of any parts of the speech that seem to drag or that simply don't work, and revise as necessary. Practice delivering your speech with a timer, and make sure you allow time for questions and interruptions. Practice delivering your speech in front of a video camera; then watch the playback and learn how to improve your performance.

Practice delivering extemporaneous remarks. You have probably marveled at how some leaders seem to be masters of the improvised remark. If you knew the truth, however, you'd probably be even more amazed at how many times they had to rehearse that "off-the-cuff" remark in order to appear so "spontaneous."

Charles P. Garcia is a venture capitalist and CEO of Garcia Trujillo LLC. He served as one of fourteen White House Fellows at the end of the Reagan administration, and also served in the US Air Force. In *Leadership Lessons of the White House Fellows*, Garcia tells of a conversation he had with General Colin Powell about communication. The general explained that he learned public speaking at infantry school at Fort Benning, Georgia. He started by taking a three-week course in public speaking that the army offered so that he could train lieutenants who were shipping out to Vietnam.

"That's where I got my basic training," General Powell recalled. "As I went through the rest of my career, I was constantly being pressed to communicate. I learned what works and what doesn't work. I learned how to use stories and gestures, how to put a simple message together, and how to take complex issues and break them down in ways that average people can understand. You can't be afraid to stand up and speak in front of people, because that's how you learn. You'll stumble and you'll mumble, but you'll gain confidence and you'll do fine in due course. In my early years, I really bombed on a few presentations, but I learned."[48]

THE POWER TO SPEAK IS THE POWER TO LEAD

My friend Richard E. Lapchick has been called "the Social Conscience of Sports." He believes that sports have a role to play in solving some of the great social problems in our society. Richard is chairman of the DeVos Sport Business Management Program at the University of Central Florida and the author of many books. He's also a compelling public speaker. He told me he discovered his ability to communicate with an audience while in high school.

During the summer after his ninth grade year, he traveled in Europe. One of his most sobering experiences was a visit to Dachau, once a Nazi concentration camp, now a memorial to those who died in the Holocaust. During that time, he also thought about the impact that numerous civil rights leaders were having on society—people like Martin Luther King Jr., Cesar Chavez, and Robert F. Kennedy.

At the end of Richard's senior year, in 1963, school officials asked him to deliver the salutatorian address at commencement. All he had to do was speak for two or three minutes and greet the graduates and their families. "But," he told me, "I decided to do something more memorable.

"I talked about racism and the civil rights movement, and how the races could work together using the model of sports. My dad [former Celtics center Joe Lapchick] coached basketball, and my friend Leroy Ellis played for him. Leroy was a six-foot-eleven-inch All-America center, and he attended the commencement.

"I gave my talk, and the audience wasn't sure how to react until Leroy rose up above the crowd, giving me a standing ovation. Seconds later, the rest of the audience joined him on their feet, clapping. At that moment, I understood that the power to speak is the power to influence—and the power to lead."

Richard Lapchick is on a leadership mission. He's a leader and a communicator. Like Abraham Lincoln, Martin Luther King Jr., Ronald Reagan, Winston Churchill, John Wooden, Vince Lombardi, Phil Jackson, Dr. Jack Ramsay, and Ernest

Shackleton, he uses the power of the spoken word to teach, motivate, inspire, communicate optimism, keep hope alive, and promote harmony and healing.

Great leaders change the world through the power of their words.

3

THE THIRD SIDE OF LEADERSHIP:
PEOPLE SKILLS

In 1999, our Magic organization founded a WNBA team, the Orlando Miracle. The team's first coach, Carolyn Peck, started as an assistant to the great Pat Summitt at the University of Tennessee. (Carolyn is now a basketball analyst for ESPN.) I asked Carolyn what she learned about coaching from Pat Summitt.

The statuesque, six-foot-four-inch Ms. Peck (who played center for Vanderbilt during her college career) replied, "Pat Summitt taught me that you've got to love your team."

It's true. Excellent leaders have a heart for people. They care about people. They have empathy and compassion for the ones they lead. To be a great leader, you have to love people.

Eddie Robinson was the longtime football coach at Grambling State University. He started coaching at Grambling in 1941, and he coached there for fifty-six years. In his auto-biography, *Never Before, Never Again*, he writes, "You can't coach a person unless you love him. I loved these guys and looked at them as though they were the ones I wanted to marry my daughter."[1]

Coach Robinson's writing partner on that book was my friend Richard Lapchick. When Eddie Robinson died in 2007 at age eighty-eight, Richard attended the funeral, along with about ninety-six hundred other people. An additional two thousand people came for the funeral but could not get inside the Assembly Center. That kind of turnout says a lot about Coach Robinson—especially when you consider that it's not easy to get to the Grambling State campus. You don't just drop in on your way to someplace else. You have to fly to New Orleans or Shreveport, rent a car, and take a two-lane road to get there. It's not an easy trip—yet nearly twelve thousand people made the trek to pay their respects.

Richard told me that, at one point, Willie Davis (who had played for Coach Robinson before going on to a Hall of Fame career with the Green Bay Packers) stood and asked all of Coach Robinson's former players to stand. An estimated twenty-four hundred men stood up. Many were elderly, having played for him early in his coaching career. They had come from all across the country.

One of Coach Robinson's former players in attendance was James "Shack" Harris, now a senior personnel executive for the Detroit Lions. Drafted by the Buffalo Bills in 1969, Harris was the first black quarterback in the NFL. "Coach Robinson promised my mother I'd go to church every Sunday and get a degree," Harris said at the funeral. "He promised me that in four years I'd get the chance to be a pro quarterback. He was true to his word."[2]

Another attendee was Hall of Fame NFL cornerback Willie Brown, now on the coaching staff of the Oakland Raiders. "I loved the man," Brown told his fellow mourners. "He made us understand that life is not about you; it's about others. If I had to choose one person in the world to pack my parachute, it would be Coach Robinson. His legacy will never die."[3]

Richard Lapchick memorialized Eddie Robinson as a black man who was never bitter about the racial injustice he endured. "He loved America," Richard said, "the same America that wouldn't let him buy a ticket to an LSU game for him and his son, but let him lie in state in the state's capitol."[4]

Coach Robinson affected literally thousands of lives

because he cared about other people. The great lesson of Eddie Robinson's life is that you can't lead people unless you love them. He loved people—and they truly loved him in return.

IF THEY KNOW YOU CARE, THEY'LL RUN THROUGH WALLS

Coach John Wooden was in his nineties when I was writing *How to Be Like Coach Wooden*, the first of two books I wrote about his life and leadership philosophy (the second was *Coach Wooden: The 7 Principles That Shaped His Life and Will Change Yours*). He graciously allowed me into his life to soak up his wisdom through hours of unforgettable conversation. On a number of evenings, I picked him up at his Encino, California, home, took him to the Valley Inn (his favorite dining establishment), and we'd share a meal together. Then we'd go back to his condo, and he'd recite his latest poem while the Mills Brothers sang close harmony on his old-fashioned record player.

That's right—Coach didn't listen to music from CDs or MP3s. Nothing but velvety smooth vinyl music for him. His apartment appeared as if it were frozen in time in 1985, the year his beloved wife, Nell, passed away—except for the late-model digital answering machine by his phone. The light on that machine was always blinking, signaling calls to be returned. Coach Wooden told me he was always getting calls from former players. This was in 2005, so Coach had been retired for thirty years. These players who were calling him might have played for him anywhere from 1948 to 1975—so they were getting on in years themselves. Why did Coach's former players care enough to check in with him after all those years? Clearly, their affection for him went deeper than championship banners hanging in Pauley Pavilion or trophies in the UCLA trophy case. These players loved Coach Wooden because he had always loved them.

Another great leader who earned this kind of love from his players is Dean Smith, whose legendary thirty-six-year tenure at the University of North Carolina at Chapel Hill stretched from 1961 to 1997. A decade and a half after his retirement, he can still tell you what almost every one of his former players is doing today—from stars like Michael Jordan, James Worthy, and Billy Cunningham to the guys at the end of the bench. He loved every one of his players, and he knew all about their families, how they were doing in their studies, their plans and dreams, everything. Even today, Dean Smith still keeps up with his former players, their children and—yes—their grandchildren. He remembers their parents, because he once sat in their living rooms, recruiting their sons to his team. Dean Smith doesn't keep up with them because he *has* to. He *chooses* to care, even in retirement, because he genuinely loves his players.

Then there's football coach Dick Vermeil. He coached at every level, from high school to college to the NFL. Dick took a lot of ribbing in the media because he's a tough-guy coach with a tender heart—a coach who cries at the drop of a hat. I got to know Dick in Philadelphia when I was the general manager of the 76ers and he was head coach of the Philadelphia Eagles. His office at Veterans Stadium was right around the bend from our facility. Ron Jaworski, who quarterbacked for Dick Vermeil during the Eagles' heyday, once told me, "If you ever played for Dick Vermeil, you'd better count on getting phone calls from him for the rest of your life. He'll usually call you around dinner time, and he'll be calling to see how you're doing."

Bill Bergey, the great Eagles linebacker of the 1970s, told me, "My wife and I invited Dick and his wife down to our home in Wilmington, Delaware. We had a lovely meal together. We broke out a bottle of wine, and Dick proposed a toast to us. And right in middle of the toast, Dick started to cry. He said, 'In all my years of coaching, this is the first time a player has ever done this for me.' After all these years, I still get a call from Dick every Christmas Day."

Broadcaster Randy Cross, who played for Dick Vermeil at UCLA before his long NFL career with the 49ers, told me, "I still get a card every Christmas from Dick and Carol Vermeil—and so does my mother. It's been decades since he met her when he was recruiting me for UCLA. I hope Coach knows he doesn't have to recruit me anymore. My eligibility is up."

In 2005, Vermeil announced his retirement as head coach of the Kansas City Chiefs, bringing his coaching career to a close. The media reported that, during the press conference announcing his retirement, he broke down and cried eight times in one hour. Sportswriter Rick Reilly has observed that Dick Vermeil "will bawl at the retirement of a blocking sled. . . . The man has the emotional stability of Judy Garland. Sometimes, Vermeil will bring a player into his office to cut him, and they'll *both* come out crying."[5]

That's what happens when a leader truly cares about the people he leads. To him, they're not just chess pieces on the board to help him win games. They are complex human beings with needs and problems, families and relationships, hopes and dreams. Great leaders love the people they lead.

I once asked Seth Greenberg, the basketball coach at Virginia Tech, "How do you get players to play hard for you?"

"Oh, that's not hard at all," he said.

"It's not?" I said, surprised. "I would think that would be the hardest part of coaching."

"Not at all," he said. "If you care about your players as human beings, if they know you *really* care, believe me, they'll play hard for you. In fact, they'll run through walls for you."

If you want to achieve your vision, you have to love your people. This principle holds true whether you're coaching a sports team, managing a company, pastoring a church, or commanding an army.

LOVE IS A LEARNED SKILL

General Tommy Franks headed the United States Central Command and commanded combined military operations in the Middle East following the 9/11 attacks in 2001. I had the privilege of interviewing General Franks by telephone shortly after his retirement in 2003. As we talked, I told the general that my son David was a marine who saw combat during Operation Iraqi Freedom, the 2003 invasion of Iraq.

There was a quaver of emotion in General Franks's voice as he said, "Tell your son that someone else loves him besides you." I proudly passed that message along to David—a message from a military leader who loves his troops.

I've seen this same principle at work in the business world: *If you lead 'em, you've got to love 'em.* In August 1997, we had an RDV Sports meeting in Grand Rapids, Michigan. Owner Rich DeVos, still recovering in London from his heart transplant, joined the meeting via teleconferencing. Even though he was "present" only as a face on a big-screen TV, his warm and genial personality dominated the meeting.

The first order of business was the need to downsize the Magic Fan Attic team store. Sixteen jobs had to be eliminated. We debated and discussed the issue for twenty minutes or so. Finally, Rich said, "This funeral has gone on long enough. It's time for the burial. Now, tell me—what happens to those sixteen employees? I want them taken care of. Either relocate them in the organization, or give them good severance checks or help them find jobs, but I want them taken care of, understood?"

We all understood. Rich didn't know any of those sixteen people, but he cared about them because they were part of his team. He loved them and had compassion for them. Love is the number one people skill every leader should have.

At this point, you might be saying, "Come on, Pat! Are you trying to tell me that loving your people is a learned skill?" Yes, that's exactly what I'm saying. Love is a people skill. It's a choice you make. It's an action you take.

"But," you may ask, "doesn't love have to come from the heart?"

No. The kind of love I'm talking about doesn't necessarily come from the emotions, though feelings are often involved. This love comes essentially from the will—from the decision-making side. And because it's a skill, you can learn it, you can improve at it, you can become better and better at loving the ones you lead.

As you get better and better at loving your players, you'll

probably find (as Dick Vermeil did) that the decision to love is usually followed by some very powerful emotions. But the *decision* comes first.

The ancient Greeks had four different words for four different kinds of love. The particular form of love I'm talking about here—love that is a voluntary and deliberate choice—is a love the ancient Greeks called *agape* (pronounced ah-GAH-pay). Agape love is a deliberate commitment to love even when the object of that love is neither lovely nor lovable. That means you've got to agape love your players (your troops, your employees, your congregation) even when they mess up, break rules, lose games, and break your heart. You have to stick with your decision to love your players even when your emotions are roiling with anger, hurt, and disappointment.

You forgive the unforgivable. You choose to say yes when your emotions say no. You love regardless of political differences, language differences, cultural differences, religious differences, or sexual orientation. It doesn't mean you don't sometimes have to sever a connection. You have to maintain discipline and enforce the rules. Sometimes the most loving thing you can do for someone is to be firm and tough in administering consequences for bad actions. But when you choose to love your players, even when you have to cut a player from the team, you can still love that player and seek the best for him or her.

James Kouzes and Barry Posner, authors of *The Leadership Challenge*, state it well: "Love is the soul of leadership. Love is what sustains people along the arduous journey to the summit of any mountain. Love is the source of the leader's courage. Leaders are in love: in love with leading, in love with their organizations' products and services, and in love with people."[6]

Swen Nater was a six-foot-eleven-inch center at UCLA who helped Coach John Wooden win two NCAA titles in the early 1970s. Swen told me that Coach Wooden once told his former players, "I didn't *like* you all the same, but I tried to *love* you all the same." Coach was talking about agape love, rooted in the will, not in feelings.

In 2002, when Jon Gruden took over as head coach of the Tampa Bay Buccaneers, he knew he had a tough assignment. The players had enormous affection for their previous coach, Tony Dungy, and many were bitter about the way Dungy had been fired and replaced. Gruden knew from the start it wouldn't be easy to build a relationship with his new team—but he forged that relationship. . .with love.

Defensive tackle Warren Sapp spoke for the team when he said that Gruden "will touch every guy with a thirty-second speech. He'll touch every guy in the room. That's just something special about him. He's got us feeling special about ourselves. Every day, he's telling us that he loves us. That's something a little strange, telling fifty-eight men that you love them. But we know that he does, and we love him, too. So we just want to go out and kill for him."[7]

Legendary NFL coach Vince Lombardi understood the power of love. His son, Vince Lombardi Jr., writes, "When we hear Jesus' prescription to 'love one another,' we accept that readily. But when Vince Lombardi says the same thing, we get a little uncomfortable. What's a rough, tough football coach doing talking about soft and unexpected things like 'love'?" Coach Lombardi himself put it this way: "When those tough sportswriters asked me what made the Packers click, I said, 'Love.' It was the kind [of love] that means loyalty, teamwork, respecting the dignity of another—heart power, not hate power."[8]

Former Chrysler CEO Lee Iacocca, in his autobiography, recounts a conversation he once had during a private dinner with Vince Lombardi. When Iacocca asked Lombardi his formula for success, Lombardi replied: "If you're going to play together as a team, you've got to care for one another. You've got to *love* each other. Each player has to be thinking about the next guy and saying to himself: 'If I don't block that man, Paul is going to get his legs broken. I have to do my job well in order that he can do his.' . . . Most people call it team spirit. When the players are imbued with that special feeling, you know you've got yourself a winning team."[9]

The love of a leader is no less important in the business world. Herb Kelleher, former CEO of Southwest Airlines, was famed for his unabashed advocacy of love when he ran the company. "We'd rather have a company run by love, not fear," he once said. Lorin Woolfe, a leadership specialist at the American Management Association, points out that Kelleher's airline "flies out of Dallas' Love Field, its stock exchange symbol is 'LUV,' the company paper is called *Luv Lines*, and its twentieth anniversary slogan was 'Twenty Years of Loving You.' . . . Ask the employees. Says one, 'Herb loves us. We love Herb. We love one another. We love the company. . . . The primary beneficiaries of our collective caring [are] the passengers.'"[10]

Love is a people skill—one of the most vital skills a leader can have.

WHAT ARE PEOPLE SKILLS?

A few years ago, I had a conversation with Howard Schultz, the man who bought a three-coffeehouse chain in 1987 and expanded it into the Starbucks coffee empire. I asked him, "In a company of that size, where do leaders come from?"

"Our leaders come from within," he said. "We're opening three stores a day, and we've got to promote from within. You can't run a Starbucks store unless you're steeped in the Starbucks culture."

"So how do you spot leadership talent in your organization? How do you know if someone is ready to lead?"

"People skills," he answered instantly. "In order to be a leader at Starbucks, you've got to have people skills. Some people think we're in the coffee business, but that's not true. We're in the *people* business—that's what Starbucks is all about."

John Friel retired in 2010 as the longtime president and CEO of Medrad, Inc., a manufacturer of medical imaging products. He once said, "I don't do anything. I don't make anything. I don't design anything. I don't sell anything, so the real work of this company is all done by other people.

My job is to create the environment for those people to be successful."[11] President Dwight Eisenhower made a similar observation: "Leadership is the art of getting someone else to do something you want done because he wants to do it."[12]

Clearly, leaders can't do it all. They can't achieve their leadership vision alone. Leaders work through people to accomplish their goals. That's why leaders need people skills.

What are people skills? They are simply the learnable skills that enable you, the leader, to understand the people you lead, to empathize with them, and to build harmonious relationships with them. People skills are the social skills that enable you to get along with people, to negotiate with people, to avoid and resolve conflict with people, and to interact with people in a way that is mutually beneficial.

A leader with excellent people skills learns not to see crowds, but faces. He or she understands the dazzling power of a smile, the music of calling people by name, the delight people feel when a leader takes a personal interest in them. A leader with excellent people skills is quick to praise, slow to criticize, and eager to serve.

There's a huge difference between a leader and a boss, and the biggest difference is people skills. Bosses intimidate; leaders motivate. Bosses give orders; leaders offer guidance. Bosses seek power; leaders seek to empower others. Bosses throw their weight around; leaders delegate responsibility. Bosses are good at fault-finding; leaders catch people in the act of doing good.

One business leader who exemplifies great people skills is S. Truett Cathy, founder of the Atlanta-based Chick-fil-A restaurant chain. He was once interviewed on *Your World with Neil Cavuto* on the Fox News Channel. Cavuto said, "I talk to some CEOs all of the time, Mr. Cathy. They say you can't be a nice guy in this business. . . . What do you say?"

"Well," Cathy replied, "I think the opposite. I think the kinder you are to your people, the more productive they will be and the more customers you will be able to attract."[13]

Truett Cathy's grandson, Don M. "Bubba" Cathy, gave a business presentation in Orlando that I attended. Bubba is the company's senior vice president, and I had a chance to visit with him after the presentation. I asked Bubba to tell me about his grandfather's leadership qualities, and he replied, "Granddad's love of people is a great motivator. We need to nurture and care for that perspective. Sometimes, we allow our egos to get overinflated, and we need to relate back to Granddad's mind-set—to glorify God, not praise ourselves, and to put other people before ourselves."

When it comes to presidential people skills, few compare with Bill Clinton. In August 2003, I spoke at an event in Tuscaloosa, Alabama. My host was John Merrill, now a member of the Alabama House of Representatives. As we drove back to the airport, John told me a story.

"It was late October 1996," John said, "with the election just a few days away. President Clinton was speaking at Birmingham Southern University. I was invited to attend, so I took my family, including my dad, who was in a wheelchair. Somehow, we got seats right next to the stage. The place was packed and it was miserably hot when the president began to work the rope lines.

"As President Clinton passed me, I quickly told him about my dad in the wheelchair. He stopped and bent close to my dad, just inches from his face. 'Tell me your name,' President Clinton said.

"'Horace Merrill,' my dad replied.

"'Mr. Merrill, you don't know how proud it makes me feel that you came out today to hear me speak in this hot sun. I know it took a lot of effort on your part to be here, but you're the reason I get up to go to work every day and fight for you up in Washington. That's why I want to go back and work for you for four more years.'

"My dad had tears rolling down his cheeks, and the rest of us misted up as well. Mr. Clinton had an exceptional ability to relate to everyday people." The ability John describes is that set of learnable skills we call people skills.

Andy Pafko is a former centerfielder who played for the Chicago Cubs from 1943 to 1951. I recently had Andy as a guest on my local sports talk radio show in Orlando, and he told me another story about President Clinton.

"In 1994," Andy said, "I was visiting the White House and had my picture taken with Bill Clinton in the Oval Office. He reminded me that his wife, Hillary, came from Chicago, and he said, 'You were Hillary's favorite old Cub.' I didn't know if that was true or if he was just saying it to make me feel good, but it was sure good to hear.

"Well, the next time I met Bill Clinton was in February 2002. I was at an old-timers game in Fort Lauderdale. Just before the game, Mr. Clinton arrived to visit with us. He went to every locker and spoke to each player. When he got to my locker, he said 'Oh, Andy Pafko! You were my wife's favorite Cub!' Hearing him say that again, eight years later, really made my day. I couldn't believe it! I went back to Chicago and told all my friends."

Clearly those presidential people skills continue to serve Bill Clinton well now that he's out of office. Those people skills obviously deserve much of the credit for getting Bill Clinton into office. Political reporter Joe Klein is probably the leading expert on Bill Clinton's political career, having covered Mr. Clinton since 1989. Klein tells the story of reporting on Clinton in the spring of 1992, during the fever pitch of the New York primary.

Klein recalls, "I dragged my five-year-old daughter, Sophie, to see Bill Clinton speak at a town meeting at Co-op City in the Bronx." The event was raucous, and the air was charged with the angry voices of trade unionists and other New York Democrats who questioned whether Clinton understood and supported their issues. The candidate was also being attacked by the liberal intelligentsia who weren't convinced that Clinton was liberal enough. "I had piled on, too," Klein adds, "with a column in *New York* magazine about the fudges and inconsistencies in his campaign."

But when Bill Clinton saw Klein's daughter, Sophie, looking small and overwhelmed by it all, he came over, bent down to her eye level, placed a hand on her shoulder, and said, "Sophie, I know that your father hasn't been home much these past few months. He's been with me. . .but he talks about you *all the time*."[14]

Mr. Clinton was talking to little Sophie—but he made an impression on Joe Klein that the journalist never forgot. That's the power of people skills.

Thomas V. Miller Jr., is the longtime president of the Maryland Senate. He tells another story from Bill Clinton's 1992 presidential campaign. "When Bill Clinton was campaigning in Maryland in 1992," Miller recalls, "my mother and I would go to every stop. . . . He would always say 'hi' to her." Miller's mother was thrilled when Clinton was elected president.

Early in Clinton's second term, Thomas Miller visited the White House at Christmastime. President Clinton asked Miller how his mother was doing.

"Well," Miller replied, "she's dying."

At that moment, President Clinton choked up and began to cry—and so did Miller. "I know he was thinking about his mother," Miller later recalled, "who'd been dead less than a year. We were in a receiving line, and he was holding my hand. My wife and Hillary had to stand there making small talk while he called for pencil and paper.

"The next day, the president called my mother and talked to her for twenty minutes. Two days later, she got a handwritten note from the president: 'Dear Esther, just wanted you to know how much I enjoyed our conversation.'

"Bill Clinton's people skills are phenomenal," Miller concluded. "He really feels your pain. When he's looking at you, there's nobody else in the world in his eyes."[15]

Another story about Bill Clinton's people skills concerns Bob Poe, a former Magic employee who went on to a career in Democratic Party politics. He was the Florida state

Democratic Party chairman from 2000 to 2003. I ran into him while Mr. Clinton was still in office. "Bob," I said, "Have you ever spent time with President Clinton?"

"Yes—recently, in fact," he said. "I was with him on Air Force One, and he gave me a tour of the plane. We came to the communications center, and he said, 'Let's call Ginny.' And Pat, I swear I never told Bill Clinton my wife's name. He said, 'What's her number?' So I gave him Ginny's number, and he dialed it, but it went to voice mail. So he said, 'What's her cell?' He called that number. At that very moment, my wife, Ginny, was pushing a cart down the supermarket aisle. Her cell phone rang—and imagine her shock when she heard the president of the United States say, 'Ginny Poe, this is Bill Clinton, and I'm calling from Air Force One.'"

Now, there's one detail in that story I hope you noticed. Bob Poe told me, "I swear I never told Bill Clinton my wife's name." And I believe him. Leaders with great people skills just seem to have that kind of information at their fingertips.

HOW TO SHARPEN YOUR PEOPLE SKILLS

Love must be genuine, love must be sincere. Love for your players is not an act, not a facade, not a technique for manipulating people into working harder for your cause. Your love for people is either real or it's nothing at all. Boston Celtics coaching legend Red Auerbach put it this way: "Players are people, not horses. You don't handle them. You work with them, you coach them, you teach them, and, maybe most important, you listen to them."[16] As a leader, do you listen to your people? Do you love them? Or do you just "handle" them?

Coach John Wooden recalled attending the press conference when the Philadelphia 76ers traded Wilt Chamberlain to the Los Angeles Lakers in 1968. A sportswriter put this question to Chamberlain: "Do you think [Lakers coach] Bill van Breda Kolff can handle you?" Chamberlain replied, "No one handles me. I am a person, not a thing. You handle things. You work with people. I think I can work with anyone."

At that time, Wooden's coaching book, *Practical Modern Basketball*, had just been published. "I had a section in this book entitled 'Handling Your Players,'" he recalled. "I left this meeting, came home and took my book and marked out, crossed out, 'handling your players,' put 'working with your players.' And anyplace that I had alluded to handling your players, I changed. I called the publisher and wanted that correction made for any future editions."[17]

Let me share with you some practical principles to help you acquire, sharpen, and improve your people skills as a leader:

People Skill No. 1: Be Visible and Available. Never isolate or insulate yourself from the people you lead. You can't lead your troops from an ivory tower. Your people need to see you and talk to you. That's why Tom Peters urges leaders to "manage by walking around"—a concept so important it is known by its initials, MBWA.

Of course, Peters didn't invent the idea of being visible and available. Twenty centuries ago, Jesus modeled that same principle. He spent a thousand days mentoring and teaching his followers. If Jesus had been a leader in today's corporate world, his staff and schedulers would have had a hard time keeping him on a timetable, because whenever someone came with a problem, he stopped what he was doing and devoted himself to that need. It didn't matter if it was a Roman military officer with a dying servant, or a little guy up in a tree, or a couple of his own disciples bickering with each other. He was visible. He was available. That's how great leaders lead.

During the eight years of the Revolutionary War, George Washington never left his troops. Though he longed to return to Mount Vernon, he didn't see his beloved plantation home for almost the entire duration of the war. (He visited only briefly shortly before the British surrender at Yorktown.)

During the Civil War, Abraham Lincoln personally visited encampments and hospitals to encourage the Union soldiers and comfort the wounded. President Lincoln sometimes rode through Washington alone, without even a bodyguard, disregarding the risk. There were a number of hospitals around Washington where wounded Union soldiers were treated—Harewood, Carver, Mount Pleasant, Columbia College Hospital, and the Soldiers' Home. President Lincoln visited them all numerous times.[18]

One of the most meaningful ways to be visible and available to your people is to share meals with them. Some of the key moments Jesus spent with his disciples involved sharing a meal—the Last Supper, the broiled fish he ate with the two disciples on the road to Emmaus, the breakfast of fish by the Sea of Galilee. There is something about breaking bread together that provides the perfect environment for relationship building between leader and followers.

Tennis coach and TV commentator Brad Gilbert offers this insight regarding former NFL coach Dick Vermeil, who was then head coach of the Kansas City Chiefs:

> Dick gave a barbecue at his house for the entire team, not just the stars. Dick did all the cooking and every bit of the cleaning up, all by himself. No caterers, no maids, no hired help. And he was happy to do it. How do you think the Chiefs' third-string defensive tackle felt after that barbecue?
>
> Like he was ready to move heaven and earth for Dick Vermeil, that's how.[19]

President George W. Bush understood the morale boost it would give to soldiers in Iraq if their commander in chief would break bread with them. So for Thanksgiving 2003, President Bush secretly flew from Texas to Baghdad. Only a handful of people knew about the covert mission. Even many of the president's security detail were caught by surprise.

An unmarked car whisked the president from his Crawford ranch to an airfield near Waco. Under the cover of dasrkness, he took Air Force One (under a false call sign) to Iraq. Along the way, the distinctive robin's egg blue 747 was spotted by a British Airways pilot, who radioed, "Did I just see Air Force One?" The president's pilot, Colonel Mark Tillman, radioed back, "Gulfstream Five." The other pilot understood and replied, "Oh," keeping the secret to himself.

Air Force One arrived in Iraqi airspace with its lights off, escorted by fighter planes. It spiraled down to the landing strip at Baghdad, which had been the target of recent mortar attacks. The military and security forces in Baghdad were told to expect a C5 cargo plane carrying a USO troupe. No one expected to see the president's airplane descending from the sky.

President Bush went to the military mess hall at Baghdad International Airport and stepped onstage to greet hundreds of astonished soldiers. He began by thanking them for their service. "You are defending the American people from danger," he said, "and we are grateful."

He stayed for two and a half hours, shaking hands, carving and serving turkey, and sharing a meal with them. Mr. Bush later recalled, "It was an emotional moment to walk into that room. The energy level was beyond belief. I mean, I've been in some excited crowds before. But this place truly erupted."[20]

If you want to make a powerful impression, if you want to build a relationship with your people, if you want to stir emotions and generate energy in your troops, then surprise them, sit down with them, break bread with them, share a meal. Great leaders know the power of being visible and available to their people.

People Skill No. 2: Be a Good Listener. We have plenty of leaders who can talk. But we can never get enough leaders who will listen. Everyone has a need to be heard. The most uplifting leader of all is a leader who listens.

Did you ever notice that "listen" and "silent" are anagrams of the same six letters? To be a good listener, you have to be silent for a while. You must stop what you're doing, put away your smart phone or your iPad, look the other person in the eye, and give your undivided attention. Don't just *kinda* listen. *Really* listen.

And let that person *know* you are really listening. Give eye contact, nod empathetically, respond in such a way that you show you are tracking and really hearing what the person is saying. That's the rarest and most meaningful of all compliments. Plus, the more time you spend listening, the more you'll know what's really going on in your organization.

Once, in the 1960s, when I was a young baseball executive, I had to go to the team owner, Bob Carpenter, and give him the news that an individual in his farm club system was alienating people and disrupting his business. No one had told him. Laying it out for him was one of the hardest things I had ever done. When I finished, Mr. Carpenter said, "Why am I always the last one to know?"

That's what often happens to the leader at the top. Underlings are reluctant to talk to the boss—and no one wants to be the bearer of bad tidings. That's why people in leadership need to make a special effort to listen, to draw people out, to encourage people to speak. Don't make your people afraid that you might punish the messenger. Always keep the lines of communication open by being a good listener.

General George Patton put it this way: "Always talk with the troops! They know more about the war than anybody. Make them tell you all of their gripes. Make sure they know we are doing everything we can to help them. The soldiers will have to win the war. We cannot do it. Talk with them. They will not trust you if you do not trust them."[21]

I had the extraordinary good fortune to be mentored by one of the legendary figures in major league baseball, owner-promoter-impresario Bill Veeck (1914–86). Bill began his executive career with the minor league Milwaukee Brewers and later owned the Cleveland Indians, the St. Louis Browns, and the Chicago White Sox in the American League. He taught me the importance of maintaining an open-door policy and always being available to everyone in his organization.

Whenever Bill Veeck would buy a ball club, his first official act was to remove the door from his office—take it right off the hinges. In fact, when he returned to the White Sox in 1976, he not only removed the door, he had his entire office wall torn down. Bill always answered his own phone, opened his own mail, and walked around the ballpark talking to the fans. After every game, Bill stood at the gate, shaking hands with fans as they left. I've modeled my own leadership style after Bill Veeck's, which is why you'll find my contact information at the end of this book.

The late Michigan football coach Bo Schembechler explained his open-door policy in his book, *Bo's Lasting Lessons*:

> When someone—anyone—in our program had a problem, I wanted to know about it. And I wanted to do something about it, too.
>
> So I had a hard-and-fast policy: Any player who needed to see me, at any time, could. . . . Is it easy? Not always. We're pretty busy! And these guys know that the most valuable thing I've got is my time, the scarcest resource I have to spend. But if they've got the guts to come down and pull me out of a meeting, it must be pretty important to them. . . .
>
> If a guy comes down to see me because he's eating his heart out over something, and my secretary says, "Bo's in a meeting right now. Can you come back tomorrow?"—well, that guy probably ain't coming back. He'll lose his nerve, and then his problem—whatever it is— isn't going to get solved, and it'll start festering inside him. And I'll lose him. . . .
>
> If they need to talk to you, they need to talk to you, not your assistant or your secretary or anyone else.[22]

Even if you are the leader of a big organization, a big corporation, or a great nation, you need to be a good listener. You may not have time to go one-on-one with everybody, but you've got to find a way to welcome ideas, information, and input. If you don't want to end up isolated from reality, you've got to be a good listener.

The absolute *worst* thing a leader can do is reprimand people for speaking up or asking questions. If you tell just one person that his or her input is unwelcome, you'll shut down communication throughout your organization. Information is the lifeblood of your organization. If that lifeblood stops circulating, it's as if your organization has suffered a massive heart attack. Keep the lifeblood flowing by being a good listener.

Let me suggest two questions that you, as a listening leader, should ask your people on a regular basis:

First question: "What do *you* think?"

I guarantee you, most people are completely unaccustomed to hearing that question from the boss. When you ask the first question, you may have to revive some people before you can ask the second question: "How would *you* make the call on this one?"

Odds are, no one has ever asked your people for their opinion. If you ask those two questions, I guarantee you'll rock your organization. People will feel *empowered* by those questions. They'll think, *Wow! The leader actually cares what I think! Maybe I really do have something to contribute!*

Reward and applaud those who give you the truth without sugarcoating—*especially* bad news. Cut through layers of bureaucracy and invite your front-line troops to come to you with important information. Coax the quiet and reserved members of your team to share their knowledge and opinions.

John Salka, battalion chief of the Fire Department of New York, observes, "If you don't listen to your people, you can't collect the information you need in order to build relationships with them or uncover their goals. And by listening, I don't just mean waiting for them to finish talking. I mean really focusing on what they have to say. Focused listening is nothing more than listening with *purpose*."[23]

General Colin Powell observes that the higher your leadership position, the more important it is to listen. High rank has a way of erecting barriers between leaders and the information they need. "In the military," he said, "when you become a four-star general, people will do anything you even suggest you want. . . . I had to work at breaking down that deference to hear from my people."[24]

The inability to listen can be a fatal flaw in a leader— and I mean *literally* fatal. You are probably familiar with the Battle of the Little Bighorn, also known as Custer's Last Stand. It was a famous battle between the Seventh Cavalry Regiment of the United States Army, commanded by George Armstrong Custer, and members of the Lakota Sioux, Arapaho, and Northern Cheyenne tribes clustered around the Little Bighorn River in eastern Montana Territory. The battle climaxed a lengthy conflict between Native American tribes and the United States government, which had repeatedly broken treaties with the tribes.

History suggests that Custer, who had served heroically in the American Civil War, had grown arrogant, self-willed, and unwilling to listen. General Alfred Terry offered Custer an additional battalion of Second Cavalry soldiers, plus a battery of Gatling guns, but Custer refused General Terry's offer, saying that the Seventh Cavalry "can handle anything."[25] Custer also ignored the advice of his Indian scouts and scout Charley Reynolds, who warned him that he should not divide his forces and scatter them so thinly.[26] Most of all, Custer refused to listen to the Cheyenne when they begged him to keep his promises so that blood would not have to be shed. Again and again, Custer refused to listen.

On June 26, 1876, General Custer led a force of seven hundred men against some eighteen hundred Native American warriors—and his troops suffered massacre and defeat. Custer himself was killed, shot in the head and chest. After the battle, two Cheyenne women walked among the dead and found a group of Sioux warriors who were planning to cut Custer's body into pieces as an act of desecration. The Cheyenne women sent the warriors away. Then they took their sewing awls—long, sharp tools used to punch holes in leather or canvas—and pushed them deep into the ears of Custer's dead body.

Custer had promised the Cheyenne that he wouldn't fight them—but he ignored his promise and refused to hear the Cheyennes' pleas. The women hoped the holes in his ears would help Custer listen better in the next life.[27]

People Skill No. 3: Empower Your People. Empowerment is the act of uplifting and encouraging people. I work for Rich DeVos, one of the most empowering business leaders in the world. Now in his mid-eighties, Rich is co-owner of the Orlando Magic. He and his business partner, Jay Van Andel, founded the Amway Company in 1959 with about forty dollars between them. They leveraged that tiny amount into a nine billion-dollar company. When Rich is asked to describe his role in Amway, he says, "I'm the head cheerleader."

For more than fifty years, Rich has been traveling the world, cheering people on, rooting for them, and encouraging them. Whenever I see him, he's a cheerleader to me. After cofounding the Orlando Magic, I invited Rich to come to Florida to help Orlando obtain a major league baseball franchise in the early 1990s. The baseball effort didn't work out, but Rich and his family ended up buying the Magic in 1991.

To this day, whenever I see Rich, he introduces me with words like these: "This is Pat Williams, who got all of this started. We wouldn't be here without him." Then he'll pat me on the back and say, "We love you and appreciate you, Pat."

Rich also sends out notes of encouragement—and those notes from Rich DeVos are framed on walls all around the world. He signs every note, "Love ya—Rich." He truly understands the power of empowerment. He has built an industry on it.

As Rich points out, the higher you are on the leadership ladder, the greater the impact of your words. A pep talk from the head of the organization does far more good than a pep talk from the guy in the mailroom. In the same way, a dismissive word, a scolding, or an insult will be magnified when spoken by a leader.

Our leadership roles give us a powerful megaphone. It amplifies the reach and effect of our words, for good or ill. We need to be aware of the power of our words whenever we speak to our children, spouses, employees, members of our team, clients and customers, neighbors, and people in our community. Every time we speak, we leave an imprint that can't be erased.

Jon Gruden earned his coaching spurs as a graduate assistant at the University of Tennessee under head coach Johnny Majors. During a home game against Auburn, Gruden noticed that Auburn's free safety played shallow against Tennessee's play-action passes on crossing routes. Gruden was sure that Terence Cleveland, Tennessee's fast receiver, could beat the Auburn safety to the post, so he scribbled a note to offensive coordinator Walt Harris: "DP8 Go? Check the post"—shorthand for "Draw-Pass 8 Go and look for the post route." Harris read the note, nodded approvingly, and called the play. Sure enough, Cleveland easily made a reception for a huge gain.

Gruden recalls what happened the next day when the coaching staff came together to watch game film:

> The moment the big pass to Terence appeared on the screen, my heart started beating fast with anticipation. "That's a good call, Walt," Coach Majors said. "That's a good job." I would have been satisfied if it ended right there, but then Coach Harris said, "Jon called that." Coach Majors walked over to where I was sitting, gave me a pat on the back and said, "Attaboy!" That

was a highlight of my career. That was one of the greatest days of my life.

I'll never forget Walt for giving me credit on that play. There are a lot of people in his position who wouldn't have done that.[28]

That's the power of empowerment. Simple words like "good job" and "attaboy," and giving credit where credit is due—these are acts of empowerment that can lift people to heights of confidence and achievement you can scarcely imagine.

Swen Nater shared with me a story that took place during the summer between his junior and senior years playing center for Coach Wooden at UCLA. Lakers center Wilt Chamberlain had agreed to work out with Swen at UCLA's Pauley Pavilion, and he arrived on campus fresh from the Santa Monica beach. As Swen greeted him, Wilt realized he had forgotten his basketball shoes.

"You want to come with me while I pick up my shoes?" Wilt asked.

Swen was only too happy to ride with Wilt in his red El Dorado convertible. When they arrived at the house, Swen was amazed at Wilt's walk-in closet. "That closet was twice as big as my whole dorm room!" he later recalled. He also remembered Wilt's generosity, because the Lakers star gave him three pairs of socks and two pairs of Converse shoes (the two men wore the same size).

Returning to campus, Wilt and Swen recruited a couple of students for a half-court game of two-on-two. Defensively and offensively, Wilt showed Swen some jukes, fakes, and dunks he had never seen before. More than once, Swen went up for a rebound and found himself blocked—and knocked flat on his back. After three or four games, Swen was feeling a bit humiliated—even if he was being schooled by one of the greatest players in NBA history.

After the last game, Wilt turned to Swen and said, "I like

the way you rebound. You can make it in the NBA if you really want to."

Swen told me that Wilt's words sent his mood soaring! If Wilt Chamberlain said it, Swen believed it. After college, Swen was drafted in the first round of the NBA draft and went on to more than a decade-long career in pro basketball, playing for the Milwaukee Bucks, Buffalo Braves, San Diego Clippers, and Los Angeles Lakers. Leaders who live to empower others never know what an impact a few words may have.

People Skill No. 4: Delegate. If there is anything in my career I'd do differently, it would be this: From the mid-1960s to sometime in the late 1980s, I did everything myself. I delegated no important responsibilities. Throughout much of my NBA career—during my time with the Chicago Bulls, the Atlanta Hawks, and the Philadelphia 76ers—I was a one-man band.

Why didn't I delegate? I was insecure. I didn't think I could trust other people to do things up to my standards—so I did it all myself. I assumed (incorrectly, by the way) that nobody was as competent and industrious as I was—that if I didn't do it, it wouldn't get done correctly. At the same time, I was so insecure that I thought if my bosses saw me handing off important responsibilities to my staff, they'd say, "What are we paying Williams for? He's got other people doing all his work for him." So, driven by a combination of arrogance, insecurity, and fear, I kept everything to myself.

When I arrived in Orlando and we began building the expansion Orlando Magic out of dreams and pixie dust, the responsibilities and challenges of running an NBA team had grown to the point where I no longer had any choice. If I tried to do it all myself, it wouldn't get done. The sport of basketball had become a worldwide endeavor, and I needed a sizable staff to tackle all the tasks of running the operation.

So I learned to delegate. Once I began sharing responsibilities, my eyes were opened to all the things a leader could accomplish by utilizing the strengths, talents, imagination, and energies of other people. It was amazing! By entrusting tasks and responsibilities to my staff, I could accomplish a hundred or a thousand times what I had once been able to accomplish.

Delegating, after all, is the essence of leadership. It means accomplishing goals through other people. It means organizing the efforts of others in order to achieve what no one person could ever achieve alone. And in the process of learning to delegate, I became very good at it.

Today I delegate *everything*. I have the cleanest desk in the state of Florida. And you know what? My staff is a lot happier, too! They feel they are truly contributing to the team effort. They get to demonstrate their own initiative and creativity. They are growing as leaders in their own right. So I've become very bullish on the idea of delegating.

Now, delegating doesn't mean that you hand off responsibility and forget about it. It doesn't mean you abandon your people or abrogate your responsibility as a leader. You are still accountable for everything your people do with the responsibility you give them. So you have to maintain communication, set benchmarks, assess performance, hold people accountable, and accept responsibility for both the achievements and the failures of the team.

Steven Sample was the tenth president of the University of Southern California, from 1991 to 2010. Under his leadership, USC became a leader in the fields of communication and multimedia technologies, and elevated its status as a leading research institution. I interviewed Dr. Sample for my book *Coaching Your Kids to Be Leaders*, and he told me, "If you want to raise leaders, then delegate real authority to your people. You can't expect people to learn to lead unless you give them the opportunity to make real decisions with real consequences."

That's wise counsel. As leaders, our job is to give our people a vision to aim for. Then we tell them, "It's up to you to take responsibility, to exercise your creativity, to make your own decisions. If there's anything you need, just ask me—that's what I'm here for. But I'm delegating my authority to you, and you don't need permission from me to make decisions. This authority is yours to do with as you see fit."

"But," you may say, "I don't know if I can trust my people with that much authority! What if they make a mistake?" Oh, they'll make mistakes. They'll make some doozies. And if you're wise, you'll let them learn from those mistakes instead of punishing them. When you punish mistakes, you punish initiative and imagination. You encourage your people to play it safe, to shift the blame, to cover up—and you lose the benefit of their leadership skills and creativity.

To delegate is to create an environment where people are free to make mistakes—and free to succeed. To delegate is to unleash the talent and imagination of your people. In the process of delegating real authority, you'll become less of a boss and more of a leader.

People Skill No. 5: Take Care of Your Troops. A leader must be loyal to those he or she leads.

In June 2005, I went to Washington DC for the twenty-fifth anniversary celebration of the Washington Speakers Bureau. There I rubbed shoulders with some of the most stellar leaders and speakers of our time: Rudy Giuliani, Tom Peters, Joe Theismann, Doris Kearns Goodwin, Lou Holtz, and many more. When I went to the dessert table, I found myself reaching for the same chocolate éclair as. . .General Colin Powell!

I said, "General Powell, I'm Pat Williams of the Orlando Magic. My son Bobby has just become a manager in the Washington Nationals farm system, and he's eager to do whatever it takes to succeed in that role. Would you have any advice for him?"

Without hesitating, the general said, "Tell your son, 'Take care of your troops.' And tell him, 'Keep your mouth shut and do your job.'" As he turned to leave the table, he added over his shoulder, "And tell him, 'Stay focused on *this* job—don't worry about your next job.'" Then he was out the door.

I took a napkin from the table and wrote down the advice General Powell had given me. It was a twenty-second course in effective leadership, and it began with the words, "Take care of your troops." In other words, be loyal to the people you lead, and they will be loyal to you.

Gen. Norman Schwarzkopf, in his autobiography, tells a story from his days in the Vietnam War. It was Christmastime and then-Lieutenant. Colonel Schwarzkopf visited some of the forward units, composed of men who had been through some of the worst fighting of the war. He brought Christmas dinner and set up a chow line to serve the men real roast turkey and dressing, cranberry sauce, and all the trimmings. He also brought with him a minister and a priest to conduct Christmas services for the soldiers.

Arriving at D Company, Schwarzkopf looked for the company commander—but the captain in charge of Delta Company was visiting wounded soldiers at a hospital in the rear. Schwarzkopf waited, but the captain never returned. Finally, Schwarzkopf went to the base at the rear and found the D Company commander in the mess hall eating Christmas dinner with some fellow officers.

"Come with me," Schwarzkopf said. He led the captain to an office and sat him down. The officer avoided Schwarzkopf's eyes. "Why didn't you go straight back out to your company?" Schwarzkopf asked.

"I wanted to have Christmas dinner," the other man replied.

"What about your troops? Don't you understand that it was your responsibility to see that they had *their* Christmas dinner?"

The captain was sullen. "Sir, I knew you were bringing them a Christmas meal, and I thought that as long as I was here, I'd shower and put on clean clothes and eat my dinner."

"Captain, do you realize what you just told your troops? You don't think they know that while they're out in the boonies on Christmas Day, their leader is in the rear? If you're not willing to go through the discomfort of spending Christmas with them in the field, how do you expect them to believe you'll be with them when they go into battle?"

"Frankly, sir, I really don't like this company command business. I don't like being responsible for the troops all the time. So sometimes I just take care of myself."

Schwarzkopf was incredulous. He offered to remove the captain from command—and to Schwarzkopf's astonishment, the captain eagerly agreed!

So Lieutenant Colonel Schwarzkopf boarded a helicopter, along with the D Company commander and a trusted staff officer, Captain Trujillo. They flew back to D Company, and Schwarzkopf assembled the men. Then, in front of all the soldiers, Schwarzkopf told the captain, "I am relieving you of command of this company immediately because you don't care about your troops. You do not deserve to be a company commander in this battalion. Get in the helicopter."

Then he turned to Captain Trujillo and said, "You are now in command of Delta Company. Take care of these men."

Looking back on the incident, Schwarzkopf concludes, "Those soldiers desperately needed to know that somebody cared about keeping them alive. The message apparently got through: as I walked toward the helicopter, the men cheered."[29]

Loyalty is the quality of being faithful to a person or cause. Loyalty is based on a commitment, a decision—not feelings. You can be loyal to a boss or a coach even if you don't like his or her personality. You can be loyal to an employee or a player even if that person has disappointed you. Your level of loyalty does not depend on whether you feel like taking care of your troops. You take care of your troops at all times because you are committed to them and loyal to them.

Always stand up for your people. If they are criticized in a meeting or in the media, speak up and defend them. You and your people will rise or fall, succeed or fail, as a team. Don't let attacks and opposition divide you from your team. No matter what happens, follow the advice of General Powell and the example of General Schwarzkopf: Always take care of your troops.

People Skill No. 6: Don't Avoid Conflict—Manage It. Great leaders don't fear conflict. They face it and resolve it. They learn the lessons of conflict and extract the benefits of disagreement. Clashing points of view can produce change and growth in your organization.

The English poet John Milton once observed, "Where there is much desire to learn, there of necessity will be much arguing, much writing, many opinions; for opinions in good men is but knowledge in the making."[30] Management consultant Peter Drucker expressed a parallel view when he formulated what has come to be known as Drucker's First Law of Decision-Making: "One does not make a decision without disagreements."[31] Great leaders understand that conflict can be a creative and constructive force in an organization.

Alfred P. Sloan Jr., was the longtime president and CEO of General Motors during GM's most exciting and innovative years, the decades from the 1920s through the 1950s. His leadership not only shaped the culture at GM, but significantly affected American culture. At one corporate meeting, after listening to the discussion around the table, Sloan said, "Gentlemen, I take it we are all in agreement on the decision here." All heads nodded affirmatively. "Then," said Sloan, "I propose we postpone further discussion of the matter until our next meeting, to give ourselves time to develop disagreement and perhaps gain some understanding of what the decision is all about."[32]

When the Walt Disney Company fell on hard times in the early 1980s, Roy Disney hired former ABC and Paramount executive Michael Eisner as the new Disney CEO. Eisner quickly revitalized the company, green-lighting such projects as *The Little Mermaid*, *The Lion King*, *Who Framed Roger Rabbit?* and the Disneyland theme park in Paris. Though Eisner's reign was controversial and he was ousted in 2005, there's no question he came in at a crucial time and saved Walt Disney's dream factory from being taken over by corporate raiders. Eisner was famous for wanting to generate as many ideas and opposing points of view as possible, because he believed that conflict stimulates creativity. At one meeting with his top managers, he said, "Why is there no conflict at this meeting? Something's wrong when there's no conflict."[33] Don't fear conflict. Embrace those times when the people on your team express strong opinions and contend for their points of view. Contention means that everyone is committed to winning. Let your people voice their opinions. Then, as the leader, make sure you have the final say and that everyone on your team buys into your decision, whether they agree or not.

Quash hidden agendas. Don't allow people to undermine you or others through rumormongering and backbiting. Make sure conflict is out in the open—a healthy exchange of views and ideas. Open communication makes an organization stronger; whispering campaigns make an organization weak and dysfunctional. Spreading rumors should be treated as a matter for discipline—and even dismissal.

As a leader, make sure you don't lose control of the situation—especially when voices are raised. People tend to shout and repeat themselves when they feel they are not being heard. If you want to de-escalate conflict, let the shouter know that you hear what he or she is saying. Echo back, in your own words, what the person is saying. Whether you agree or disagree, make sure the person knows you get the point.

Instead of trying to shout over others to make yourself heard, try lowering your voice. People will realize they have to be quiet in order to hear what the leader is saying. (Also, there's something a little ominous about a leader who speaks in a lowered tone!) Demonstrate your control of the situation by remaining calm and authoritative.

Have you ever been stopped for speeding? How did the traffic cop treat you? Most likely, he respectfully called you "Sir" or "Ma'am," remained frustratingly calm, and after writing the ticket and ruining your day, said, "Have a nice day."

Police officers are trained to maintain a calm, professional demeanor in confrontational situations. They de-escalate conflict by showing that they are in total control. So, in times of conflict, be the traffic cop. Lower your voice, lower your emotions, and maintain control.

People Skill No. 7: Level with Your People. I first became acquainted with George "Sparky" Anderson when we were both in the Western Carolinas League. (He was a manager in the Cardinals farm system; I was a general manager in the Phillies system.) He went on to a Hall of Fame career managing the Cincinnati Reds and the Detroit Tigers, becoming the first manager to win a World Series with both a National League team (the Reds in 1975 and '76) and an American League team (the Tigers in 1984). One of Sparky's unbreakable rules throughout his career was *be honest with your players.*

"The first rule," Sparky once said, "and thank God I learned it in my very first year, is you have to have the players to win. The most important thing is to be honest with them. If you do that, they'll be yours. But if a player finds you've lied to him, you'll not only lose him but ten others in the clubhouse."[34]

Another sports leader famed for his integrity and honesty is former NFL coach Mike Holmgren, now president of the Cleveland Browns. As an assistant coach and head coach, Holmgren shaped the careers of such legendary quarterbacks as Joe Montana, Steve Young, and Brett Favre. Sports agent Bob LaMonte describes Holmgren's absolute honesty:

> I've known Mike Holmgren for a long time, and you'll never meet a more straightforward guy. Everyone knows he'll always be truthful with them, and he often says, "Look, if you ask me a question, make sure you want to know the answer." One thing is certain—he will let you know where you stand with him. Sometimes you might not like the answer he gives you,

but he'll be honest with you. I've never known him to tell a lie. For instance, if a player says, "Coach, why aren't I starting?" he'll give him specific reasons. If a player asks why he got cut, he'll tell him exactly why. He doesn't mince words. He doesn't do it in a harsh way, and it's not personal. The bottom line is that the players respect him because he will tell the truth.[35]

LaMonte goes on to relate the story of a free agent wide receiver recruited by Mike Holmgren when he coached the Seattle Seahawks. The player was wary because he felt the previous coach he played for had lied to him. Before signing with the Seahawks, this player wanted to make sure that Holmgren would be truthful.

"Look," Coach Holmgren said, "we want you here. We have a role for you on our team, but you're not going to be a starter. We have two young players that we plan on giving every opportunity to be the starters. Now if one of them gets hurt, or he can't do it, then yes, absolutely, you'll get an opportunity to start. But I'm not going to tell you what you want to hear so you'll sign."

That's all the man needed to hear. He respected Holmgren's candor—and he signed a one-year contract. As it turned out, he often started in games with three-wide-receiver formations, and he went on to sign for additional seasons and enjoyed a successful career in Seattle.

"I never lied to a player or a coach," Holmgren reflects, "not even to the press. My philosophy is that honesty has to permeate your entire existence. You must live your life this way, at the office and away from the office. This is where you start, because if you lose trust, you can't teach. You can't communicate. Your people won't listen to you and you'll never be able to get them to do what needs to be done."[36]

One of my favorite Sam Walton quotations comes from Rule 4 of what he called "Sam's Rules for Building a Business."

He said, "Communicate everything you possibly can to your partners [that is, your employees]. The more they know, the more they'll understand. The more they understand, the more they'll care. Once they care, there's no stopping them."[37]

If you want to lead people, you've got to level with them. Leaders of excellence are leaders who speak the truth.

THE GREATEST PEOPLE SKILL OF ALL

You'll recall I previously said that love is the first and most foundational people skill of all. If you truly show *agape* love to the people you lead—a love that is rooted in your will, not your feelings—then every other people skill I've listed will come naturally.

If you love your people, you will be visible and available to them as a leader. If you love them, you'll be a good listener, and you'll empower them. If you love them, you'll delegate to them and entrust real responsibility to them. You'll be loyal to your people—you'll take care of your troops. You'll manage conflict, and you'll level with your people. All these other people skills are simply facets of the greatest people skill of all, the people skill of agape love.

In *The Greatest Communicator*, former presidential pollster Dick Wirthlin tells a story about President Ronald Reagan that is truly the last word about the people skill called love. In February 1984, near the end of Reagan's first term, Wirthlin walked into the Oval Office and found the president standing beside his desk with a photograph in hand.

"Mr. President," Wirthlin asked, "what's that you've got there?"

"Well, Dick," said the president, turning the photo so that his aide could see it, "I just got off the phone with this young man."

Wirthlin looked at the photo—and winced. It was a portrait of a twelve-year-old boy who had suffered severe burns while rescuing his two younger brothers from their burning home. He'd found the first brother quickly and had passed him out through a window. But while frantically searching for his second brother, then carrying the young boy to safety, he sustained disfiguring burns to his face and body.

"I called this little fella," Reagan said, "to see how he was doing and to tell him how proud I was of his heroism. . . . At the end of our conversation, the youngster said, 'President Reagan, I sure wish I would have had my tape recorder on so I could remember our call together.' So I said, 'Well, son, turn it on and let's chat some more.'"[38]

Here was the most powerful leader on the entire planet— and he was willing to give unstintingly of his time to one heroic twelve-year-old boy. President Reagan didn't do it for the publicity, even though he faced a reelection challenge later that year. The story didn't become public until twenty years later, when Wirthlin published his book. President Reagan did a favor for a twelve-year-old hero because the third side of leadership excellence is *people skills*, and the greatest people skill of all is *love*.

4
THE FOURTH SIDE OF LEADERSHIP: CHARACTER

When I was thirteen, I tried out for a summer sandlot baseball team. I made the cut—the youngest player on the team. I was elated to be selected, but I wondered if I could really perform at the same level as the older players.

When my mother drove me to my first game, my grandmother came with us. They sat in front, and I was in the backseat. On the way to the ballpark, we talked about the challenges I faced as the youngest player on the team.

"Well," I said, "if it doesn't work out, I can always quit."

My grandmother whirled around and looked me in the eye. "You. . .don't. . .quit!" she said. "Nobody in this family quits!"

I got my grandmother's message—loud and clear. It was a tough summer, and I had to work hard to keep up. But I didn't quit.

I'm so grateful for my grandmother's stern message. That early lesson in the character trait of perseverance has been the foundation for everything I've accomplished in my life. That lesson was never more important to me than when I was forty-six years old, working eighteen-hour days, seven days a week, trying to build an NBA expansion team in Orlando. My life was an endless whirl of giving speeches, attending meetings, talking to the media, selling, and promoting.

During that time, there were many days when I thought, *I'm fooling myself. What have I gotten myself into? There's no way this team is ever going to happen.* But it never, *ever* occurred to me to think, *If it doesn't work out, I can always quit.* In fact, there were definitely times when I could hear my grandmother saying to me, "You don't quit! Nobody in this family quits!"

And I *didn't* quit. I truly believe the Orlando Magic exist today because my grandmother once told me that quitting is not an option, and because my partners in that effort, Jimmy and Bobby Hewitt, had the same nobody-quits attitude. I'll always be grateful for my grandmother, who pounded a steel rod of *character* into my young spine that day.

I can personally testify that character is essential and indispensable as the fourth side of leadership excellence.

"WE NEED SOME CHARACTER PEOPLE!"

I once heard Norman Schwarzkopf give a speech in which he said that leadership consists of two vital ingredients: *strategy* and *character*. Then he added, "If you must do without one or the other, do without the strategy." As John Maxwell reminds us, "You can only go as high on the leadership ladder as your character will allow you."[1] So what is character?

Your character is the array of personality traits you have built into your life over time. These personality traits determine how you will behave in a range of situations, including times of pressure, danger, stress, and temptation. Are you honest through and through—or will you resort to lies and evasions when your character is put to the test? Are you courageous—or cowardly? Are you loyal—or unfaithful? Are you self-sacrificing—or self-serving? Are you hardworking—or lazy? Are you upright—or corrupt?

When people get caught behaving selfishly, disgracefully, and immorally, they often excuse their behavior by saying, "Oh, I behaved out of character. I don't normally behave that way. I was under pressure. I was tempted. That's not who I am." In reality, who we are under pressure is *exactly* who we are, period. What good is it to say, "I have excellent character—as long as it's never tested. I'm a great person—as long as I'm not under pressure or being tempted"? The only true character any of us possesses is the character we demonstrate in times of testing.

Bill Walsh, the late, great 49ers coach, put it this way: "Some define character as simply aspiring to high ideals and standards. I disagree. Many people have lofty aspirations. Unfortunately, aspiring isn't enough. You must also have the strength of commitment and sacrifice to adhere to those standards and ideals in good times *and* bad."[2]

I lived in Philadelphia from 1974 to 1986—the glory years of Philadelphia sports. I was general manager of the 76ers, and our team got to the finals four times and won the NBA Championship in 1983. During that time, the Eagles got to the Super Bowl, the Flyers won two NHL crowns, the University of Pennsylvania basketball team got to the Final Four in 1979, Villanova won an NCAA title in 1985, and the Phillies won their first-ever World Series in 1980. The Phillies manager at that time was Dallas Green, my longtime friend from Delaware. (He holds a senior adviser position with the Phillies to this day.) At six feet five inches tall, with a voice like a foghorn, Dallas is an imposing figure. In the clubhouse with his players, he could often be heard to bellow, "We need some *character* people on this team!"

The fact is, every team, every company, every military unit, and every religious organization needs some character people—especially at the leadership level. I've been researching and thinking about the issue of character for more than three decades, and I have concluded that leadership is rooted in character. A leader is not just someone who takes charge. A leader is someone who takes charge *and does the right thing*. It's not enough to make a decision; it needs to be the *right* decision resulting from strong character. It's not enough to take action; it needs to be the *right* action, prompted by strong character.

How do we become people of good character? We build character gradually, moment by moment and year after year, by making moral decisions. We accumulate character strength by consistently choosing the harder path instead of the easy way out, by taking responsibility instead of shifting blame, by sacrificing our own welfare in order to serve others. Every good, moral choice we make, especially those choices we make when no one else can see, helps to build the habits of good character. As the English statesman Thomas Babington Macauley observed, "The measure of a man's character is what he would do if he knew he never would be found out."[3]

The people on your team must be able to trust you as their leader. Trust is based on character. If your people can't rely on your integrity, your word of honor, how can they trust you, respect you, and follow where you lead? I once heard former congressman J. C. Watts speak at a conference in Arizona. The theme of his talk: character. "How many of you husbands think the character of your wife is important?" he asked. "And how many of you wives think the character of your husband is important? Yes, I thought you would. Now, don't tell me that the character of our leaders doesn't matter. You can no more have leadership without character than you can have water without the wet."

There are many character traits we can focus on, but I'm going to zoom in on just a few that are especially relevant to the leadership role.

INTEGRITY: "HONESTY WITH A LITTLE OOMPH"

In February 2006, my son Bobby and I were in Houston for the NBA All-Star Weekend. Our first day there, we left the hotel for a jog. On our way back, we saw a phalanx of TV reporters with cameras and boom mikes in front of an office building up ahead. Jogging closer, we saw a man and woman emerge from the crowd and head our way. Even from a distance, I instantly recognized the man.

"Bobby," I said, "that's Ken Lay."

It was indeed Ken Lay, the former CEO of Enron. He was two weeks into the federal securities fraud trial that was making headlines from coast to coast. As the couple stepped up on the curb near us, I put out my hand. "Mr. Lay," I said, "I'm Pat Williams with the Orlando Magic."

We shook hands and he introduced the woman at his side, his wife, Linda. We chatted briefly—but we avoided talking about the trial. Then I added, "I just want you to know we're praying for you."

He seemed surprised. "Well, thank you," he said. "I appreciate your prayers."

His wife said proudly, "And I'm standing with him all the way."

Then the light changed, and they crossed the street.

"Dad," Bobby said, "he seems like a really nice guy."

He did indeed. And I had to wonder—was Ken Lay innocent? Guilty? Had he been set up? Or had he succumbed to the arrogance of power and greed? Here was a man who had been a friend and confidant to presidents. Then, in 2001, he urged Enron employees to buy stock in the company while he unloaded his own holdings. When the company collapsed, investors and pension funds lost billions—but Ken Lay had already cashed out. The fraud case seemed ironclad.

I did pray for Ken Lay over the coming days. I was pulling for him as I followed the trial. I hoped he'd produce the evidence to clear his name. But on May 25, the jury found him guilty. Then, on July 5, before he could be sentenced, Ken Lay suffered a massive heart attack and died.

How did this man's life take such a tragic turn? Ken Lay was the son of a minister, raised to live by the moral precepts of the Bible—yet he was at the center of one of the worst corporate scandals in US history. Somewhere along the line, he abandoned his moral foundation. He lost his integrity.

The life and death of Ken Lay serves as a sobering lesson to you and me: Never let go of your integrity. Guard it with your life.

This word *integrity* is widely used and widely misunderstood. According to John M. Morse, the publisher of Merriam-Webster's online dictionary, *integrity* was the most frequently looked-up word of 2005. He attributed the heightened interest in the word to a string of ethics scandals in government, the corporate world, and the sports world.[4]

The origin of the word *integrity* helps to make the meaning clear. The word comes from the Latin *integer*, which means "whole" or "complete." You may remember from your high school math classes that an integer is a number without any fractional part. Similarly, a person of integrity is honest and complete—he or she does not have any fractional part and is not compartmentalized or divided. People of integrity demonstrate wholeness and completeness because their actions match their beliefs. They are the same person in public and in private. Their inner reality matches their outer reputation.

Optimize magazine (*Information Week's* magazine for corporate investment officers, which ceased publication in 2007) published a ten-point description of integrity in its May 2005 issue:

The Ten Universal Characteristics of Integrity
1. You know that little things count.
2. You find the white when others see gray.
3. You mess up, you fess up.
4. You create a culture of trust.
5. You keep your word.
6. You care about the greater good.
7. You're honest but modest.
8. You act like you're being watched.
9. You hire integrity.
10. You stay the course.[5]

When I was researching my first book on John Wooden, *How to Be Like Coach Wooden*, I interviewed one of Coach's former student managers, who by that time was a businessman in Pittsburgh. He told me, "Here's the deal with John Wooden. The John Wooden on the practice floor was the same John Wooden in the locker room, and the John Wooden in the locker room was the same John Wooden on the campus at UCLA, and the John Wooden on the campus was the same John Wooden at home. He didn't change from place to place and situation to situation. There was an absolute consistency and integrity to his life."

When a leader has the character trait of integrity, his walk and his talk are totally aligned. Leaders who compromise their integrity may get away with it for a while. They can maintain a false facade for years. But no one gets away with it forever. Leaders who lack integrity are eventually exposed.

A few years ago, I had lunch with my youngest son, Michael, who was nineteen at the time. As we chatted, he used the word *integrity*. I said, "Michael, what's your definition of integrity?"

He replied, "Integrity is honesty with a little oomph." I thought that was a great definition. Integrity and honesty certainly go hand in hand, but integrity and character are a lot more than honesty alone. As John Wooden once wrote: "You can be as honest as the day is long and still be short on character. How? You can be honest and selfish, honest and undisciplined, honest and inconsistent, honest and disrespectful, honest and lazy. . . . There's more to character than just being honest."[6]

To be a leader of excellence, you must be a leader of integrity—a leader like Bobby Jones. Bobby was one of our outstanding players when I was general manager of the Philadelphia 76ers. He played in Philly from 1978 through 1986, when we had some great teams. Bobby didn't talk much, but everyone looked up to him as a leader and a role model. He was one of the toughest defenders in the game, yet he played clean—no hip-checking or elbow-throwing. The Sixers never missed the playoffs while Bobby was on the team, and he was a major factor in our championship season of 1982–83.

Despite health problems that included an irregular heartbeat, asthma, and epilepsy, Bobby enjoyed a successful twelve-year career, first with the Denver Nuggets and then with the Sixers. His teammate Charles Barkley once said, "If everyone in the world was like Bobby Jones, the world wouldn't have any problems."

Immediately after Bobby joined the Sixers, he approached me with a new idea—pre-game chapels. I thought it was a terrific idea, and we held the first chapel in NBA history in February 1979, before a game against the Milwaukee Bucks at Philadelphia's Spectrum Arena. We invited Melvin Floyd, an African-American youth worker from inner-city Philadelphia, to be our speaker. Only three players showed up—Bobby, Julius Erving, and Milwaukee's Kent Benson, plus assistant coach Chuck Daly. Even though the congregation was small, Mel got as wound up as if he were preaching to a packed arena. We only had twelve minutes for the chapel, and after eleven minutes, Mel showed no signs of slowing down. So I had to tell him the game was about to start.

From that modest beginning, the tradition of team chapels continued and spread throughout the NBA. Today, there's a chapel before every NBA game, usually drawing ten or twelve players from both teams. In the pressure-packed, temptation-charged world of pro sports, many players appreciate a time of spiritual renewal and prayer before they go out and compete with intensity. This tradition can be traced to the quiet leadership of Bobby Jones.

One of Bobby's most notable traits was his spotless reputation for integrity. One night, we were playing the Spurs in San Antonio. Bobby went racing after a ball that was heading out of bounds. The referee was blocked and couldn't see whether Bobby touched it before it went out. "Bobby, Bobby!" he called. "Did you touch that ball?"

Bobby said, "No, sir, I didn't."

And the ref called, "Sixers' ball!" Just like that—he simply took Bobby's word for it.

A week or ten days later, we were back home at the Spectrum in Philadelphia. And it happened that this same referee was assigned to this game. Once again, right in front of our bench, the ball headed out of bounds and Bobby went for it. Again, this ref was blocked and couldn't see if Bobby touched it or not. "Bobby," he said, "did you touch that ball?"

And Bobby said, "Yes, sir, I did."

So the ref gave the ball to the other team.

Our coach, Billy Cunningham, launched himself from the bench and slammed his foot on the floor. "Bobby!" he shouted. "Let the referees call the game!"

Bobby calmly replied, "Coach, I'm not going to compromise my integrity over one call."

Fact is, Bobby wouldn't have compromised his integrity for a million bucks. He had earned a reputation from a long career in the NBA, and because Bobby was renowned for his honesty and integrity, the refs knew they could trust anything Bobby said.

As inspirational writer M. H. McKee observed, "Integrity is one of several paths. It distinguishes itself from the others because it's the right path, and the only one upon which you will never get lost." To which management guru Tom Peters adds, "There is no such thing as a minor lapse of integrity."[7] It's true. Integrity must be absolute and uncompromised. If you stay on the path of integrity, you will always know where you are.

How do you maintain your personal integrity in a world filled with pressures and temptations? Dr. Billy Graham, in his autobiography, *Just As I Am*, explains the steps he and the other leaders in his organization took to safeguard their integrity for more than half a century. In 1948 Dr. Graham and his top-level team—Cliff Barrows, George Beverly Shea, and Grady Wilson—drove to Modesto, California, for a series of outreach events. Dr. Graham recalls:

> From time to time Cliff, Bev, Grady, and I talked among ourselves about the recurring problems many evangelists seemed to have, and about the poor image so-called mass evangelism had in the eyes of many people. . . .

> One afternoon during the Modesto meetings,
> I called the Team together to discuss the problem.
> Then I asked them to go to their rooms for an
> hour and list all the problems they could think
> of that evangelists and evangelism encountered.
> When they returned, the lists were remark-
> ably similar, and in a short amount of time, we
> made a series of resolutions or commitments
> among ourselves that would guide us in our
> future evangelistic work.[8]

In these resolutions, the Graham team pledged not to manipulate audiences with emotional appeals, nor misuse funds, nor exaggerate successes. The most important resolution dealt with the issue of moral and sexual integrity. Dr. Graham explained, "We pledged among ourselves to avoid any situation that would have even the appearance of compromise or suspicion. From that day on, I did not travel, meet, or eat alone with a woman other than my wife." He added that this pledge, which came to be known as The Modesto Manifesto, served to "settle in our hearts and minds, once and for all, the determination that integrity would be the hallmark of both our lives and our ministry."[9]

This is what I called the "firewall" approach to maintaining your moral integrity. A firewall is a barrier designed to prevent fire from spreading aboard a building or ship. There's also a firewall between the engine compartment and passenger compartment of your car. You hope you never need a firewall—but if a fire ever starts, you're certainly glad it's in place.

A moral firewall is a zone of protection you build to keep from getting scorched by temptation. You put certain rules in place in your life—"I will never cheat on my taxes," "I will never place myself in a compromising position with someone of the opposite sex"—so that the "fire" of moral temptation never even comes close to you.

But remember, the firewall you put in place in your life is

only as good as your commitment to maintaining your integrity. Your moral firewall could be compared to the Great Wall of China, which was built more than two thousand years ago to keep China secure against invasion by barbarians from the north. The Great Wall seemed invincible and indestructible, so the people of ancient China believed they were secure against invasion. However, their enemies managed to invade China three times during the first century of the wall's existence. The barbarians didn't break through the wall, and they didn't climb over it. They simply bribed a gatekeeper and walked through the open gate unchallenged.

As you guard your own integrity, make sure your internal "gatekeeper" doesn't let his guard down and open the gate to temptation. In other words, don't ever say to yourself, "I can handle a little moral compromise. I can flirt with temptation and still be okay. I can give in to a little immorality or dishonesty now and then." The moment you say that to yourself, you've opened the gate. You've breached your integrity. Make sure the moral firewall of your integrity stands firm at all times.

DILIGENCE: "IF YOU'RE LAZY, STAY AWAY"

Leaders of character work hard. They have a strong work ethic. Leaders of excellence are usually the first to arrive and the last to leave. This is not to suggest that leaders must be driven workaholics who neglect their families. But leaders do need to set a good example of a strong work ethic. Your followers are watching you, and your example of diligence sets the tone for your entire team or organization.

If you want to lead people, be prepared to outwork them. I call it having a "what else?" mind-set. A diligent leader is always thinking, "What else can I do? What else can I offer?"

TV and radio impresario Art Linkletter was one of Walt Disney's closest friends. I interviewed Art for my 2004 book on Walt Disney, *How to Be Like Walt*. Art also agreed to write a wonderful foreword for the book, and he told me the story of how he first met Walt Disney.

"It was 1940," Linkletter said, "and I was working at a local radio station in San Francisco. Walt had come to introduce his new motion picture, *Fantasia*. I arrived early for the press conference and found the place empty except for one fellow who was busily arranging chairs. I said, 'When is Walt Disney supposed to arrive?' He grinned and said, 'I'm Walt Disney.' I said, 'You are? Why are you arranging chairs?' He replied, 'Well, I like to have things just-so.' That was quite an introduction, because it gave me a glimpse of the kind of person Walt was."

What does that personal glimpse of Walt Disney tell us? It tells us that the leader of a major Hollywood studio wasn't too self-important to set up chairs. Walt Disney had worked hard all his life, so as far as he was concerned, no job was too big, too small, or too menial. As Peter Drucker said, "No leader is worth his salt who won't set up the chairs."[10]

Grant Hill played seven seasons with the Orlando Magic, and I came to know him as a young man of exceptional character. During his college career, Grant played for Coach Mike Krzyzewski at Duke. He told me about an experience he had during his college days—an experience in which Coach K set an example of a strong work ethic.

"When I was a freshman," Grant said, "I got my nose broken. It was in December and Coach K invited me to stay in his home over the Christmas break. Because of the pain from my broken nose, I had trouble sleeping. I'd wake up, and I couldn't get back to sleep. So I'd come out of my room at four or five in the morning—and Coach was already up! He got up early every morning and watched game film. That said a lot about the way Coach K approached this game. Whenever I'm tempted to slack off, I remember Coach K watching game film at five in the morning."

Pat Summitt has been head coach of the University of Tennessee Lady Vols since 1974, when she was just twenty-two years old. When she started coaching, she earned $250 a month, and her duties included washing the players' uniforms and driving the team van. Coach Summitt's strong work ethic was shaped by her early years growing up on a farm. She preaches the same tough work ethic to her players that her parents taught her, saying, "If you're lazy, stay as far away from me and our program as you can, because you'll be miserable. We work hard."[11]

Another coach who was legendary for a hard-nosed work ethic was the late, great Alabama football coach Paul "Bear" Bryant. In fact, as I studied his life (in the course of writing a book called *Bear Bryant on Leadership*), I found him to be one of the most driven and hardworking coaches in the history of collegiate football. He believed that every day is a gift from God, and we owe it to God to work hard and fulfill the promise of that gift. He had a plaque on his office wall that read:

> WHAT HAVE YOU TRADED FOR WHAT
> GOD HAS GIVEN YOU TODAY?

And on the wall of his home, he had another plaque that read:

> ASK GOD TO BLESS YOUR WORK.
> DO NOT ASK HIM TO DO IT FOR YOU.[12]

Andy Seminick spent most of his career with the Philadelphia Phillies organization. He filled an assortment of roles—player, scout, coach, and manager. I first met Andy when I was a young Phillies fan hanging around the ballpark. Years later, I played for Andy during my minor league career with the Miami Marlins. Andy managed or coached ninety players who got to the major leagues, including Ferguson Jenkins, Bob Boone, Greg Luzinski, Mike Schmidt, and John Vukovich.

I got to know John Vukovich in 1967 when I was general manager of the Spartanburg Phillies, and he shared with me a story about playing for the great Andy Seminick in the Pacific Coast League.

"Andy was old-school," Vuke said. "He had a cast-iron work ethic, and he expected everyone to keep up with him.

When I played for him in the PCL, we'd play a game in Hawaii then take an all-night flight back to Portland, Oregon, then take a bus to Eugene. Everybody on the team was lagged out because of the travel and the three-hour time difference. But we didn't go home. We went straight to the ballpark—Andy's orders. We put in a full day of batting practice and infield.

"Andy was older than the rest of us, and you'd think he'd want to get some sleep. Nope. He didn't need sleep, and he figured the rest of us didn't either. And you didn't hear anybody complaining. Everyone on the team knew that Andy had caught in the 1950 World Series with a broken ankle. So no one was gonna tell *that* guy, 'I'm tired.'"

Andy Seminick had a work ethic that just wouldn't quit—and he set an example for his players that inspired them to work harder, too. When a leader exemplifies that kind of work ethic, followers can't help being inspired.

My writing partner, Jim Denney, once interviewed Bob Griese, the Hall of Fame quarterback who led the Miami Dolphins to an undefeated season in 1972, plus back-to-back Super Bowl wins (VII and VIII). Griese told Jim this story about the indefatigable work ethic of Dolphins head coach Don Shula, and Jim related it to me as we were writing this book:

"The Miami Dolphins became an expansion franchise in 1966," Jim told me, "and Bob Griese was drafted by the Dolphins the following year. Coach George Wilson was an easygoing guy who demanded little from the team. Practices were neither grueling nor strenuous. Bob knew they had great talent on the team, yet his first three seasons under Coach Wilson were losing seasons. Bob is a fierce competitor, and he couldn't stand being on the worst team in the league.

"Bob told me, 'I liked George, but we needed some discipline, some tail-kicking.' They got that in 1970 when the Dolphins hired Don Shula, replacing Wilson as head coach. When Shula was asked to describe his coaching style, he said, 'I'm as subtle as a punch in the face.' In just one season, Shula completely turned the Dolphins around. They went from a

3–10–1 finish in 1969 to a 10–4–0 finish in 1970. The year after that, they went to the Super Bowl. What made the difference? Don Shula's work ethic.

"As Bob Griese explained it, Shula immediately increased the practice schedule to four tough workouts a day. Bob told me, 'My attitude was, "Bring it on! I want to win as much as you do, Coach!"' It was a football boot camp, and Bob said he'd never worked harder in his life. They did scrimmages, Oklahoma drills, and murderous drills called 'gassers.' They ran gassers at the end of every practice. Shula broke the team into squads, and each squad would sprint flat out from sideline to sideline and back again, rest thirty seconds, run it again, rest thirty seconds, and run it a third time. Shula ran the gassers with them, usually with the quarterbacks and kickers.

"I asked Bob if any of his teammates complained about the workouts. 'No,' he said. 'Shoes [Shula] had pared the team down to a hard-core bunch of guys who wanted to win. We knew we needed to be tougher than the guys on the other side of the ball.' Though Bob didn't say so, I suspect that having Shula running gassers with the team was a big motivator. As a player, you can't complain that a drill is too hard if your coach is running alongside you. Don Shula had an incredible work ethic, and he challenged his players to match it.

"Though Shula turned the team around in his first year as head coach, all that hard work really paid off in his second season, 1971. On Christmas Day, the Dolphins went to the divisional playoffs against the Kansas City Chiefs. The Dolphins never had the lead and only managed to tie the game, 24–24, near the end of regulation. They went into overtime, set up a fifty-two-yard field goal attempt—and missed. So they went into a *second* sudden-death overtime.

"Bob Griese recalled thinking, *Wow, Kansas City can't beat us! They're tiring out, and we've still got plenty of steam!* He was glad that Coach Shula had put them through those drills. The Dolphins were the better-conditioned team. In the second overtime, the Dolphins marched to the Chiefs'

30-yard line, kicked a field goal, and won.

"The Dolphins went on to Super Bowl VI, which they lost to Dallas. That was the first of three consecutive Super Bowl appearances, and they won Super Bowls VII and VIII. They went 14–0 in 1972—the NFL's only unbeaten season— and 12–2 in 1973. They accomplished all of this with essentially the same talent pool that had been winning three or four games a season under the previous coach. What made the difference? Hard work and superior conditioning. If you want to win, nothing beats hard work."

SELF-CONTROL: "THE HARDEST PERSON TO LEAD IS YOURSELF"

The 1986 NBA draft brimmed with talent, yet few players from that class went on to stellar NBA careers. Tragically, one of the most promising picks of '86 died before his NBA career even began. I'm talking about Len Bias—the six-foot-eight-inch All-America forward from the University of Maryland. Many sportswriters believed this amazing player had as much raw talent as a young Michael Jordan, maybe more. Bias was selected second overall by the Boston Celtics, and Coach Red Auerbach believed that Bias would extend the Celts' dominance far into the 1990s.

Less than forty-eight hours after his selection in the draft, Len Bias lay dead in a dorm room on the Maryland campus. After apparently consuming large quantities of cocaine, he was sitting on a sofa when he suffered a massive seizure and a fatal cardiac arrhythmia.

This tragedy impressed NBA recruiters with the need to examine a player's *character* as well as his talent. Specifically, we needed to examine whether a given player possessed the character trait of *self-control*.

Looking back on the 1986 draft, it turns out that very few first-round picks in that talent-heavy draft went on to greatness. (The number one pick, Brad Daugherty, was a good character player whose career with the Cleveland Cavaliers was cut short by injuries.) Half of the top fourteen picks of

1986 washed out or were severely hampered by drug or alcohol abuse. They squandered their golden opportunity because they lacked self-control.

If you want to achieve great things, if you want to turn your leadership vision into reality, you must be a person of self-control. The trait of self-control is also known as self-discipline or the ability to lead oneself. Thomas J. Watson, the longtime chairman of IBM, said, "Nothing so conclusively proves a man's ability to lead others as what he does from day to day to lead himself."[13] William Penn, the Quaker leader who founded the Commonwealth of Pennsylvania, wrote in 1669, "No man is fit to command another that cannot command himself."[14] And Bill George, in *True North: Discover Your Authentic Leadership*, writes:

> Authentic leaders know competing successfully takes a consistently high level of self-discipline in order to produce results. They set high standards for themselves and expect the same from others. This requires accepting full responsibility for outcomes and holding others accountable for their performance. . . . Self-discipline should be reflected in their personal lives as well, because without personal self-discipline it is not possible to sustain self-discipline at work. . . . The hardest person you will ever have to lead is yourself.[15]

Swen Nater tells a story from his UCLA basketball days. One day, just minutes before practice, he saw one of his teammates enter Pauley Pavilion in street clothes. The player stepped up to Coach Wooden and chatted privately with him for a few moments.

Players were almost never late to Coach Wooden's practices, because Coach made practice so enjoyable. His practices were mostly competitive, and competition is *fun*. His players always looked forward to basketball practice. So when a player was late, something was *really* wrong.

Swen turned to a teammate, Kenny Booker, and asked, "Why is that guy late?"

"You didn't hear?" said Booker. "He has fifteen unpaid campus parking tickets. Campus police finally caught up with him." Booker gestured toward the rest of their teammates. "We all knew he was going to be late today."

"Did Coach know?"

"Are you kidding?" said Booker. "Coach knows everything before we do."

Some coaches discipline tardiness with physical punishment—a certain number of laps or wind sprints or push-ups. Others discipline tardiness with chores, such as sweeping the gym or picking up trash on campus. Coach Wooden had a tardiness policy that every player understood and accepted: "If you know you are going to be late for practice, don't change into practice gear. Instead, come down to the floor in your street clothes and give me your excuse. If I buy it, you'll be able to practice. If I don't, I have the option of dismissing you for the day. Practice is a privilege." And it was.

Coach Wooden's approach to discipline was not to impose discipline from on high, but to motivate his players to be disciplined from within. He used a player's natural desire as an incentive to develop self-control and self-discipline. A person who is self-controlled within never needs to be punished from without.[16]

Leaders also motivate players by being role models of self-control. Vince Lombardi put it this way: "A good leader must be harder on himself than anyone else. He must first discipline himself before he can discipline others. A man should not ask others to do things he would not have asked himself to do at one time or another in his life."[17]

One of the most effective ways to build self-discipline and self-control into your life is to permit a few trusted friends to hold you accountable. Seek out a few people of trusted character with whom you can meet on a regular basis—weekly, biweekly, or monthly. Agree together that you want to meet on a regular basis to talk honestly about your self-control goals, and hold each other accountable for your progress in character growth. The best foundation for such an accountability group would be a number of covenants that everyone in the group would adhere to:

A covenant of confidentiality: Everything shared in the group stays in the group. This covenant is an absolute requirement for mutual trust.

A covenant of time: You mutually agree to set aside a regular day and time, and to make that meeting time a priority.

A covenant of honesty: You mutually agree to speak truthfully and candidly to each other, to answer honestly when asked about your own life, and to share your honest response to what others say.

A covenant of prayer: Especially if your accountability group is faith-based, you promise to support each other daily in prayer.

A covenant of accountability: You mutually agree to allow others in the group to ask you probing, realistic questions about your actions and moral decisions. These questions might include:

- Are you experiencing problems with temptation or moral choices?
- Are you fighting a moral, ethical, or spiritual battle right now? Are you winning or losing that fight?
- Have you done anything in the past few weeks that, if uncovered, would harm your reputation as a leader?
- Are you moving forward in your character growth right now? Are you moving backward? Are you just coasting?

- What shape is your marriage in right now? Would your spouse agree with your answer?
- How is your relationship with your kids?
- Is there anything going on in your life that makes you feel angry?
- Is there anything that makes you feel defeated or discouraged?
- Are there any steps or actions you need to take this week? Someone you need to forgive? Someone from whom you need to ask forgiveness? What would you like us to check in with you about at our next meeting?

Making yourself accountable to others is a great way to speed your own character growth—especially in the realm of self-control and self-discipline. Behavior that is observed changes. Let a few trusted people into your life to observe your behavior, and you'll begin to see real, steady growth in your character.

PERSEVERANCE: "IT'S A LEAGUE RULE"

Leaders of character don't quit. As a leader, you are a role model, and the way you respond to adversity sets the tone for your entire organization. If you fold your tent in tough times, how will your followers respond? When the shepherd falls, the sheep scatter. As the shepherd of your organization, you've got to keep going, no matter what. You've got to outlast any trial of adversity that comes your way.

Brian Piccolo was a freshman football player at Wake Forest when I was a senior, and I got to know him there. I reconnected with Brian in the fall of 1969 when I was general manager of the Chicago Bulls and Brian was the starting fullback for the Chicago Bears. Tailback Gale Sayers was Brian's roommate.

During a game in Atlanta on November 16, Brian took himself out of the game because he was having trouble breathing. He was diagnosed with an aggressive embryonal cell carcinoma in his chest. Brian underwent several surgeries in an attempt to arrest the cancer. During that time, he had business cards printed up that read:

YOU CAN'T QUIT. IT'S A LEAGUE RULE.
BRIAN PICCOLO

I still have the card Brian gave me.

In May 1970, Gale Sayers (who came back from knee surgery to become the NFL's leading rusher in 1969) was honored with the George S. Halas Courage Award at the Pro Football Writers Association annual banquet in New York. As Sayers got up to receive the award, there were tears in his eyes. "You flatter me by giving me this award," he said, "but I'll tell you here and now that I accept it for Brian Piccolo. Brian Piccolo is the man of courage who should receive the George S. Halas Award. I accept it tonight, but I'll present it to Brian tomorrow. I love Brian Piccolo. And I'd like all of you to love him, too. And tonight, when you hit your knees, ask God to love him, too."[18]

I don't doubt that God loved Brian Piccolo. Nevertheless, on June 16, 1970, Brian Piccolo died at age twenty-six. But even though he died, he never quit. He couldn't. It's a league rule.

What are the trials and setbacks that make you want to quit? Do you need some inspiration and motivation right now to keep you in the game? Then take a page from the story of Coach Bear Bryant and the Junction Boys.

The Junction Boys were the victorious survivors of Coach Bryant's football camp in Junction, Texas, during ten incredible days in September 1954. Sportswriter Jim Dent wrote a book about the Junction Boys, and ESPN made a movie about them. It's a story of character and perseverance.

Paul "Bear" Bryant took over as head football coach at Texas A&M in 1954. Arriving on campus in February of that year, he met his players and found them to be undisciplined, out of shape, and in serious need of an attitude adjustment. So

Coach Bryant set up a football camp on a tract of university-owned land just outside a dusty little town called Junction.

There was nothing to do in Junction—and thus, no distractions. The region was going through the worst drought and heat wave anyone could remember. Every day of football camp topped 100 degrees Fahrenheit, which compounded the misery of Bear Bryant's grueling workouts. Practice lasted from dawn to dinnertime, with meal breaks and team meetings to relieve the physical agony of the workouts.

Today, of course, we know that such intense training methods pose a risk of heatstroke and even death due to exhaustion and dehydration. In Coach Bryant's day, however, these intense practice regimens were designed to increase the stamina and endurance of the team—and to weed out any players who lacked the commitment to persevere. If any of his players were going to quit on him, Bear Bryant wanted them to quit during training camp—not during a game. It worked.

He started day one of training camp with nearly a hundred players. By day ten, he was down to around thirty or so. Those few rugged survivors became known as the Junction Boys.

Now, did the Junction Boys go out and win every game on their schedule that season? Nope. In fact, after all of that suffering, they went on to a miserable 1–9 season. That's right—one win, nine losses.

But that first season was the *only* losing season of Bear Bryant's thirty-seven-year coaching career. The Junction experience laid a strong foundation for future seasons. The A&M Aggies went 7–2–1 in 1955, and 9–0–1 (with a conference championship) in 1956. The Junction Boys formed the durable, won't-quit nucleus of those teams.

One of the Junction Boys, Jack Pardee, recalled that his Junction experience helped prepare him for life after football. He said, "Coach Bryant compared the fourth quarter to getting ready for life. . . . He'd say, 'What are you going to do when you're thirty-five years old, you get your pink slip at work, you go home, your kids are hungry and your wife has run off with the shoe salesman? That's the fourth quarter. Are you going to quit then? Is it going to be too tough for you? Or can people count on you?'"

Pardee credits his Junction experience for preparing him for a cancer diagnosis when he was just twenty-eight years old, playing for the Los Angeles Rams. He noticed a fast-growing mole on his arm, which turned out to be malignant. Fortunately, he caught it in time and has now been cancer-free for decades, but facing a cancer diagnosis at that early age gave him a new perspective on life. That's when he realized, more than ever before, what Coach Bryant had tried to teach him about persevering through "the fourth quarter."[19]

I believe perseverance is a more important indicator of potential success than intelligence, skill, education, talent, or luck. It's hard to defeat a person who simply won't give up.

To date, I have run fifty-eight marathons—one of the most punishing things you can do to the human body. People sometimes ask, "Why do it? Why put yourself through that kind of torture?" My reply: "Running a marathon is the best way I know to practice perseverance." After the first ten miles, my body is screaming, "Stop! You're killing me!" But my will to endure drives me on.

Unless you have run a marathon, you probably can't imagine the euphoria you feel the moment you cross the finish line. Part of that feeling comes from knowing you have passed a punishing physical test. When you pass that test, you *know* you can persevere.

The character trait of perseverance is just as important in the business world as in the sports world. Just ask Tom Monaghan.

When Tom was four, his father died and his mother (who wasn't up to the challenge of single parenthood) sent him to a Catholic orphanage in Michigan. He grew up in a series of foster homes. Tom didn't do well in high school, graduating at the bottom of his class. He attended college at the University of Michigan for a while but dropped out due to lack of funds, and joined the marines.

In the marine corps, Tom gained confidence and leadership skills. He also saved his pay, hoping to start a business. After his discharge, however, a swindler conned him out of his money with a get-rich-quick oil drilling scheme. Two more times he tried going back to college but had to leave due to lack of money.

In 1960, Tom's brother told him about a pizza parlor called DomiNick's, in Ypsilanti, Michigan. The owner wanted to sell out—cheap. So Tom and his brother put five hundred dollars down and borrowed another nine hundred dollars. The owner gave Tom a fifteen-minute lesson in the art of pizza making. Tom Monaghan knew nothing about running a business—not even that he was supposed to collect sales tax. His brother originally agreed to split shifts with him, but Tom soon found himself doing all the work while his brother kept his job as a letter carrier. Finally, Tom bought his brother out—by signing over the VW Bug they used for pizza deliveries.

In time, Tom learned he could make his business more profitable by simplifying the menu and locating pizzerias near college campuses. He changed the name from DomiNick's to Domino's and focused on hiring young people who were willing to work hard and maintain his standards of excellence. "I had great people," he recalled. "I was the best man at just about every wedding for an employee who got married."

In the late 1960s, he attended a franchise seminar and met Ray Kroc of McDonald's and John Y. Brown of KFC. At that time, Tom's Domino's pizza stores were pioneering the concept of pizza delivery. Most pizza shops at that time were dine-in places. "Nobody thought you could make money on delivery," Tom said. "I decided to focus on that, and it was the best thing I've done." In 1969 he began franchising the Domino's brand and quadrupled the number of Domino's shops.

As Domino's expanded, however, Tom lost control of the concept that had made the chain successful—fast delivery from pizzerias located near universities. "I kept selling the franchisees food they couldn't pay for," he said, "and they weren't paying royalties. . . . I ended up losing 51 percent of the company to the bank, which brought in a so-called expert and made things even worse. He ran roughshod over the franchisees—raised prices on the food, cut back on service, cut back on the quality. . . . There was nothing I could do." Finally, after running the franchise into the ground, the bank handed it back to Tom. "I returned to a disaster," he said.

The franchisees filed suit against Tom's company. He owed more than a thousand creditors—and many filed lawsuits against him. Unable to afford an attorney, he handled his own defense in each lawsuit. He spent two years working eighteen-hour days—and each day he expected to be his last day in business. He was determined to pay back all of his creditors, even if he could only pay a few dollars a week—and in time he paid every one of them in full.

Soon he began franchising new stores again, using a completely different franchise model than before. By the end of 1983, Domino's had more than eleven hundred stores. "I was making money like I never had in my life," he said—so much money, in fact, that he bought the Detroit Tigers in 1983, a team he had idolized since his boyhood. The Tigers were good to Tom Monaghan, winning the World Series in 1984. He bought collector cars—244 of them. He bought several landmark houses designed by Frank Lloyd Wright.

And then something happened.

"I read a book by C. S. Lewis called *Mere Christianity*," Tom recalled. "There's a chapter in there on pride, and it hit me right between the eyes. It basically said that sometimes when you work harder than other people and set higher goals than other people, you do it for the wrong reasons—so you have more than other people. And that's pride. . . . So I changed. I took a millionaire's vow of poverty and sold most of my big possessions. I don't drive luxury cars, I don't fly first-class, I don't own yachts, airplanes, any ostentatious things. It was a tremendous sense of freedom. I even sold the Tigers."

Tom Monaghan became increasingly involved in his faith. He founded an organization for Catholic CEOs called Legatus. He built a cathedral in Managua, Nicaragua. He founded a Catholic college and law school. And in 1999 he sold Domino's to Bain Capital and devoted himself completely to serving the church.[20]

Born with nothing, cheated by a con man out of what little he had, Tom Monaghan seemed an unlikely candidate for success. He built up his company—only to have it taken away by the bank. He got the company back—only to discover that he was hopelessly in debt, facing scores of lawsuits. Refusing to go bankrupt, he patiently earned the money to pay back his creditors and go on to become an amazing success story. Now, after years of serving pizzas, he's living out his vision of serving God and serving the church. Not bad for a guy from nowhere who started life in an orphanage.

Tom Monaghan is a living tribute to the power of perseverance. If you refuse to quit, no matter how many setbacks life throws at you, there's no limit to how far you can go or what dreams you may achieve.

RESPONSIBILITY: "THE RULE OF THE RIVER"

Many so-called leaders today make "deniable decisions." If the decision turns out well, they take credit. If the decision flops, they deny they had anything to do with it. But leaders of excellent character don't make excuses and don't shift the blame. They own their decisions, whether good or bad. They are people who possess the character trait of responsibility.

When Mike Krzyzewski was a lowly plebe at West Point in 1965, he discovered a West Point tradition the cadets called "Beast Barracks." He recalled that for two months "they really stripped you of your individual identity." One of the first things he learned was that there are only three possible answers when an upperclassman asks a question: "Yes, sir," "No, sir," or "No excuse, sir."

On one occasion, Krzyzewski was walking on the West Point campus with his roommate. Both were in full uniform. The roommate stepped in a puddle of mud, some of which splashed on Krzyzewski's shoes. Moments later, Krzyzewski saw two upperclassmen approaching. "Halt!" one of them said.

Mike Krzyzewski groaned inwardly and came to a full stop. The two upperclassman looked Mike and his roommate up and down. To the roommate, they said, "You're okay." But when they saw Mike's name tag with the seemingly unpronounceable word *Krzyzewski* printed on it, they demanded, "What kind of name is that?"

Well, that was not the kind of question that could be answered "Yes, sir," "No, sir," or "No excuse, sir," so Mike Krzyzewski said nothing.

"Your shoes are all cruddy," one of the upperclassman pointed out. "How did that happen?"

Krzyzewski wanted to say that his knucklehead roommate splashed mud on his shoes. But at West Point, that was not acceptable. Standing at attention, he replied, "No excuse, sir."

The upperclassman verbally read him the riot act then wrote him up and gave him demerits for the mud on his shoes. At first Mike was furious with his roommate for getting him in trouble. But soon he began to view the situation differently.

> When my roommate stepped in that puddle and splashed mud on my shoes, I had a choice to make. Do I continue or do I go back and change my shoes? What my roommate did was something I had no control over. But the next event was my decision to make. They were my shoes and I was responsible for them. I kept walking and took the chance that I wouldn't be caught. I could have gone back but I didn't. That was my choice. The truth is that I had no right to be mad at my roommate. I should have been mad at myself. And later, when I under-

stood the reality of the situation, I was angry with myself. That was a huge lesson for me.

So how does that lesson translate to what I do now as a coach, as a leader?

Well, no matter what happens, it's my team. I'm responsible. There's no excuse. That's how I feel and that's how I act.[21]

That encounter with a mud puddle was a huge turning point in Mike Krzyzewski's character growth and his growth as a leader. He learned a valuable lesson in taking responsibility for his own actions—a lesson he has carried with him throughout his leadership career.

In 1943, at the height of World War II, British prime minister Winston Churchill came to the United States and delivered a speech at Harvard University—a speech about the shared values that linked the American and British peoples in friendship. In the course of that speech, one especially memorable and quotable line stands out: "The price of greatness is responsibility."[22] It's true. If you want to be a great leader, if you aspire to leadership excellence, then the price you must pay is the price of responsibility. You cannot escape it or evade it. There is no authentic leadership without the character trait of responsibility. There is no such thing as an "irresponsible leader," because the very phrase is a contradiction in terms.

Mike Westhoff, then the special teams coach of Don Shula's Miami Dolphins, was forty years old in 1989 when he was diagnosed with cancer. In surgery, his doctors cut into his thigh and removed an egg-sized tumor from his left femur.

When I interviewed Mike, he told me, "You really find out what you're made of when you're diagnosed with a life-threatening disease. Fighting bone cancer changed my life. It took eight major surgeries to help me beat the cancer. One of those surgeries saved my leg from being amputated by removing the femur."

It took twenty-five screws, two metal plates, and seven inches of leg bone from a cadaver to repair his femur. "I had a serious illness," Mike said, "but I didn't want to sit around and think about how sick I was. Even though you're fighting for your life, you still have day-to-day troubles. Everything is still there—your job, family and friends, stress and bills. How do you handle all of these issues as well as the cancer? I had to dig deep and find new strengths within myself in order to beat the cancer."

Westhoff told Coach Shula he wanted to stay on the job, even though he had weeks of chemotherapy ahead of him. "Fine," Shula said, "but let's get back to work."

Mike recalled, "Coach Shula wasn't going to tuck me in and go easy on me just because I was sick. He's an intense coach, and he has high demands for his staff and players. While I was battling cancer, Coach was supportive, but he didn't treat me any differently than he had before.

"He was treating me the way I *could* be, not the way I was. He never looked at me as if I was handicapped. That helped me see myself as Shula saw me—not a guy on his back in a hospital bed, but as a coach who was going to get the job done. That, as much as anything, helped me get past the cancer."

When Westhoff arrived at training camp, he was pale, thin, and bald from the chemo, and he was walking on crutches. But he went right to work, just as he had before the cancer.

"It's all about responsibility," he said. "I was responsible to do my job—and I was responsible for my own recovery from cancer. Going through that experience has made me a better coach. I preach and teach personal responsibility to my players. They're accountable to learn the system and do it right. As a result, my teams have traditionally been among the least penalized teams in the NFL."

After recovering from his health crisis, Mike took on some new physical challenges. "I went whitewater rafting on the Snake River in Wyoming," he told me. "Each raft holds six or eight people. The guide explained that if someone got thrown from the raft, all attention must be directed toward rescuing that person.

"But he also explained something called the 'Rule of the River,' which states that if you fall into the water, you must be active in your own rescue. You can't just sit there in the water waiting for someone to pull you out. Do that and you may end up floating all the way to Mexico. You have to take responsibility and work with your fellow rafters to get back to safety.

"Responsibility in the NFL is a lot like the Rule of the River. Every player has to know and execute his assignment. If one player fails to shoulder his share of the load, even for one down, the whole effort collapses."

Today Mike Westhoff is a special teams coach for the New York Jets. He demands the same character trait of responsibility from his players that he has always demanded from himself. The Rule of the River is also the Rule of the Football Field and the Rule of the Cancer Ward. In fact, it's the rule of whatever leadership arena you work in. The price of leadership greatness is responsibility.

HUMILITY: "ABSENCE OF ARROGANCE"

Again and again, I've seen leaders get promoted and move up the ranks. They start inhaling the rarefied air of the leadership role. They start believing they are in a special category, a cut above mere mortals. They start thinking, "By divine right, this is all mine." They become narcissistic and they feel entitled to all the perks of leadership—the country club membership, the parking privileges, the executive washroom key. They begin to enjoy having people bowing and scraping before them and fearful of them. These people now have *power*—and their power feeds their ego.

The arrogance that so often comes with promotion and success inevitably begins their downfall. It has ruined more leaders than anything else I could name.

The antidote to this syndrome is a commitment to humility, to maintaining a humble spirit. I've had so many wonderful opportunities throughout my career to meet legendary sports figures, political figures, and media figures. When I see famous people on TV, I often wonder, "Am I seeing the real person—or am I only seeing a carefully crafted image? What is this person *really* like, away from the cameras and microphones?"

Often, when I meet famous people in person, I'm disappointed to discover they are as phony as a three-dollar bill. But whenever I meet someone who is genuine, unaffected, and authentically humble, it is so gratifying and heartwarming.

I once had an author, Sheila Murray Bethel, on my Orlando radio show, and she told me about the late Katharine Graham, longtime publisher of the *Washington Post*. Sheila said that whenever the famous and powerful came to Washington DC from anywhere around the world, they would inevitably end up at Katharine Graham's office or home. She met them all—the great celebrities, the heads of state, the captains of industry, the movers and shakers of the world.

When Sheila interviewed the *Washington Post* publisher, she asked, "Is there a common trait you've noticed in the great leaders you have met?"

"Yes," Katharine Graham replied, "absence of arrogance. All the truly great leaders possessed a humble spirit."

Another guest on my local Orlando radio show was Ruth Graham, Dr. Billy Graham's youngest daughter. She had written a book called *Fear Not Tomorrow, God Is Already There*. In the course of our conversation, I asked her about her famous father. In her rich North Carolina accent, she said, "My Daddy knows who he is, a flawed human being. In Daddy's mind, he's still just a farm boy from Charlotte, North Carolina."

I said to myself, "Dr. Billy Graham has preached to a billion people, and his face and voice are known all around the globe—yet in his mind, he's still just a farm boy from North Carolina."

In April 2011 Dr. James Merritt was a guest on my show. Dr. Merritt, the host of the *Touching Lives* broadcast ministry, had just spent four hours visiting with Billy Graham in his North Carolina home. I asked Dr. Merritt to describe his impression of the ninety-two-year-old evangelist. "The man's life is marked by total humility," he replied. "His home is neat but not ornate at all. I looked at his wrist and saw his watch. It was an inexpensive Timex, at least fifty years old. I also got a sense that Dr. Graham is still overwhelmed that God has used him all these years to touch the world with the gospel."

Another recent guest on my radio show was Michael Reagan, son of President Ronald Reagan. I asked Michael, "What would you say was your dad's greatest strength as a leader?" Without hesitating, he replied, "It would have to be his humility. He was never focused on himself, but was always focused on you. He kept the plaque on his desk in the Oval Office that read, 'There's no limit to what a man can do or where he can go if he doesn't mind who gets the credit.' That wasn't just a slogan to my father. That's who he really was."

Another man who represented leadership greatness along with great humility was Coach John Wooden. As broadcaster Billy Packer once said to me, "John Wooden is the humblest famous person I have ever met."

When I was preparing to write a book called *How to Be Like Coach Wooden*, I wrote him a letter asking for his blessing on the project. A few days later, the phone rang, and I heard an age-mellowed voice say, "Mr. Williams, this is John Wooden, the former basketball coach at UCLA."

I thought to myself, *Coach, I do know who you are, sir.*

He said, "I received your letter, and even though I'm not worthy of a project like this, if you would like to write this book, you go right ahead."

That was the beginning of a decade-long relationship with Coach Wooden that resulted in not one but two books about his life. In every encounter I had with the man, I always came away amazed by his absolute humility—the humility of the number one ranked coach of all time, in all sports, both collegiate and professional. He was a world-class leader—and a world-class, humble servant.

I recently had a chat with Ken Whitten, senior pastor of Idlewild Baptist Church in Tampa, Florida, about another world-class, humble leader—Tony Dungy. Ken is Coach

Dungy's pastor, and he shared a couple of fascinating stories that say a lot about the coach's character.

"When Tony first arrived in Indianapolis to take over as head coach of the Colts," Ken said, "one of the stadium janitors stopped him in the hall. He told Tony he had prayed for years that a Christian coach would come to Indianapolis. When Tony told me that story, he said in all seriousness, 'Pastor, do you realize that I am the coach of the Colts because of the prayers of a janitor?' And you know, Pat, that is how God moves heaven and earth to answer prayers—and that's also a great example of the humility of Tony Dungy."

The other story Ken Whitten told me took place shortly after Tony Dungy suffered a great personal loss. A few days before Christmas 2005, Tony's son James took his own life at the age of eighteen. Not long after James died, a man came to Tony and said, "I'm desperate to keep my son from taking his life. His fiancée committed suicide, and he's depressed and sees no way out. Could you call him and find some way to help him?"

Coach Dungy called this man's son and said, "My name is Tony. Your father asked me to talk to you." They talked for a long time, and Tony told the young man how much he suffered and grieved after James committed suicide.

"You know, son," Tony concluded, "I don't know why God allowed my son to die. But maybe God allowed it just so I could talk to you now and tell you, 'Don't do that to your daddy.'" Dungy shared his faith with the young man and asked him to promise to call him in the morning. The young man gave his word that he would call.

Tony continued having daily talks with this young man for about a week. And each day, he had the young man promise to call him the next day. Finally, the young man reached a point where he promised he would not take his own life. Then he asked, "Tony, what do you do for a living?" This young man didn't even know he'd been speaking to one of the most famous sports leaders on the planet.

"I'm a football coach," Tony replied.

"You coach high school or college football?"

"I coach the Indianapolis Colts," Tony said simply.

Only then did this young man realize who he'd been talking to.

Great leaders are people of character, exemplifying such virtues as integrity, diligence, self-control, courage, perseverance, responsibility, and humility. Of all of these virtues, perhaps the most paradoxical is humility. The greater the leader, the deeper the humility.

As leaders, we set the tone for our teams, our organizations, our military units, our churches, and our families. Leadership is influence, and we inevitably leave the imprint of our personalities on the organizations we lead and the people we meet. So the questions we have to ask ourselves are, "What kind of imprint am I leaving on this team? Do I want this organization, and everyone in it, to be just like me? Do I really want the people in this organization to exhibit all of my character traits—including my flaws?"

Our character is our leadership legacy. The legacy we leave tomorrow is the legacy we are building today.

5

THE FIFTH SIDE OF LEADERSHIP: COMPETENCE

As this book was being written, I had a speaking engagement at a college campus in Northern California. I flew to Sacramento and rented a car from the Hertz facility at the Sacramento airport. At the college, I spoke on—what else?—the seven sides of leadership. Afterward, I drove back to the airport, parked the car in the Hertz lot, grabbed my luggage, and went to catch the bus to the terminal.

I hadn't taken more than a half dozen steps when an attractive young lady with a Hertz name tag approached. She smiled and said, "I hope you had a nice trip."

"Very nice, thank you."

"You know, the two items customers most frequently leave behind in rental cars are cell phones and keys."

I slapped my pockets—my *empty* pockets. "Oh no," I said, looking back at the car. I knew exactly where my cell phone and house and car keys were: the center console of the rental car. If the Hertz manager hadn't reminded me, I probably wouldn't have missed them until I was winging my way back to Orlando. "Miss," I said, "you have saved me from a terrible mistake."

"Glad I could help."

After retrieving the items from the car, I turned to the

young lady and read her name tag—Nicole Machado, manager of the Hertz car rental facility at the Sacramento airport. She walked with me to the bus area, and I said, "Nicole, you have leadership written all over you! You're competent, you're available to the public. You don't hide in an office somewhere, but you're out among the customers, making sure our needs are met. I think you have a great leadership career ahead of you. Give me your card, and when I get home, I'm going to send you some leadership materials."

The following day, back home in Orlando, I mailed her a couple of my recent books, and I plan to send this book to her as soon as it's published. I also called Nicole's boss and said, "You have a young leader in your district who did me a huge favor when I returned my rental car yesterday." And I told him the story.

For Nicole Machado, it probably was a small thing to remind a customer not to forget his cell phone and keys—but for *this* customer, it was a very big deal! The fifth side of leadership is competence. Nicole Machado's competence in her leadership role at Hertz really made my day.

LEADERS ARE MADE, NOT BORN

A few years ago, I spoke at an event in Arkansas hosted by Arvest Bank, which was founded by the Walton family. Not the TV Waltons, the Walmart Waltons. After I delivered my talk, I walked to the back of the room and sat down next to a man dressed in khaki slacks and a golf shirt.

He leaned toward me and said, "Nice job."

"Thank you."

He put out his hand and said, "I'm Jim Walton."

Wow! By sheer chance, I had managed to sit down next to James Carr Walton, the chairman of Arvest Bank and the youngest son of Sam Walton. With an estimated net worth of more than twenty-one billion dollars, Jim Walton is ranked by *Forbes* as the twentieth-richest individual in the world.

"Glad to meet you, Mr. Walton," I said.

"Call me Jim," he said. "Would you like to join me for lunch?"

Lunch with a billionaire? Count me in! What's on the menu—pheasant under glass, perhaps? As it turned out, we ate at an outdoor food court and I had an excellent turkey sandwich on whole wheat.

We chatted for a while, and I said, "Jim, are you aware that a group of Harvard professors published a thick book ranking the hundred greatest business leaders in American history, and they ranked your dad number one?"

"How about that?" he said. "I'll have to get the book."

"Jim, what was your dad's greatest strength as a leader?"

"You know, that's a great question—and I'm surprised nobody ever asked me that before. I'd have to say his greatest strength was his passion for the retailing industry. Dad loved the merchandise. He was always going here and there, looking for the latest item, trying to get the best price. 'Stack it high and sell it low,' he'd always say. For example, that shirt you're wearing—"

(I wore a Hawaiian shirt that day. Why a Hawaiian shirt? Well, have you ever seen anyone in a Hawaiian shirt having a bad day?)

Jim said, "Dad would have been fascinated by your shirt. He would have wanted to examine the material and the weave. He'd want to know where the material came from. He'd turn your sleeve inside out and check the quality of the stitching. He was curious about everything, knowledgeable about everything, constantly learning and reading up on every aspect of the retail business. That's why he was so good at what he did—and that was his greatest strength as a leader."

Business writer Robert Slater came to the same conclusion in *The Wal-Mart Decade*, observing that Sam Walton "was perhaps the greatest merchant of his era. He had an uncanny instinct for sensing what products would sell, at what prices they would sell; where to locate stores, and what those stores should look like. . . . He thought of himself first and foremost as a merchandiser, as someone who had a knack for creating the kind of store environment that would appeal to the customer."[1] I believe the qualities that Jim Walton and Robert Slater saw in the late Sam Walton are expressions of his high level of *competence* as a leader.

I would define *competence* as "the ability to perform the leadership role in a highly effective way." A leader of competence displays the attitudes, skills, abilities, and behaviors needed to function at a very high level and to take the organization to increasingly higher levels of success. Competence is not a static condition. It's a state of one's continual dynamic growth, both as a person and a leader.

A few years ago, while researching my book *Coaching Your Kids to Be Leaders*, I sent a questionnaire to leaders across the country, and asked, "Are leaders born or made?" About 85 percent of the respondents replied that leaders are *made*. That was great news! If they had all told me that leaders are born, not made, I would have had to call my publisher and say, "Never mind. There's no need to write the book. We're either born leaders or we're not, end of story."

Ever since I moved to Florida, I've been going out to the end of my driveway each morning and picking up my copy of the Orlando *Sentinel*. I have yet to see a headline that reads, "Great Natural Leader Born Yesterday at Florida Hospital!" I'm sure that a few individuals are born with a natural talent for leadership, just as a few seem to have a natural gift for mathematics or music or athletics. But for the rest of us, leadership is a learnable skill. No matter how our personalities have been shaped by DNA, parentage, education, and life experiences, we can all acquire and improve the skills of a leader—and great leadership experts agree. In *Learning to Lead*, Warren Bennis and Joan Goldsmith write:

> Leaders are made, not born, and are created as much by themselves as by the demands of their times. They have a talent for continually learning about themselves. They seek to know who they are, what they want, why they want

it, and how to gain support to achieve it. They live on the frontiers, where tomorrow is shaped. They avoid cookie-cutter patterns, come from diverse backgrounds, are of different ages and types of intelligence, have a variety of occupations and accomplishments. They are committed to continually growing throughout their lives. Some blossom only in their later years, like George Bernard Shaw, Margaret Mead, Charles Darwin, Eleanor Roosevelt, Elie Wiesel, Nelson Mandela, Mohandas Gandhi, Golda Meir, Jean Piaget, and Martha Graham. The glittering accomplishments of these great leaders demonstrate to us that it is never too late to begin.[2]

The late religious leader and author Leonard Ravenhill offers a short parable to make the point: "A group of tourists visiting a picturesque village saw an old man sitting by a fence. In a rather patronizing way, one of the visitors asked, 'Were any great men born in this village?' Without looking up, the old man replied, 'No, only babies.'"[3] Leaders aren't born. Leaders are made—and each of us can choose to be leaders-in-the-making—constantly learning and improving our leadership skills throughout our lives.

The overall competence of a leader can be broken down into a number of specific "competencies" or traits. In the next few pages, we'll examine fifteen leadership competencies:

1. The competency of problem solving

If you are not a problem solver, you are not a leader. Many people avoid problems. Great leaders eat problems for breakfast. General Colin Powell put it this way: "Leadership is solving problems. The day soldiers stop bringing you their problems is the day you have stopped leading them. They have either lost confidence that you can help them or concluded you do not care. Either case is a failure of leadership."[4]

So as long as problems keep landing in your "In" basket, your leadership job is secure.

I learned a big lesson in problem solving during my early days as a minor league general manager in Spartanburg, South Carolina. If you want to lead the league in problems, that was the job to have. The whole season was one crisis after another. I'd have my promotions set up; then a big rainstorm would hit. Or the front office would move our best player up to the next level. Or I was struggling with the manager, who had his own way of doing things. Or the hot dog vendor was a no-show on our biggest attendance night.

The team co-owner, Mr. R. E. Littlejohn, was a wonderful teacher. I still rely on the principles he taught me. When I had a problem, I'd spread it out on Mr. Littlejohn's desk and say, in effect, "Please solve this problem for me."

I can still hear him say, in that gentle South Carolina twang, "Don't run from your problems, Pat, because they give you a wonderful opportunity to sell yourself to others. Anybody can lead when conditions are perfect. If you want to be a leader, then you need to show that you are a problem solver. Problems just come with the job."

When Hall of Fame NBA coach Chuck Daly was head coach of the Orlando Magic in the late 1990s, he told me about a conversation he once had with his assistant coach, Bob Zuffelato, when Chuck coached men's basketball at Boston College. "Bob came into my office one time," Chuck said, "and he was really steamed about something. Boiling mad. So I let him get it out of his system. Then I said, 'Wait a minute, Bob. You want to be a head coach someday, right? Well, you see the problems you have now? When you're a head coach, multiply that by ten.' He didn't say another word."

Fox News Channel anchor Neil Cavuto knows about problems. In the late 1980s, he battled and overcame stage IV Hodgkin's lymphoma. In the late 1990s, Cavuto was diagnosed with multiple sclerosis—a crippling and progressive neurological disease. Today Cavuto courageously defies his

MS, exercising on a treadmill to arrest the muscle atrophy that is common among MS sufferers.

He often does his show while suffering headaches, exhaustion, hoarseness, and vision impairment. He memorizes his scripts in case his vision blurs to the point he can't read the teleprompter.[5] He once said, "I don't hide that I have had a tough life in many respects. I fought back a near-life-ending cancer, only to end up with multiple sclerosis years later. Doctors have since told me that the odds of contracting both diseases in the same life are something like two million to one! Yet here I am, marching on, continuing to do my job when doctors who've examined my scans and MRIs tell me I shouldn't be walking or talking."[6]

On one occasion, Cavuto addressed a gathering of patients with MS. His message to them: "Quit being a victim. You are sick. Some of you are *very* sick. It's not fair. It's not right. I'm telling you it just *is*. . . . You—we—just got dealt a bad deck of genetic cards. End of story. Move on."

When he recounted that story on his Fox News show, *Your World with Neil Cavuto*, he used it to make a broader point—a point that every leader should take to heart. "My point," he said, "is to address this bigger trend in our society to play victim—to play the 'woe is me' card."

Cavuto noted that President Obama frequently talks about the problems he inherited from the previous administration, or that were thrust upon him after he came into office. "But I think you have a choice in life," Cavuto observed. "You can play the victim, or you can be a leader. It's fair to say that this president had a lot thrown at him. It's also fair to say a majority of voters looked to him to fix it. And he hasn't. Life is unfair. . . . But I think that just means we buckle down. . . [and] show the world that there is more to us, that our hardships haven't made us bitter—but better."

In other words, we need leaders who are problem solvers, not finger pointers. Instead, all we get from our elected leaders, from our business leaders, and yes, from ourselves, is more finger pointing. Cavuto said, "Republicans [are] pointing at Democrats for budget cuts that aren't real, then submitting cuts of their own that aren't much better. Wall Street is bemoaning big government then griping if they don't get help themselves from the government. Mortgage victims say they were forced to sign documents they didn't read to get a house they knew they couldn't afford. . . . It's time to stop pointing fingers and saying 'woe is me,' and time to start saying, 'Follow me.'"[7]

Neil Cavuto's advice to the Republicans and Democrats, to Wall Street and to all of us, is essentially the same advice Mr. R. E. Littlejohn gave a young Pat Williams so many years ago. Stop bemoaning your problems and start using them as opportunities to show what you're made of. Stop saying, "Woe is me," and start saying, "Follow me." That's what leaders do.

2. The competency of selling

When Chuck Daly was head coach of the Magic, he'd sometimes come to me looking flustered. "Pat," he'd growl, "I'm not a coach—I'm a salesman! All I do is sell. I'm selling these ballplayers on my game plans and strategies. I'm selling the front office on improving our facilities and personnel. Every time I talk to the media, I'm selling them. And I'm constantly selling to the fans. All I do is sell!"

Chuck was right—and former NBA coach Phil Jackson agrees. Jackson, who won eleven NBA titles as head coach of the Bulls and Lakers, once observed, "Coaching is salesmanship. Coaching is winning players over and convincing them that they have to play together."[8]

What Daly and Jackson say about coaches is true of *all* leaders in *every* arena. Leadership is selling. Turn on the TV or pick up a newspaper, and what do you see? The president of the United States is selling his domestic policy agenda, his foreign policy agenda, his health care agenda, or his tax policy. Every time the president makes a public appearance, whether he's giving the State of the Union address or pardoning the Thanksgiving turkey, he's selling. If the leader of the free world is always selling, shouldn't you and I become competent salespeople as well?

In our Orlando Magic organization, people sometimes come to me for advice. They say, "I'm in sales, and I really want to get out of sales and into management." I'll bet I've heard a hundred variations on that statement. I always say, "Oh, you want to get into management. Well, then you'll *really* be in sales. Even if you reach the pinnacle of the organization, you will never leave sales—because leadership is all about selling."

So what are you selling? A message? An idea? A candidate? A product? My friend, it all starts with you. To be a leader, you must sell *you*. No one person represents a team, a company, a military unit, or a church as much as the leader. You are the personification of your organization. When people think of your organization, they don't think of a building or a logo; they think of a leader.

Former presidential speechwriter James C. Humes is credited with helping to write (along with William Safire and Patrick Buchanan) the text on the Apollo 11 lunar plaque. In his book *Speak Like Churchill, Stand Like Lincoln*, he writes:

> Leadership is selling. And selling is talking.
>
> The ability of a chief executive to talk for and promote his company is a chief factor in determining the worth of that company in the marketplace. Harold Burson, founder and head of one of the nation's biggest public relations agencies, Burson & Marsteller, commissioned a survey that found that 86 percent of analysts said they "would buy stock based on the CEO's reputation." Burson concluded that it's the winning personality and selling ability of the CEO that is crucial to the growing health of the corporation. If a company's chief executive cannot persuade, convince, and sell the unique strength and future of his company, his company stands in jeopardy.[9]

Mr. Littlejohn was one of the greatest salesmen I ever met. He started out selling equipment to gas station owners and later used those same selling skills to acquire a fleet of tankers and build a fuel hauling company. He built his minor league baseball team on selling, because in the sports business, that's all you do. Mr. Littlejohn taught me that if you can't sell minor league baseball to the fans, whether you're winning or losing, you will fail, period.

In minor league baseball, you can't expect to win all the time. Having a winning team helps to draw the fans—but what if your team is losing? You have no control over how well your ball club performs, because the major league organization calls the shots. They send players down and move players up. The moment you have a player on a hot streak and becoming a crowd-pleaser, what happens? The team moves him up to the next level!

So, in minor league baseball, you have to sell a good time, whether the team wins or loses. You have to keep the fans entertained with promotions and pregame shows. People need to feel that they're going to get their entertainment dollar's worth at the ballpark. And believe me, *that* can be a tough sell! But selling is also fun. Those days of selling minor league baseball to the fans in Spartanburg were some of the happiest days of my life.

Jack Kent Cooke (1912–97) was a Canadian-born self-made billionaire whose holdings once included the Chrysler Building in New York, the Los Angeles Lakers, and the Washington Redskins. Cooke learned the essential rules of selling at the age of fourteen during the Great Depression.

His mother needed $2.50 to pay the phone bill, so Jack got a job selling encyclopedias door-to-door. The encyclopedias came with a booklet on successful salesmanship. Jack flipped through the book but didn't think he needed the sales tips. He could sell encyclopedias with charm alone.

Cooke made his first call on a store owner named Mr. Pickering. The encounter went so badly, it shook Jack's confidence. So he went home and studied the salesmanship book for two hours. Then he went out and approached another customer. This time he made the sale. Then he went back to Mr. Pickering—and sold a set of encyclopedias to the man who had already turned him down.

After that, he made the rounds of his neighborhood, and by the end of his first day, he had earned $24.50—almost ten times as much as his mother needed to pay the phone bill. "That was the proudest moment of my life," he later said. In fact, he added, it was even better than winning a Super Bowl.[10] That early lesson in salesmanship was the defining moment of his life—the moment when the course of his future life was set.

If you want to be a leader, you have to be a salesman. And as Mr. Littlejohn often told me, the first thing you must sell is yourself.

3. The competency of continuous learning

Once, when I was visiting Coach John Wooden at his condo in Encino, California, he quoted an adage he had lived by throughout his life: "Live as though you'll die tomorrow. Learn as though you'll live forever." Coach gave the credit for his love of learning to his father, Joshua Hugh Wooden. "There is no book that compares to the Bible," Coach Wooden once wrote, "but Dad also read Shakespeare to his sons, and lots of poetry. I continued reading—the philosophers, biographies of great individuals, and other good literature. Dad reminded me often, 'Johnny, you'll never learn a thing that you didn't learn from someone else.' Good books help us do that."[11]

Leaders must fall in love with learning. Author Andy Stanley observes, "Great leaders are great learners."[12] And President John F. Kennedy reminded us, "Learning and leadership are indispensable to each other. If we stop learning today, we will stop leading tomorrow."[13] Leaders who excel over time are always learning, always striving to stay current, always scanning the horizon for new insights and ideas.

How do you become a lifelong learner?

First, you can continue your formal education. You may think, *I've always wanted to get my master's degree.* Or, *I never really finished college—but why not do so now?* Or, *Why not go for that PhD I've always thought about?* You can do it. You don't have to drop out of life and spend the next few years of your life on a college campus. There are fully accredited extension and online universities, and there are many ways you can finish your education while you continue your life.

My wife, Ruth, is completing a doctorate in organizational leadership at Walden University—and when she does, I'll be married to Dr. Ruth. (That should make life interesting.)

Second, you can be a lifelong learner by hanging out with really smart people. Seek out those who are a rung or two above you on the achievement ladder. Take them to lunch, ask questions, and take notes. Soak up their knowledge and ideas, their curiosity about the world, their wisdom and understanding.

Third, seek out mentors. These are people who have already been down the path you are on, people you'd like to meet with on a regular basis, people you approach anytime with a question or a problem. You might think, "I'd like to ask so-and-so to be my mentor—but I'm sure he or she is too busy to take that kind of time for me." Well, maybe so—but what do you lose by asking?

Most people would be honored that you asked—particularly those who are retired. You could not pay them a higher compliment than to ask, "Would you consider mentoring me?" Seek them out. Nine times out of ten, they'll be eager to invest in your future.

Fourth, if you happen to encounter an accomplished person by chance, don't waste the opportunity. Speak up! Shyness is no excuse.

I remember times when my kids would say to me, "Hey, I saw Ken Griffey Jr., downtown today," or, "I saw Monica Seles at the mall." I'd ask, "What did you ask them?" And they'd reply, "Nothing—I didn't want to intrude."

They didn't want to intrude! Haven't they ever seen their dad in action? When I see accomplished people, I *leap* at the chance to talk to them. I'm always eager to have some of their wisdom and success rub off on me. If there's only enough time for a handshake, I'll settle for the handshake. If there's time for a few questions, I'll grab my pen and a paper napkin, and I'll fire away: "What's the most important word of advice you ever got? Who were your role models when you were growing up—and why?"

Over the years, I've crossed paths with many famous people—sometimes for just a few seconds. I always seize the opportunity. Sure, I've been rebuffed a few times—but so what? I've also accumulated a vast treasure trove of insights, many of which are contained in this book.

One opportunity took place a few years ago at a book convention in Chicago. I had nearly finished writing *How to Be Like Walt Disney*, my motivational biography of the beloved entertainment mogul. I'd spent years trying to track down every living person who had known Walt. There were a few people I was unable to reach, including the lovely Julie Andrews.

So there I was at the book convention, waiting in the greenroom for my turn to go out and speak. I looked up, and there, about twenty feet in front of me, was Julie Andrews! I had no idea she was at the convention. I raced over to her and said, "Miss Andrews, I'm Pat Williams, and I'm writing a book called *How to Be Like Walt Disney*. Could you please tell me—what's your most vivid memory of Walt?"

"Oh, Pat," she said in her lilting Mary Poppins voice, "it was his sparkling eyes!"

This was great! I wanted to know more! But just then, one of her handlers said, "Miss Andrews, it's time to go."

They whisked her away, and she was gone. I had gotten only ten seconds with Julie Andrews—but I picked up a little insight into Walt Disney that no one else had shared with me. Just a few words—"his sparkling eyes!"—said so much about Disney's enthusiasm, his energy, his childlike wonder. That was pixie dust sparkling in his eyes—and Julie Andrews had given me the gift of that insight.

I added that little story to the book, and I was happy.

Fifth, become a voracious reader. Harry Truman, one of my favorite presidents, once wrote, "Readers of good books, particularly books of biography and history, are preparing themselves for leadership. Not all readers become leaders, but all leaders must be readers."[14] After graduating high school in 1901, Truman went to work for the Santa Fe Railroad. Though never formally educated at college, Truman was one of our brightest presidents. He had a quick and ready wit and possessed a deep understanding of world history. Truman could study a situation and render a keen and perceptive decision within moments.

How did a mere high school graduate possess such a great mind and a thorough understanding of the world around him? I believe it's because Harry Truman out read all of his contemporaries. He didn't have a diploma to hang on his wall, but he was a highly educated man. He earned his education from books.

If you hold a university degree but you've stopped reading and learning after you graduated, you're not a well-educated person. Really, how much of what you learned in college can you recall right now? How much has the world changed since you left college? You have to keep discovering new ideas and insights about the world around you. The way you do that is through reading.

People magazine, *USA Today*, and the *Wall Street Journal* are all fine publications, but most of what they contain is of fleeting importance. Novels are entertaining but contain little that will enlarge your leadership capacity. If you truly want to grow as a leader, I urge you to invest an hour a day in reading books about great lives, great events, and great ideas.

If you read an hour a day, you can usually get through one book in a week. At the end of one month, you will have read 4 books. In one year, 52 books. In ten years, 520 books. If you read five authoritative books on any one subject, you can be a leading authority on that subject. You'll be a sparkling conversationalist, requested as a dinner companion all over town. You'll fascinate people and take your leadership skills to the next level. There are other benefits to lifelong reading and learning as well. If you want to be good to your brain, keep learning and keep reading. In his book *The Anti-Alzheimer's Prescription*, Dr. Vincent Fortanasce writes:

> Studies show that people who have higher education or continue to learn throughout their lives may be at a lower risk of Alzheimer's disease than those who have less education. Please note that by education, researchers are not referring to the number of years of formal education. . . . People who continue to learn—by traveling to new places, reading books, visiting art galleries and museums, and discussing their findings with family and friends, doing crossword puzzles daily, playing a musical instrument or learning a new language—boost the size of their brain reserve and reduce their chance of Alzheimer's disease.[15]

Whenever I go to speak, I always promote the joy of reading. After my talks, people often come to me and ask, "What books should I read?" This is an important question. When you buy a book, you make a financial investment—and when you sit down to read that book, you invest a piece of your life in its pages. So invest wisely.

Check for current releases in the book review section of the *New York Times* or your local newspaper. For the latest books on science, culture, history, and politics, watch *Book TV* on C-SPAN2. Look up your favorite books on Amazon. com and see what other titles are suggested under "Customers Who Bought This Item Also Bought. . . ." Ask for recommendations from people whose interests you share. Personally, I like to browse in bookstores, pick up the books, and scan a few pages to see if a book "speaks" to me or not.

When you see someone reading on a flight or in the park, be bold and say, "Excuse me—is it a good book? What do you like about it?" I always find that book lovers enjoy talking about their latest finds. And when you meet someone new, here's the perfect conversation starter: "What books have you read lately?" Or, "Who's your favorite author?" You'll find out more about someone through the books they read than any other way—and you'll come away with some life-changing recommendations.

I have a library at home of about seven thousand books. They are like friends to me because I've spent quality time with them. I enjoy their company, and I revisit them again and again. My books are an investment I've made in energizing and revitalizing my mind so that I will be a sharper, smarter, wiser leader. I identify with artist Michele Oka Doner, who writes, "Our accountant nearly dropped dead when he saw what I spent on books last year. My husband said, 'I guess he doesn't know too many people who would spend more money on books than on clothes.'"[16]

To get the most out of books, schedule a daily reading time, at least an hour a day if you can. Even if you read for as few as fifteen minutes a day, it adds up to at least seven hours per month. I guarantee that those seven hours will make a big difference in your life. Keep books handy at all times. Keep a good book on your bedside table, in your den, and in your living room. Take books with you whenever you travel. You can keep hundreds of books at your fingertips by loading e-books on your iPad, smart phone, Kindle, Nook, or other e-readers. If you commute, listen to audio books in your car.

Have an interactive experience with your books. Mark them, highlight them, write notes, ideas, and questions in the margins. Cheer the author on—or rant and shout at the author in the notes you write. Join a book discussion club and share your reading experiences with other book lovers. As bookseller Nathan Pine once observed, "There's something special about people who are interested in the printed word. They are a species all their own—learned, kind, knowledgeable, and human."[17]

Books are windows into great minds and grand ideas. So be a continuous learner and a lifelong reader.

4. The competency of teaching
The greatest leaders are also outstanding teachers. In July 2009, *The Sporting News* ranked the fifty greatest coaches of all time, in every sport, both collegiate and professional. The number one coach on that list was John Wooden, the longtime basketball coach of the UCLA Bruins. One of the legendary players he coached, Kareem Abdul-Jabbar, wrote these words of tribute to Coach Wooden in 2000:

> Thirty-five years ago, I walked into John Wooden's office at UCLA and began a special relationship that has enriched my life. . . . He was soft-spoken and serious. . .more a teacher than a coach. He broke basketball down to its basic elements. He always told us basketball was a simple game, but his ability to make the game simple was part of his genius.
>
> I never remember him yelling on the court, but there was no need because he never had trouble getting his point across. I remember a close game in my sophomore year against Colorado State. During timeouts, his instructions were clear and precise. I had never doubted him before, but when the game ended, it was obvious he had been thinking three moves ahead of us, calm and cool as always.[18]

Over the years, I have written two books about Coach Wooden, and I had the chance to interview him extensively about his life, his values, and his leadership philosophy. I discovered that he considered himself, first and foremost, a teacher. If you asked him, "How many years have you spent in coaching?" he'd gently correct you and say, "I was a *teacher* for forty years, eleven in high school, twenty-nine in college."

That's a perspective every leader should adopt in every field of endeavor: *Leadership is teaching.* Presidents, governors,

CEOs, coaches, military leaders, opinion leaders—all should see themselves as teachers. Our job is to take the complex and make it simple, take the arcane and make it understandable. We should never assume that our people "get it." If they don't "get it," it's because we failed to teach them.

Another great coaching legend who was both a leader and a teacher was Vince Lombardi, who led the Green Bay Packers to five NFL championships, including victories in Super Bowls I and II. Like John Wooden, Lombardi started teaching at the high school level. He spent eight years coaching football at St. Cecilia High School in Inglewood, New Jersey, while also teaching Latin, chemistry, and physics. He also taught at Fordham and West Point before moving on to the NFL.

In a book about Coach Lombardi's leadership principles, *The Lombardi Rules*, written by his son, Vince Lombardi Jr., we see the same emphasis on clear, concise, correct teaching that we see in the leadership philosophy of Coach Wooden:

> Lombardi often used the words "teaching" and "coaching" interchangeably. . . .
>
> As both a teacher and a coach, Lombardi concentrated on the whys. "I never tell a player, 'This is my way, now do it,'" he once said. "Instead, I say, 'This is the way we do it, and this is why we do it.'" . . .
>
> Lombardi taught to the bottom of the "class," going slowly enough—and being repetitive enough—so that no one was left behind. . . . The risk in this style of teaching/coaching, of course, is that the top of the class—or even the teacher—will get bored. Lombardi avoided this in part by the simple force of his personality and convictions. He had a way of making even a routine task sound important, as if there were no routine tasks. . . .
>
> "I loved it," recalled Packers quarterback

Bart Starr. "I never, ever was bored or tired at any meeting we were in with Lombardi. I appreciated what he was trying to teach. He was always trying to raise the bar."[19]

Condoleezza Rice served as national security adviser and secretary of state in the George W. Bush administration. Before joining the Bush White House, Rice taught political science at Stanford, where she also served as provost from 1993 to 1999. Secretary Rice is a leader—and a teacher. In *Condi: The Condoleezza Rice Story*, biographer Antonia Felix examines Rice's teaching role at Stanford:

> One of Condi's colleagues remarked that the passion she brought to teaching was obvious even after she left the classroom. "Anyone who has had the good fortune to have a meeting with Professor Rice immediately after one of her lectures can sense the excitement she brings to the classroom," he said. "Just by the way she talks about the lecture she has just given, it is obvious that she is still completely engaged in her subject and in her students to a truly extraordinary degree." Students who had Condi as an academic advisor knew that she was seriously committed to them. . . . [A graduate student] described her as a marvelous facilitator, a teacher in an ancient Socratic sense.[20]

It should amaze no one that Professor Rice the teacher and Secretary Rice the government leader are one and the same person. Both leaders and teachers inspire and motivate. Both are role models. One of Professor Rice's students offered this assessment of her as both a teacher and a leader:

> "She. . .treated us all as if we were her favorite students. . . . Several of the students were wist-

fully thinking about how much we wanted to be like her. This was not idle hero-worship. She seemed to be the embodiment of everything we admired about academia. She was knowledgeable without being closed-minded, prestigious without being pompous, and her lectures were complex without being dry."[21]

That is an excellent role model for us all to emulate, whether we are leaders in academia, in government, in the corporate world, in the religious world, in the sports world, or in any other leadership field. As Noel Tichy and Eli Cohen observe:

Teaching is at the heart of leading. In fact, it is through teaching that leaders lead others. Leading is not dictating specific behavior. It is not issuing orders and commanding compliance. Leading is getting others to see a situation as it really is and to understand what responses need to be taken. . . . Simply put, if you aren't teaching you aren't leading.[22]

To become the fully competent leader you were meant to be, lead by teaching and teach by leading.

5. The competency of team-building

Human beings are social beings. We're designed to achieve our goals through teamwork. Mike Krzyzewski put it this way: "People want to be on a team. They want to be part of something bigger than themselves. They want to be in a situation where they feel that they are doing something for the greater good."[23]

This is true whether the team is a sports, business, non-profit, religious, academic, or military organization. People need a sense of connection to other people and to a greater cause. I have given thousands of speeches before audiences in the corporate world, and the number one topic I'm asked to speak on is teamwork. One of your most important priorities as a leader is to enable people to function together as a team.

Coach Bill Curry is the founder and architect of the Georgia State University football program. He knows about team building from the ground up. He calls teamwork "the miracle of the huddle." Why is teamwork a "miracle"? Because when a group of individuals come together and fuse themselves into a dynamic organism called a team, all differences between individuals are magically transcended, and these teammates are bonded together in a tightly knit brother- or sisterhood.

Curry says, "The most important thing about sports is the miracle of the huddle. Players of all races, nationalities, religions, backgrounds, and creeds come together as one to accomplish a common goal as a team."[24] That's why I truly believe that teamwork is the ideal environment for solving all the problems that plague humanity, from racial division to a troubled economy to conflicts between nations. Teamwork is the power to leverage individual competencies and abilities into a force far greater than the sum of the parts.

At the 1980 Winter Olympics in Lake Placid, New York, the United States fielded a hockey team of young amateurs and college players. Team USA was seeded seventh in a twelve-team field. On February 22, they faced off against a Soviet team of so-called amateurs, who were actually paid by the Soviet government to train year-round in world-class hockey facilities. The Soviets had not lost a single Olympic match since 1968, and had won the gold at every Winter Olympiad since 1960.

USA hockey coach Herb Brooks knew his team was completely overmatched by the Soviets. To beat the USSR, Team USA would have to display superior teamwork. In assembling his team, he cut several highly talented players from the team in favor of less-talented players who understood teamwork. He said he was looking for players who believed the team name on the front of the sweater was more important than the player's name on the back.

As the match began, the Soviets scored quickly—but USA forward Buzz Schneider answered with a tying goal. The Soviets scored again—but USA forward Mark Johnson evened the score again with one second remaining in the first period. In the second period, the Soviets went ahead once more—and Johnson fired back, tying the match at three. Goalie Jim Craig smothered thirty-six of the Soviets' thirty-nine goal attempts. Team USA played at a level that astounded even Coach Brooks. Finally, with ten minutes remaining, USA's Mike Eruzione blasted the puck into the net for a 4–3 USA lead.

That's when Coach Brooks really began to sweat. He'd seen other teams achieve a one-goal lead over the Soviets—only to see them collapse before the final buzzer. Brooks shouted to his team, "Play your game!" His team played its game, clinging to its slim margin as the crowd counted down. ABC sportscaster Al Michaels made the historic call: "Morrow, up to Silk, five seconds left in the game!"

The arena shuddered with noise and raw emotion.

"Do you believe in miracles?" shouted Michaels. The buzzer sounded, and Michaels answered his own question. "*Yes!* Unbelievable!"

The crowd cheered, wept, and waved American flags. People sang "God Bless America." On the ice, Team USA whooped, hugged, and wept. They had accomplished the impossible—and they had done it by the power of teamwork.

Now, fast forward twenty-four years to the 2004 Summer Olympics in Athens, Greece. In men's basketball, the United States fell short of the goal for the first time since NBA players were permitted to participate. Puerto Rico defeated the highly touted, highly talented Team USA, 92–73. When the US team returned home with only a bronze medal, a sports reporter asked retired UCLA coach John Wooden why the United States lost. Coach Wooden replied, "We send great players; they send great teams."[25] Talent is important, but as Coach Wooden reminds us, it's teamwork that brings home the gold.

In my 2009 book *Extreme Dreams Depend on Teams*, I discuss what I believe to be the eight essential keys to building great teams:

1. Acquire top talent.
2. Be a great leader.
3. Be committed (you must persuade your team to commit to each other, to commit to your leadership, and to commit to the team vision).
4. Be passionate (you and your people need to have an intense passion for the game, whether your "game" is a sport, a business, a nonprofit organization, a church, or a military unit).
5. Think *teamwork* (everyone must be in it for the team, not the ego).
6. Empower individuals (cheer them on and entrust them with real decision-making power).
7. Build trust and respect.
8. Focus on character.

If your people display all of these essential ingredients, you can't help but have a great team.[26]

Dr. Noel M. Tichy, currently at the Ross School of Business at the University of Michigan, was head of management education at the General Electric Leadership Center (the legendary Crotonville facility) during the Jack Welch era at GE. Dr. Tichy once told interviewer Lan Liu: "Welch grew up as a working-class kid. As he grew up, he was always putting a team together. He was captain of the hockey team in high school. His view of the world was that you win by building a team."[27]

Other leadership experts agree: "Teamwork is so important," writes Brian Tracy, "that it is virtually impossible for you to reach the heights of your capabilities or make the money that you want without becoming very good at it." Industrialist-entrepreneur Andrew Carnegie said, "Teamwork is the ability to work together toward a common vision—the ability to direct individual accomplishments toward organizational objectives. It is the fuel that allows common people to attain uncommon results." And Ken Blanchard offers this concise nugget of teamwork wisdom: "None of us is as smart as all of us."[28] Patrick Lencioni, in *The Five Dysfunctions of a Team*, writes, "Not finance. Not strategy. Not technology. It is teamwork that remains the ultimate competitive advantage, both because it is so powerful and so rare."[29]

Even our military is discovering the transformative magic of teamwork. As Nebraska athletic director Tom Osborne writes in *Beyond the Final Score*:

> I had lunch one day with the Commandant of the Marine Corps, General Charles Krulak. We were comparing basic training in the Marines with preseason football training. General Krulak told me that the Corps had changed its approach to its new recruits: In times gone by, the point of basic training was to break down each recruit's will so that he or she would follow orders no matter what. But, he said, the focus now is on building teams.
>
> Why? Because somewhere along the line, the Corps did its research and found that the reason Marines would go charging up a hill in the face of machine-gun fire wasn't because they were trained to follow orders no matter what; the reason was that they cared so much for their fellow Marines, and they didn't want to let them down. In light of this new understanding, the Corps changed its approach to basic training to focus much more on building strong relationships among the Marines and forming cohesive teams.[30]

The competency of teamwork is undoubtedly one of the most important and foundational of all leadership competencies.

If a leader cannot persuade his people to become a genuine team, then in what sense is that leader truly leading? The cohesion and unity of purpose within the team must be constantly monitored. Skills and personality traits must be balance and optimized. Conflict must be managed to keep constructive differences of opinion from turning into corrosive personality clashes. As Phil Jackson, one of the greatest team builders in sports history, once observed, "Teamwork is a nebulous thing. It is as ephemeral as love, disappearing at the latest insult."[31]

To be a leader of excellence, become a great team builder.

6. The competency of organization and planning

A leader of excellence starts with a vision and creates a plan to achieve that vision. That plan—which lists priorities and goals that must be met along the way—is a road map to the fulfillment of that vision. The plan should also anticipate pitfalls and roadblocks, along with solutions wherever possible.

On February 22, 1988, then-colonel Tommy Franks was working at his desk, listening to a classical radio station, when the radio announcer interrupted to report that an Army CH-47 helicopter had crashed in north Texas. Several soldiers were dead.

For a moment, Colonel Franks found it hard to think. Those soldiers were under his command. What should he do? Whom should he call? His paralysis lasted only a few seconds, but it made him realize that he didn't have a clear-cut plan of action for dealing with such an emergency.

Franks immediately had his executive officer call the Aviation Brigade for confirmation, then he and his wife, Cathy, along with the chaplain, began visiting the widows of the dead soldiers. (He found it especially hard to comfort one distraught young widow with a crying toddler in her lap.) The colonel also made phone calls to the parents of the dead soldiers and attended to several other related duties. Later, when the immediate crisis had passed, Franks felt he had not done his best for his soldiers and their families—that he should have been better prepared for an unexpected tragedy, even in peacetime. He later recalled, "I couldn't get over the thought that I had failed as a leader."

The next morning, even before he had his first cup of coffee, Franks took a three-by-five card and printed on it, "23 Feb '88—The biggest challenges I may face today." Underneath, he listed the five most important problems, crises, or contingencies that could arise within the following twenty-four hours. Then, turning the card over, he wrote, "Opportunities that may appear today."

Those three-by-five cards became a regular morning habit with Col. (later Gen.) Tommy Franks. In his autobiography, he writes, "Every morning since that Thursday in February 1988, I noted the 'Challenges and Opportunities' that might occur on that day. More than five thousand cards later, I still do. The card itself isn't important; preparing myself for each day definitely is. Through complex operations in Afghanistan and Iraq, the process helped me to anticipate any number of problems. . .and solutions."[32]

Archie W. Dunham was CEO of Conoco, Inc., from 1996 to 2002, and chairman of ConocoPhillips until 2004. He said, "My four years of service in the United States Marine Corps were years of tremendous personal growth. I was privileged to lead at an early age and consequently learned much about leadership. I have never forgotten the five P's. . .Prior Planning Prevents Poor Performance. . . . Early in my career, I learned the importance of always being prepared. This single lesson helped me become an effective manager early in my career and a good leader later in life. Preparation helps you take care of your employees, meet the needs of your customers, and create wealth for your shareholders."[33]

From 1934 to the start of World War II, John Wooden taught English and coached at South Bend Central High School in Indiana. In South Bend, he was mentored by Notre Dame football coach Frank Leahy. Coach Wooden thought he ran a pretty good basketball practice—until he visited Leahy's football practice. When Wooden saw how the Notre Dame players shifted instantly from drill to drill at the sound of Leahy's whistle, he realized he could adapt this same well-planned, fast-paced approach to his basketball workouts. He later reflected:

> Organization became a primary asset of my coaching methodology—the ability to use time with great efficiency. Practices were taut and fast-moving. I was able to accomplish this with three-by-five cards and the meticulous advance planning that went into what was written on them. . . .
>
> There wasn't one second in the whole practice when anybody was standing around wondering what would come next. . . . The whole thing was synchronized; each hour offered up sixty minutes, and I squeezed every second out of every minute.
>
> Players felt, at times, that the actual game against an opponent was slower than our practice in the gym. That's exactly the way I designed it.[34]

Organization, preparation, and planning are crucial competencies for every leader of excellence.

7. The competency of managing change

Change is stressful because change brings with it turmoil, uncertainty, instability, anxiety, and risk. We prefer *sameness*—though we prefer to call it stability. A leader proves his or her mettle not in calm, stable circumstances, but in times of uncertainty and rapid change when the ground is shifting underfoot. Great leaders are flexible in the face of change.

James Kouzes and Barry Posner write about change as a *challenge* the leader must rise to. "Challenge is the crucible for greatness," they observe. "Exemplary leaders—the kind of leaders people want to follow—are always associated with changing the status quo. Great achievements don't happen when you keep things the same. Change invariably involves challenge, and challenge tests you. It introduces you to yourself. It brings you face-to-face with your level of commitment, your grittiness, and your values. It reveals your mindset about change."[35] Dr. Greg Morris once said, "Change is the context for leadership, as well as the goal of leadership."[36]

If you don't want change, why are you in leadership? Your job as a leader is to *make change happen*. You can't bring a vision into existence without changing a piece of the world. A leader who resists change is not a leader at all. Leaders are called to provoke change, manage change, respond to change, and prepare the organization for change. The one thing a leader should almost *never* do is oppose change.

The late Bill Walsh coached the San Francisco 49ers to three Super Bowl championships (XVI, XIX, XXIII). He believed that leaders are to be flexible and adaptable in the face of rapidly changing circumstances and situations. Walsh's biographer, David Harris, explains, "Bill wanted the Niners to be resilient and always change their approach as the situation required." And Walsh himself said, "As soon as you set your mind hard and fast, you limit your value [as a leader]. You have to account for the ebb and flow. Every football game is full of it and you have to account for it. . . . If you adapt to each shift and continue to concentrate, continue to work at it, the momentum will flow back to you."[37]

Change is coming at you, ready or not. How are you going to respond? How are you going to manage it? How are you going to leverage change to your advantage? Your answers to these questions will largely determine your competence as a leader.

8. The competency of balance
Leaders have to balance competing, paradoxical demands on their lives—action versus reflection, risk versus prudence,

logic versus intuition, managing today versus envisioning tomorrow, work versus play, exercise versus rest, family demands versus leadership demands—and leaders have to maintain this balancing act on the fly. As Albert Einstein once told his adult son, life is like a bicycle, and you can only keep your balance if you keep moving forward.[38]

Coach Wooden defined balance as "keeping all things in perspective, maintaining self-control, and avoiding excessive highs or lows that occur because of luck or misfortune. Balance means not permitting the things over which you have no control to adversely affect the things over which you do have control, and it means retaining your poise during times of turmoil *and* triumph."[39]

One player who learned the importance of balance from Coach Wooden was Gail Goodrich, who helped the UCLA Bruins win two national championships (1963–65). Goodrich had to learn about submerging his individualism and becoming part of a balanced and cohesive team. Goodrich recalls:

> [Coach Wooden] always talked about balance: body balance, scoring balance, team balance, and most of all, mental and emotional balance. Your feet have to be in balance. Your body has to be in balance over your feet. Your head needs to be in balance with your body and your arms. He said if you're not in balance, you'll eventually fall over, and he meant it in more ways than one.
>
> I came to see balance as one of the keys to success, not only in basketball, but in life. When things get out of balance, it's generally not good. Everything needs balance. That one word he kept drilling at us—balance—has stuck with me.[40]

Phil Jackson credits his coach and mentor, Red Holzman, for his own coaching success. Phil played for Holzman and the

Knicks from 1967 to 1978. "The pivotal moment in my life," Phil recalls, "was when I was injured, a career-ending type of injury with a spinal fusion necessary for recovery. . . . Red took me under his wing. He didn't have an assistant coach, so he made me his assistant coach and taught the game to me."

Holzman continually preached *balance*. "He talked about the importance of staying not too high, not too low," Phil recalls, "and not letting victories or defeats send you tumbling one way or the other. He believed in what was called the middle path."[41]

One middle path all leaders need to find is the path of balance between career and family. All great leaders must weigh the demands of a strong work ethic against the need for rest, relaxation, and family time. The leadership role is hard on marriages and families, so learn the competency of finding the right balance—then guard that balance with your life.

9. The competency of charisma

The most memorable leaders have charisma—a personal style that appeals to people. Charismatic leaders are personable and outgoing, carry themselves with an air of confidence, and are positive and optimistic in the face of adversity. Charismatic leaders attract followers, inspire loyalty, and mobilize support.

Many people assume that charisma is a gift. Some people have it, others don't. The word itself actually reinforces this notion, because *charisma* comes from the Greek word *charis*, meaning "a gracious gift." Don't be fooled. You can *learn* to be a more charismatic leader.

Much of what we call charisma can actually be distilled to a few simple skills: Make good eye contact with others. Smile warmly and sincerely. Project optimism and enthusiasm. Show some sparkle. Give people a firm handshake. Maintain a confident posture. Dress well. Show that you care about people by asking them about themselves. Lean into the conversation. Listen carefully to what others say. Be gracious and humble. In short, practice good people skills (see chapter 3). Charisma is nothing more than an array of learnable skills.

One of the most charismatic presidents in US history was John F. Kennedy. He was the handsome scion of a powerful political family. His charming, stylish wife completed the picture that came to be known as Camelot. But as John Barnes tells us in *John F. Kennedy on Leadership*, Kennedy was not always the charismatic figure of political legend:

> Charisma is widely believed to be a sort of innate trait; you either have it or you don't. The weight of the evidence, however, does not support this view. We have all known people who seemed to be naturally charismatic, possessing an enviable kind of innate confidence in their abilities and judgment. But it is equally true that many people who do not appear charismatic early in their lives subsequently come to be seen that way.
>
> John F. Kennedy was among the latter. A glance at one of his earliest appearances before a newsreel camera shows an awkward, self-conscious, almost impossibly young-looking man explaining his vague and inchoate plans to one day work for the government. "Charismatic" is not a word that would leap immediately to the viewer's mind.[42]

So how did the uncharismatic young John F. Kennedy come to acquire the charm and charisma for which he is now universally remembered? Peter Collier and David Horowitz disclose the source of JFK's charisma in *The Kennedys: An American Drama*:

> JFK had a friend, Chuck Spalding, who lived in Hollywood and was an assistant to actor Gary

Cooper. JFK visited Spaulding in Hollywood, and his friend took him around pre-WWII Hollywood, taking him to film colony parties and nightclubs, introducing him to such stars as Gary Cooper and Clark Gable. Spalding later said, "Charisma wasn't a catchword yet, but Jack was very interested in that binding magnetism these screen personalities had. What exactly was it? How did you go about acquiring it? Did it have an impact on your private life? How do you make it work for you? He couldn't let the subject go.[43]

So learn from JFK. Study the people skills that give famous, influential people their aura of charisma—then work on acquiring those skills. Don't be surprised if people start calling you "Kennedyesque."

10. The competency of poise
Poise is the ability to remain cool, calm, and collected in emotional or stressful situations. A poised leader keeps such emotions as anger, frustration, impatience, and panic under control. Poise gives you the power to think, focus, and find solutions.

Hall of Fame point guard Walt Frazier had a thirteen-year career in the NBA—a decade with the Knicks and three years with the Cavaliers—before retiring in 1980. During his long career, he never received a single technical foul—a remarkable achievement for any NBA player. In *The Game within the Game*, Frazier recalls:

When a ref made a poor call on me, I never talked back. . . . To me, a look is worth a thousand words. I'd just put my hands on my hips and fix the ref with a look that said, "You stupid guy. What are you doing?" but I'd never say a word. I kept my emotions within. I kept my cool be-

cause I knew that I couldn't look like I was losing it. I was the leader on the floor and the other
players on the Knicks—as well as Red Holzman,
our coach—looked to me to keep my cool. . . .

When I was in the eighth grade—when everything would be in disarray on the court and
my team started to discombobulate—my coach
would pull me over and say, "Frazier, don't lose
your head, son. Your brains are in it." It was funny,
but I never forgot those words of wisdom.[44]

The ability to maintain poise in a crisis is the key to effective
leadership on the basketball court—and on the world stage.
During the thirteen-day Cuban Missile Crisis in October 1962,
the remarkable poise of President John F. Kennedy may have
been the only thing that prevented World War III. In the fall
of 1962, the Soviet Union, under Premier Nikita Khrushchev,
shipped 20,000 troops, 150 jets, and 700 antiaircraft guns to
Cuba, an island just ninety miles from our shores. American
spy planes flew over the island, keeping tabs on the Soviet military buildup. The spy planes brought back shocking evidence
that the Soviets had also installed medium-range nuclear missiles capable of reaching 85 percent of the United States within
minutes.

The Soviet premier was putting President Kennedy to
the ultimate test, provoking a confrontation that could,
if mishandled by either side, destroy the world by nuclear
annihilation. As President Kennedy discussed the crisis
with his advisers, it seemed that there were only two options
available: The United States could attack Cuba militarily and
destroy the missiles—and possibly provoke the Soviets to
nuclear war. Or the US could simply do nothing and accept
the existence of a Soviet nuclear presence in its own backyard.
The two alternatives were equally unacceptable.

Then someone suggested a third option: the United States
could quarantine Cuba with a naval blockade, preventing

Soviet ships from delivering anything, even grain shipments, to Cuba. President Kennedy green-lighted the idea. He laid out the facts before the American people and sent his ambassador, Adlai Stevenson, to the UN General Assembly to make the case before the world.

Around the globe, millions braced for Armageddon. Fear was palpable. Yet President Kennedy seemed calm, poised, and totally in control whenever he spoke to the media or the American people. He projected total confidence in his decision.

Mark Updegrove, in *Baptism by Fire*, notes that the JFK White House had reached the only logical course of action. The president's brother, Attorney General Robert F. Kennedy, explained: "We all agreed that if the Russians were willing to go to nuclear war over Cuba, they were ready to go to nuclear war, and that was that. So we might as well have the showdown then as in six months."[45]

Kennedy aide Theodore Sorenson recalled that President Kennedy "insisted on knowing all his options and what [solutions] were possible. He did not do anything rash. He did not panic or overreact, did not yield to the military. He was calm—never lost his sense of humor, perspective, modesty."[46] Kennedy also maintained direct communication with Khrushchev, which helped to reduce tensions. By talking directly with his adversary, Kennedy was able to talk the Soviets down from the ledge of nuclear miscalculation. Khrushchev began to replace bombastic rhetoric with expressions of peaceful intentions and pleas for restraint.

Some historians argue that Kennedy made too many compromises in order to get the Soviet missiles out of Cuba. Even so, the fact remains that Kennedy's poised approach to the crisis helped restore a sense of calm to a panicky world.

If President Kennedy could maintain his calm in that crisis, then you should be able to remain cool and poised in any leadership crisis you face. Just tell yourself, "It's not the end of the world." People look to you, the leader, to see how you respond in a crisis, and they take their cues from you. If you want your organization to weather any storm, then commit yourself to remaining cool in heated situations.

11. The competency of historical awareness

Great leaders are as fascinated by the past as they are by the present and future. They want to understand the context of history—the history of great lives and great leaders, and the history and traditions of their own team or organization. History is filled with patterns that have a way of repeating themselves. The better we understand the cycles of past history, the more quickly we recognize the events that come our way. History not only reveals the past, but points the way into the future.

Nazi Germany invaded France in May 1940 and had conquered France by the end of June. A few days after the fall of Paris, British prime minister Winston Churchill gave a speech before the House of Commons, saying, "The Battle of France is over. I expect that the Battle of Britain is about to begin."[47] He was right, of course. The German Luftwaffe staged a brutal bombing campaign against the United Kingdom throughout the summer and autumn of 1940. Hitler hoped to bomb Great Britain into submission—and for a while, it was working.

In the darkest days of the war, Churchill's cabinet urged him to "make peace" with the Nazis. But Churchill knew that "making peace" with Hitler was nothing less than surrender— and he utterly rejected surrender. Asked why he was so insistent about fighting on, Churchill replied, "Because I study history. And history tells you that, if you hold on long enough, something always happens."[48]

And Churchill was proved right. On December 7, 1941, Imperial Japan attacked Pearl Harbor. The United States of America, which had remained neutral to that point, came into the war against the Axis powers, Germany, Italy, and Japan. When America added its industrial and military might to Britain's war effort, the course of the war and the course of history were changed. Churchill's awareness of history gave him the will to fight on against overwhelming odds.

In May 2003, historian David McCullough delivered the Jefferson Lecture in the Humanities at the Ronald Reagan International Trade Center. This talk was called "The Course of Human Events," and it included these remarks, which Churchill would have approved:

> History is filled with voices that reach out and lift the spirits, sometimes from the distance of centuries.
>
> Is it possible to imagine not learning from the wisest, most thoughtful people who shaped the world, or to fail to take heart from manifest courage?
>
> Is life not infinitely more interesting and enjoyable when one can stand in a great historic place or walk historic ground, and know something of what happened there and in whose footsteps you walk? . . .
>
> History is a larger way of looking at life.[49]

Another great student of history was Harry S. Truman. Reflecting on his love of the past, he writes, "Reading history, to me, was far more than a romantic adventure. It was solid instruction and wise teaching which I somehow felt that I wanted and needed. I could see that history had some extremely valuable lessons to teach. I learned from it that a leader is a man who has the ability to get other people to do what they don't want to do, and like it."[50]

On another occasion, Truman wrote, "Not only must a president be fully informed, but he must be constantly alert to what lies ahead. And he can see ahead only if he has a sense of history and understands the times he lives in."[51] Truman's deep insight into history helped him to make sound, time-tested decisions. When a leader sees the present through the lens of the past, seemingly murky choices become clearer and decision-making becomes much easier. Truman observed,

"One of the things that intrigued me in reading history has been to find out how the great leaders of the world reached decisions."[52] This is undoubtedly why, when the buck stopped at Truman's desk, he knew exactly what to do with it.

It's equally important for leaders to understand the history and traditions of their own organizations. Whether you are the leader of the free world, the leader of United Way or General Electric, or the leader of Scout Troop 10, if you want to know where you're going, it helps to know where you've been.

Dr. Kurt Senske is chairman of Thrivent Financial for Lutherans and CEO of Lutheran Social Services of the South, Inc. In *Executive Values*, he writes, "Leaders today sometimes tend to ignore the history of their organization, as they look to the future. In order to devise a forward-looking plan, it is vital to understand where you have come from. Including such a 'history lesson' in the planning process is time well spent."[53]

To be a leader of vision, remember your past. Nurture the competency of historical awareness.

12. The competency of authority

You are a leader, not a boss. Authority has been conferred upon you so that you can serve the organization. Followers grant authority to leaders by agreeing to follow—and they can withdraw that authority by simply refusing to follow. A follower can reject authority through outright defiance or through passive-aggressive insubordination.

Followers grant authority only to those who demonstrate the character and competence to lead well. If people lose confidence in your competence, your authority will evaporate. Authority is your stock-in-trade as a leader. Wielding that authority is one of the most important things you do as a leader, so it's critically important to wield it well.

Great leaders understand that a leader's authority should never be used to bully or intimidate. It should never be used to feed the leader's ego. Authority exists for the sake of achieving organizational goals and the leader's vision, and should be used sparingly. A great leader doesn't always "flash his badge." Leaders lead best when they inspire and motivate rather than command. People work harder, longer, and more energetically when they are willing participants in your vision, not slaves to the lash of your authority.

That being said, leaders must sometimes issue commands and enforce the rules. If you don't use your authority when authority is demanded, you'll appear weak and indecisive—and you'll lose that authority. It's a delicate balancing act, and knowing when and when not to use your authority is one of the key competencies of leadership.

A classic case of misused authority is the story of Napoleon Bonaparte. Born on the island of Corsica, Napoleon suffered from chronic childhood illnesses that hindered his physical growth. In adulthood, he stood five feet two, and his short stature is thought to have given him a lifelong sense of inferiority. He probably compensated by attempting to glorify himself through wars of conquest. History records that Napoleon spent the lives of no fewer than 860,000 French soldiers in his wars—and countless enemy soldiers.

A commoner, Napoleon schemed to attain royal status by marrying a princess. Viewing Czar Alexander I of Russia as a friend, Napoleon asked the czar for permission to marry his daughter. Through a "blood pact" with Russia, Napoleon hoped to legitimize himself as an equal to the other crowned heads of Europe. But Czar Alexander rejected Napoleon's proposal.

Humiliated, Napoleon invaded Russia in 1812—a disastrous military exploit that led to his undoing. As leadership experts Henry Blackaby and Richard Blackaby observe, tens of thousands of lives were sacrificed on the altar of Napoleon's ego:

> It could be argued that hundreds of thousands of Europeans died in one man's vain attempt to achieve satisfaction through the brutal acquisition of power and fame. Ego-driven people become desensitized to the suffering

of others. It is acknowledged that few commanders suffered military casualties with greater indifference than Napoleon. The Duke of Wellington lamented the loss of thousands, but Napoleon boasted he would readily sacrifice a million soldiers to attain his goals.[54]

The purpose of authority is to serve people, to serve the team or organization, and to meet the goal of achieving the vision. The misuse of authority to serve a leader's ego ultimately destroys people, organizations, and visions.

13. The competency of good judgment

All great leaders possess the competency of good judgment—the capacity for making wise, moral, effective decisions. Leaders with good judgment know which opportunities to seize and which to pass up, which people to hire and which to avoid, and which path to take among a number of competing options.

The competency of good judgment is rooted in strong character, knowledge and wisdom, common sense, courage, and experience. It's said that good judgment comes from bad experience, and bad experience comes from bad judgment. So to have good judgment, we must have the capacity to learn and grow from our mistakes. As Noel Tichy and Warren Bennis observe:

> The essence of leadership is judgment. The single most important thing that leaders do is make good judgment calls. In the face of ambiguity, uncertainty, and conflicting demands, often under great time pressure, leaders must make decisions and take effective actions to assure the survival and success of their organizations. This is how leaders add value to their organizations. They lead them to success by

exercising good judgment, by making smart calls and ensuring that they are well executed.[55]

Leaders of excellence are leaders of good judgment. This is one of the core competencies of your leadership role.

14. The competency of authenticity

What does it mean to be authentic? Very simply, it means *be yourself.*

Coach Vince Lombardi coached the Green Bay Packers to three consecutive NFL championships, 1965 through 1967, and never had a losing season in the NFL. He was such a popular leader that 1968 presidential candidate Richard Nixon put Lombardi on his short list as a possible running mate.

Lombardi became head coach of the Washington Redskins in 1969. The first thing he did as coach was meet one-on-one with Redskins quarterback Sonny Jurgensen. "Sonny," he said, "I just ask one thing of you: I want you to be yourself. Don't emulate anyone else. Don't try to be someone you're not. Just be yourself."[56]

Be yourself. That was Coach Lombardi's message to his players, and the rule he lived by as a leader and coach. Lombardi didn't try to emulate other coaches. He coached from within the zone of his own self-awareness and self-confidence. "In all my years of coaching," he once said, "I have never been successful using somebody else's plays."[57]

The competency of authenticity—the ability to simply *be yourself*—is a key trait of great leaders in every arena, from the ballfield to the battlefield. *BusinessWeek* once asked baseball manager Sparky Anderson, "What one piece of advice would you give to a CEO about to take over a company for the first time?" Sparky replied: "You are who you are. . . . Always be yourself. . . . You can't learn to manage by copying [other leaders]. Take [former Miami Dolphins coach] Don Shula. He's the greatest coach. Shula is Shula. It's his way. . . . You've got to do it your own way."[58]

Learn from other leaders, but don't imitate them. Know your own strengths and abilities, and lead from within your own unique personality. Lead according to your core principles and values—and never give in to outside pressure, the sniping of the critics, or the temptation to be popular. Lead your own way. Be yourself.

15. The competency of patience

As the general manager of the Spartanburg Phillies, I was young, ambitious, and impatient. I couldn't wait to get on with my career and move up to the majors. My boss, Mr. Littlejohn, understood my impatience and continually preached to me, "Patience, Pat! Pay your dues. Learn the ropes. You can't come into a new situation and jump right to the top." It was hard for me to get that advice through my young noggin.

My first season in Spartanburg, we had a mediocre team, but an outstanding season in terms of tickets and advertising sold and community excitement. I was named Executive of the Year in the Western Carolinas League—and it went right to my head. There I was, a mere stripling at age twenty-five, yet I was convinced that the Yankees, Cubs, and Dodgers would all be begging for the services of this Class D manager with one good season behind him.

At the end of the season, I sat with Mr. Littlejohn in his car, and I said, "It's been a great season, sir. Thank you for all your help and encouragement."

He knew what I was thinking. "Patience is the key to your future," he said. "Pat, you have a right to be proud of what you've accomplished. But your job here isn't done."

"I dunno," I said, "I've left the place in good shape for the next guy. I'm ready to step up."

Mr. Littlejohn sighed. "Pat, you think you're ready to move on, but I'm telling you it could have been an even better year. The real measure of success is how well you build on what you've begun. Stay here and prove yourself. Show the league what you're *really* capable of."

I didn't think much of that advice—but after a few weeks went by and the big league teams didn't call with any offers, I faced the fact that Mr. Littlejohn was right. The next year was even better—and we had a great team that year as well. We even had a twenty-five-game winning streak at one point.

Finally, in 1968, during my fourth season in Spartanburg, I received a call from Jack Ramsay, the general manager of the NBA's Philadelphia 76ers. He had been following my successes in Spartanburg, and he invited me to join the 76ers organization as business manager. That job eventually led me to serve as general manager for the Chicago Bulls, then the Atlanta Hawks, and (in a move back to Philadelphia) the 76ers. And from there, it was on to Orlando and the founding of the Magic. But I don't know if that path ever would have opened up to me if I hadn't learned patience from Mr. Littlejohn.

Looking back, I can see that he liked my eagerness and aggressiveness—but he knew I needed to temper my charge-ahead attitude with maturity and patience. Every leader needs the competency of patience.

Coach John Wooden used to tell his players, "Be quick, but don't hurry." He understood the importance of patience in leadership:

> Most of us are impatient. As we get a bit older, we think we know more, and that things should happen faster. But patience is a virtue in preparing for any task of significance. It takes time to create excellence. If it could be done quickly, more people would do it.
>
> A meal you order at a drive-through window may be cheap, it may be quick, it may even be tasty. But is it a great dining experience? That takes time. Good things always take time, and that requires patience.
>
> Competitive greatness requires patience.

Excellence requires patience. Most of all, success requires patience.[59]

An impatient decision led to the explosion of the space shuttle *Challenger* seventy-three seconds into its tenth mission on January 28, 1986, killing all seven members of the crew. Engineers at the Utah solid rocket booster factory warned NASA not to launch in extreme cold. The rubber O-rings that sealed the joints of the boosters became brittle under icy conditions and could leak hot gases just like a blowtorch. The booster casing temperature on the morning of the launch registered 8 degrees Fahrenheit—well below the factory recommendations.

Engineers pleaded with NASA managers, trying to delay the launch. But the space agency was impatient to maintain its schedule and prove that the shuttle was dependable. As *Challenger* lifted off from the launch pad, the factory engineers watched on television, silently praying. Seventy-three seconds later, their fears were realized.

Impatience destroyed the *Challenger* and took seven brave lives. Don't let impatience destroy your organization or your dreams. Build the competency of patience into your leadership life.

QUALIFIED TO LEAD

There are many other leadership competencies we could name. For example, we could talk about the *competency of inner security*—also known as the hide of a rhinoceros. To be secure within yourself means that you are able to absorb constructive criticism and deflect destructive attacks without becoming angry or defensive. You don't let the words and actions of others disturb your inner serenity.

Or we could talk about the *competency of obedience*. Benjamin Franklin said, "He that cannot obey, cannot command." It is a rare leader who does not have to answer to some higher authority. Even dictators are held accountable for their crimes, as Saddam Hussein found out. The president of the United States may be the leader of the free world, but he is accountable to the Constitution, the Congress, the Supreme Court, and the American people. If the president cannot obey, he cannot lead.

We could also talk about the *competency of physical health*. How can we do our jobs as leaders if we are sleep-deprived zombies, if we feel sluggish from overeating and lack of exercise, or if we're in the hospital due to neglecting and abusing our bodies? As leaders, we need to get up and walk at least ten thousand steps a day, stay hydrated, consume plenty of protein and whole grains, cut our intake of sugar and fat, avoid alcohol and tobacco, and get rid of processed foods. Daily low-impact exercise is great for our backs, helps build bone and muscle mass, slims our midsections, balances our hormones, increases our pain tolerance, regulates our sleep patterns, helps us look and feel better, keeps us young longer, and enables us to manage stress.

I'm sure you can think of at least a few more areas of leadership competence, including some that are specific to certain arenas, such as the corporate world or the military. There might even be competencies specific to your own market sector or organization. It's vital that you identify those competencies so you can lead people to the successful achievement of your vision.

The first seven letters of "competence" are *c-o-m-p-e-t-e*. The goal of every competent leader is to prepare his or her team to compete and win. People want to know that you can lead them to victory. Your *competence* gives them *confidence*. Confident teams win championships, and confident organizations accomplish great goals and achieve big visions.

Your competence as a leader is measured by the accomplishments of your team or organization. A leader's competence in the business world is measured by profit and loss, return on investment, and stock value. A leader's competence in the sports world is measured by wins, losses, and championships. A leader's competence in the religious world is measured by church growth, communities served, and lives changed. A leader's competence in the military world is measured by low casualty rates and success on the battlefield.

"Competence goes beyond words," writes leadership guru John C. Maxwell. "It's the leader's ability to say it, plan it, and do it in such a way that others know that you know how—and know that they want to follow you."[60] As Warren Bennis observes, "The leader hasn't simply practiced his vocation or profession. He's mastered it. He's learned everything there is to know about it, and then surrendered to it. . . . Mastery, absolute competence, is mandatory for a leader."[61]

Your competence qualifies you to lead. Competent leaders produce winning teams and organizations, and make visions and dreams come true.

6

THE SIXTH SIDE OF LEADERSHIP: BOLDNESS

When I was general manager of the Philadelphia 76ers, I heard that Julius Erving—the legendary Dr. J—was unhappy with his team, the New York Nets, and was going to sit out training camp in the fall of 1976. So I called the Nets' general manager, Bill Melchionni, and said, "Billy, if you decide to trade Dr. J, please let me know."

A couple of weeks later, Billy phoned me. "If you want to buy out Erving's contract," he said, "we can talk—but we want cash."

"How much?"

"Three million."

My jaw hung loose on its hinges. "Three million. . .dollars?"

"And that's just to buy his contract. I can tell you right now that Erving is going to want another three million for his services."

"*Six* million?" I whistled. "Billy, I'll get back to you."

The 76ers had a new owner, Fitz Dixon, who had just purchased the team from Irv Kosloff for eight million dollars. That's right, Mr. Dixon had just paid eight mill for an entire NBA team, and I was about to ask him to spend three-quarters of that amount on just one player! I didn't think he'd go for it, but I had to try. I was sure if we could land Dr. J, we'd have an NBA championship in the bag—maybe a few of them.

So I went to Fitz Dixon's office and said, "Mr. Dixon, we have an opportunity to get a really special player on our team. The player I'm referring to is"—I paused for dramatic effect—"Julius Erving."

I waited for Mr. Dixon to come out of his chair with excitement. Instead, he looked at me in befuddlement. "Oh?" he said. "Well, tell me, Pat, just who *is* this Julius Erving fellow?"

Who is Julius Erving? *Who is Julius Erving!*

Then I remembered that Fitz Dixon was fairly new to the sports world. He was an educator, a philanthropist, a Harvard man, the son of a wealthy banker, the husband of an heiress of the "old money" Widener family of Philadelphia. He had become a basketball fan mere weeks before buying the team. No wonder he had no clue who Julius Erving was! How could I explain Dr. J to Fitz Dixon in a single sentence? Then inspiration struck.

"Julius Erving," I said, "is the Babe Ruth of basketball."

Mr. Dixon's eyes lit up, and I knew we understood each other. He said, "How much will it cost to bring Mr. Erving to Philadelphia?"

I gulped hard then squeaked, "Six million dollars."

He didn't even flinch. "Are you recommending this deal?" he asked.

"Yes, sir, I am," I said firmly.

Fitz sat back in his chair and nodded slowly. Then he smiled at me and said, "Well, go get it done." Then he added an expression he always used when he felt pleased: "That'll be just fine and dandy."

I was stunned. On the strength of my recommendation alone, he had just made a bold six-million-dollar decision. And you know what? Fitz Dixon never regretted a nickel of it.

Bold leaders make bold decisions. On every team, in every organization, somebody has to make the decisions. That's what leadership is all about. The role of a leader is to gather as much information as practicable, consult with key people, reflect on all the options, upsides, downsides, risks, and rewards. . .

Then *decide.*

And once the leader decides, he or she does not look back, does not agonize, does not second-guess. Having decided, the leader now does whatever it takes to make that decision work for the good of the organization.

MANY DECISIONS, NO REGRETS

David Gergen, who served as an adviser to Presidents Nixon, Ford, Reagan, and Clinton, once observed that President Harry S. Truman "never thought of himself as a leader, nor did anyone else. . . . [Due to poor eyesight], Truman couldn't try out for school sports and mostly stayed at home, working the farm, reading, or playing the piano. . . . [He was] the only president of the twentieth century who never went to college."[1]

Truman joined the Missouri Army National Guard in 1905, passing the vision portion of his physical by memorizing the eye chart. He served until 1911 then rejoined at age thirty-three when World War I broke out. He shipped out to France as the commander of an artillery battery that was infamous for disciplinary problems—D Battery, 129th Field Artillery, 60th Brigade, 35th Infantry Division.

Truman later recalled, "When I first took command of the battery, I called all the sergeants and corporals together. I told them I knew they had been making trouble for the previous commanders. I said, 'I didn't come over here to get along with you. You've got to get along with me. And if there are any of you who can't, speak up right now and I'll bus you right back now!' . . . We got along."

Captain Truman whipped his unit into shape. In field maneuvers, D Battery quickly became the fastest-loading, best-disciplined unit in the 129th Field Artillery. But the biggest test of Harry Truman's early leadership ability came during an incident that became known as "The Battle of Who Run." On the evening of August 29, 1918, Captain Truman's unit was positioned on the slopes of Mount Herrenberg in the Vosges Mountains.

Just after dark, the soldiers moved the horses away from the artillery pieces, and D Battery fired a massive barrage of poison gas shells at the Germans—about five hundred rounds. The horses were supposed to be brought back immediately after the last round was fired so that the artillery could be moved out of range of the German artillery. But after almost half an hour, the soldiers hadn't returned with the horses. Frustrated by the delay, Truman ordered the artillerymen to pull the artillery pieces out of the mud by hand. Then he got on his own horse to ride to the rear and retrieve the horses—but his horse stumbled in a shell hole and rolled over on him.

Just then the German artillery retaliated with a combination of high explosives and poison gas. As Truman crawled out from under his fallen horse, he heard the sergeant call out to the other artillerymen, "Run, boys! They've got a bracket on us!"

Captain Truman leaped to his feet and ordered the men back to their posts, cussing them out with every epithet in his vast reservoir of profanities. As he later recalled, "I got up and called them everything I knew. . . . Pretty soon they came sneaking back." The artillerymen returned, hauled the guns back from their original positions, and camouflaged them with branches for safekeeping. The soldiers who returned to their posts after Captain Truman's haranguing were later cited for their "cool courage" under fire. (The truth was that they feared Truman more than they feared German explosives and poison gas.)

Truman's superiors wanted him to court-martial the sergeant. "I didn't," Truman later recalled, "but I busted him and afterwards I had to transfer him to another battery. Later in the war, he stood firm under the fiercest fire." He added, "I didn't care for court-martials. I'd get myself back of a table and I'd look as mean as I could. Then I'd tell them, 'You can have a court-martial or, if you prefer, you can take what I give you.' That worked."[2]

David Gergen observes that it was Truman's trial by fire in the Vosges Mountains that proved him to be a leader.

"There for the first time in his life he was forced to lead men through moments of mortal danger," Gergen writes. Truman rallied his panicked troops, called them back to their posts, got them through that night—and got them through the war. Under Truman's command, not a single man of D Battery was lost. For the rest of their lives, Gergen notes, the men of D Battery "were loyal to Harry Truman, their leader who refused to back down. . . . Truman discovered two vitally important things about himself that night. First, that he had plain physical courage; and second, that he was good at leading people." Gergen also quotes historian David McCullough, who writes that Truman learned through that experience that "courage is contagious. If the leader shows courage, others get the idea."[3]

Truman became president on April 12, 1945, after the death of Franklin D. Roosevelt. Soon after taking the oath of office as president, Truman turned to reporters and said, "Boys, if you ever pray, pray for me now. I don't know if you fellas ever had a load of hay fall on you, but when they told me what happened yesterday, I felt like the moon, the stars, and all the planets had fallen on me."[4]

Though the demands of the office weighed heavily on him, Truman had confidence in his own leadership ability— and he intended to take charge. David McCullough records that Truman told his Cabinet that he "welcomed their advice. He did not doubt that they would differ with him if they felt it necessary, but final decisions would be his and he expected their support once decisions were made."[5]

Truman went on to complete Roosevelt's term, then was elected to a term of his own in 1948. He presided over the Allied victory in Europe and made the decision to drop the atomic bombs over Hiroshima and Nagasaki, ending the war in the Pacific. In the postwar period, he dealt with the transition to a peacetime economy; record high inflation; a crippling national railway strike; the creation of the United Nations; the beginning of the Cold War; Soviet attempts to destabilize Iran, Greece, and Turkey; the Marshall Plan for rebuilding postwar

Europe; the creation and recognition of the state of Israel; the Berlin Airlift; the invasion of South Korea by North Korea, and much more. On some issues that he fought for—national health insurance, repeal of the Taft-Hartley Act, and an aggressive civil rights agenda—he suffered major defeats. But he fought hard, he made bold decisions, he took charge.

In 1960, Truman said, "I have been asked whether I have any regrets about any of the major decisions I had to make as president. I have none."[6] In his book *Mr. Citizen*, he reflects:

> Whenever I felt a mistake had been made, I always tried to remedy the mistake by making another decision. Everybody makes mistakes and the important thing is to correct them, once they are discovered. Sometimes you have a choice of evils, in which case you try to take the course that is likely to bring the least harm.
>
> I am not one who believes it does any good to cry over past mistakes. You have got to keep looking ahead and going straight ahead all the time, making decisions and correcting the situation as you go along. This calls for a fundamental policy, a basic outlook, for the making of major foreign and domestic decisions. Otherwise the operations of the government would be reduced to improvisation—and inevitable trouble. . . .
>
> The man who keeps his ear to the ground to find out what is popular will be in trouble. I usually say that a man whose heart is in the right place and who is informed is not likely to go very far wrong when he has to act.[7]

For some reason, President Roosevelt, even though he knew his own health was failing, never saw fit to draw Vice President Truman into his confidence. During Truman's eighty-two days as vice president, he was never briefed on plans for the conduct of the war and was never told about the existence of the atomic bomb. In fact, Truman was not fully briefed about the bomb's capabilities until almost two weeks after he became president.

Throughout the postwar years, and long after he left the White House, Truman was often asked if he agonized over the atomic bomb decision. He always replied that the decision to drop the bomb was not a difficult one. The atomic bomb, he said, "was merely another powerful weapon in the arsenal of righteousness. The dropping of the bombs stopped the war [and] saved millions of lives. It was a purely military decision."[8] Much more difficult and agonizing, he said, was the decision to enter the Korean War.

Even though Harry Truman appeared to make decisions quickly and firmly, historian Alan Axelrod points out that Truman was never hasty or arbitrary in his approach to decision making:

> There was never anything "automatic" about the decisions he made. But he was so incisive and absolute a decision maker that it often appeared as if he breezed through the process. He was not a man who agonized, at least not visibly. The president's job, Truman believed, was to make decisions, and he was very good at his job. Instead of a nameplate on his desk, he had his famous sign proclaiming, "The Buck Stops Here." He explained in 1952: "The papers may circulate around the government for a while but they finally reach this desk. And then, there's no place else for them to go. The president—whoever he is—has to decide. He can't pass the buck to anybody." . . .
>
> The idea, of course, was always to make the right decision. But this was less important than making some decision. . . . Truman wrote,

"Presidents have to make decisions if they're going to get anywhere, and those presidents who couldn't make decisions are the ones who caused all the trouble." Of course, the right decision was the best decision, but the worst possible outcome did not result from a wrong decision. It resulted from the failure to decide.[9]

In the early 1990s, I hosted my radio show live from a restaurant in Orlando. My guest was Col. Paul W. Tibbets Jr., who flew the atomic bomb mission over Hiroshima. It was fascinating—and sobering—to hear him talk about the fateful mission that ended World War II. He told me that when the bomb exploded, he felt a tingling in the fillings of his teeth. He recalled a sense of shock when he saw the towering mushroom cloud and realized that an entire city had disappeared underneath it.

I asked him what his thoughts were as he flew back to Tinian Island. He told me he was relieved that the bomb would end the war and stop the killing. There was no doubt in his mind that millions of Americans and Japanese would get to live out their lives because of what he and his crew had done that day.

"Did you ever meet Harry Truman?" I asked.

"Just once," he said. "After the war ended, President Truman invited me to the White House, and we had a short talk. He thanked me for completing my mission, and then he said, 'Don't lose any sleep over it. You did what you had to do. The decision to send you was mine.'"

The words of Harry Truman—a man who firmly understood the meaning of leadership in wartime. He had learned it under fire on a mountainside in France.

WHEN PLACED IN COMMAND, TAKE CHARGE

The leadership mettle of President John F. Kennedy was also tested and refined by war. In the predawn hours of August 2, 1943, twenty-six-year-old Lieutenant Kennedy commanded an eighty-foot patrol torpedo boat, *PT-109*. He and his twelve crewmen were patrolling the Blackett Strait in the Solomon Islands on a moonless night, eager to locate and sink a Japanese warship. Suddenly, they found themselves in the path of the Japanese destroyer *Amagiri*. The destroyer collided with *PT-109*, slicing the patrol boat in two and setting off an explosion. Burning fuel sprayed in every direction.

Two American crewmen were killed in the collision. Two others were burned and badly injured. The stern half of the boat sank immediately, but the watertight bow section stayed afloat. Lieutenant Kennedy, who had been a varsity swimmer at Harvard, organized the survivors and towed the most badly burned seaman on his back, clenching the man's life-jacket strap in his teeth. The other survivors swam as a group, clinging to floating debris. After four hours of swimming, the eleven survivors reached Plum Pudding Island, a deserted rock about the size of a football field.

Kennedy eventually led his men to Olasana Island, which had coconuts and freshwater. He carved a message into a coconut and gave it to some islanders to deliver to the Allied base at Rendova Island in the Solomons. A week after their boat was sunk, Kennedy and his fellow survivors were picked up by *PT-157*. The carved coconut hull was returned to Kennedy, and he had it preserved under a glass dome as a paperweight, keeping it on his desk throughout his presidency.

In 2001 Gerard Zinser, the last survivor of the sinking of *PT-109*, died at the age of eighty-two. Zinser, who had been a machinist's mate first class, rode with other *PT-109* crewmen in JFK's 1961 inaugural parade—and attended JFK's funeral in 1963. Years after President Kennedy's assassination, Zinser said, "I served twenty years in the Navy, and I never had an officer that would ever come close to what I saw Kennedy do."[10]

For his own part, JFK was—like all great leaders—self-effacing. When asked how he became a war hero, Kennedy replied, "It was involuntary—they sank my boat."[11]

After being tested under fire in World War II, Kennedy

ultimately had to make decisions that affected whether atomic weapons might be unleashed upon civilian populations. The wrong decision could have brought about the end of civilization.

Great leaders don't waste time and don't get bogged down by "the paralysis of analysis." Though thoughtful analysis is a necessary component of decision making, too much study can quickly become a *substitute* for decision making. Former presidential aides James Carville and Paul Begala warn:

> When analysis leads only to the conclusion that you need further analysis, look out. You're heading into paralysis mode.
>
> Harry Truman understood that. He once said he was looking for a one-armed adviser, because he was sick of Washington sharpies telling him, "On the other hand. . . ."
>
> And John F. Kennedy understood something even more important: that delaying a decision is itself a decision; a decision with risks as well. "There are risks and costs to a program of action," he once said, "but they are far less than the long-range risks and costs of comfortable inaction."
>
> You want to be the smartest person at the big meeting? Be the first person to demand that your organization move quickly. Acknowledge the risks and costs of doing something, then outline the myriad risks and manifest costs of doing nothing. You'll find that JFK was right.
>
> Do something. . .now. If it works, do more of it. If it doesn't work, do something else. But do something—quickly.[12]

On May 28, 1970, when then–Lt. Col. H. Norman Schwarzkopf Jr. was nearing the end of his second tour of duty in Vietnam, he received a call that a unit under his command, Bravo Company, had entered a minefield and touched off several mines. Two men were wounded. The minefield was on the notorious Batangan Peninsula, which Schwarzkopf described as "a horrible, malignant place," strewn from one end to the other with mines and booby traps. Schwarzkopf immediately boarded a helicopter and flew to the scene.

Upon arrival, he found a number of soldiers in the minefield, paralyzed with fright, unable to go forward or backward for fear of stepping on a hidden charge. The helicopter took off with the wounded soldiers, leaving behind Schwarzkopf, Schwarzkopf's artillery liaison officer, Tom Bratton; company commander Tom Cameron, and the rest of Bravo Company. Standing at the edge of the minefield, Schwarzkopf and Cameron pored over a map, trying to figure out how to get the men out of the minefield, when—*Bam!*—a mine went off, blowing one of the soldiers into the air. The man landed with a broken leg. He flailed and thrashed, screaming in pain. At the same time, some of the other men yelled to each other, "We're never gonna get out! We're gonna die here!" Schwarzkopf saw panic spreading through the company, and he feared that the man on the ground might cut an artery and bleed to death. Just then, Harry Truman came to his aid. Schwarzkopf recalls:

> One of the things I thought about was the sign on Harry Truman's desk that said "The Buck Stops Here." I really didn't have any choice in the matter. Somebody had to go over there and calm that kid down and I was the senior ranking man there and it was my responsibility. Besides that, I wanted the company commander, who was standing next to me, to. . .get his leadership working, talk to them and get the company calmed down. So I went over to help this kid. . . .
>
> That's the only time in my life my knees have ever shaken, but man, they were shaking! I

had to grab my knee with both hands, it would shake so badly. . . . I got over to the kid. I was a pretty big guy then, as I am now, and I laid down on top of him. I literally pinned him and was talking to him, saying, "Come on, you've got to calm down now. You're going to cut an artery. You're going to kill yourself. You're scaring the hell out of all the rest of the troops". . .and I got the kid calmed down.[13]

Next order of business was to splint the wounded man's leg. So Schwarzkopf turned to his artillery liaison officer, Tom Bratton, and said, "Cut a limb off that bush and throw it to me so I can splint this guy's leg." Bratton took one step—and detonated a mine. When the smoke cleared, Bratton was on the ground missing an arm and a leg, and bleeding profusely from his head—but he was alive. Schwarzkopf himself had taken a load of shrapnel in the chest. The mine had been in the helicopter landing zone, which had been considered safe.

The men in the minefield started to panic. Schwarzkopf ordered, "Nobody moves! Stand where you are! We're going to get you out!"

He removed the wounded man's belt and lashed his legs together to immobilize the broken one. Then he eased his way over toward Bratton. Schwarzkopf and the company commander bandaged Bratton, and soon a medevac helicopter arrived and took Bratton and the other wounded man away.

Then Schwarzkopf called for a team of engineers to come and mark the mines to make a path for the Bravo Company to safely exit the minefield. Thinking quickly, Schwarzkopf also ordered HQ to send shaving cream—as many cans of shaving cream as they could round up. When the man on the other end of the radio asked if Schwarzkopf was *sure* he wanted shaving cream, Schwarzkopf swore and shouted, "Don't argue with me! Get the shaving cream out here *now!*"

Soon the engineers flew in—and so did the shaving cream.

The engineers spent a couple of hours clearing a path through the minefield with metal detectors. Whenever a metal detector indicated the presence of a potential mine, the engineer would place a dollop of shaving cream on the site. The foamy shaving cream was too light to set off a mine, yet it made a white mark that was visible for hours.

Schwarzkopf later recalled, "When the last kid was off the hill, I had them fly me to the hospital. After they dug seven or eight pieces of shrapnel out of my left pectoral muscle and bandaged me up, I bullied the doctor into letting me go."[14]

He went to the emergency room and found Bratton lying on a gurney, conscious and in no apparent pain. This scared Schwarzkopf. "I'd seen badly wounded men rally that way," he recalled, "only to die minutes later."

"Hang in there, Bratton," Schwarzkopf told him. "You're going to make it." And as it turned out, Bratton did survive.[15]

Schwarzkopf's shaving cream idea, which he improvised on the spot, came to be the accepted method for marking land mines and is still used to this day by American soldiers in Iraq and Afghanistan.[16] Schwarzkopf was awarded a Silver Star for bravery (his third), but the medal was less important to him than the fact that his men trusted him as an officer who would take charge—and would lay down his life for them.

Schwarzkopf once explained what he calls "the secret to modern leadership" in an interview for the online Academy of Achievement:

> Leadership is not managing an organization. . . . Leadership is motivating people. . . . So I tell people that the secret to modern leadership is two rules. Rule 13: When placed in command, take charge. The leader is the person who is willing to take the responsibility. . . .
>
> Okay, I've got it. When placed in command, I take charge. But what do I do? The answer is Rule 14: Do what's right. Because we all know

. . .when placed in those circumstances, what the moral, what the ethical, what the correct thing to do is. . . . So, the true modern leader of today is the one that's, number one, willing to take charge, and [number two] willing to do what's right. That's the secret of leadership.[17]

I don't know what happened to Rules 1 through 12, but it sounds to me as if Rules 13 and 14 are all you need to be a bold, take-charge leader. So, leader, take charge—and do what's right.

THE LONELINESS OF LEADERSHIP

I mentioned before that Dr. Jack Ramsay hired me to my first job in the NBA in the summer of 1968. Jack was general manager of the Philadelphia 76ers, and he was also taking over the coaching duties, so he asked me to serve as business manager. Shortly after the team announced that Ramsay would coach the 76ers, he got a call from an old friend—Eddie Donovan, general manager (and former coach) of the New York Knicks. Eddie welcomed Jack to the NBA coaching fraternity (Jack had previously coached at St. Joseph's University in Philly). The two men had a nice chat, and then, just before he hung up, Eddie said, "One more thing, Jack—be the boss!"

Jack Ramsay told me he never forgot that simple yet profound piece of advice.

I've used that same advice in my own leadership counseling over the years, particularly with my son Bobby, who is a manager in the Washington Nationals farm system. As I write these words, Bobby is finishing his twelfth year in organized baseball. He left the Cincinnati Reds organization, where he had been a coach, and in 2005 the Nationals named him a manager in their farm system. At twenty-seven, Bobby was one of the youngest managers in the history of baseball. I remember when he called me to give me the news—and then his voice jumped a couple of octaves as he asked me, "Dad, what do I do now?"

Remembering the advice Eddie Donovan gave Jack Ramsay

in 1968, I said, "Bobby, be the boss."

I didn't say "be bossy"—there are far too many bossy bosses in this world. I simply said, "Be the boss." In other words (as Stormin' Norman Schwarzkopf would say), take charge and do what's right.

When the great Packers quarterback Bart Starr was entering his senior year in high school, his football coach, Bill Moseley, gave him a life-changing gift. Moseley arranged for young Bart to be personally tutored by Kentucky quarterback Vito "Babe" Parilli. For two weeks in the summer of 1951, Starr was personally instructed by the quarterback who had led the Kentucky Wildcats to an upset victory over national champion Oklahoma in the 1951 Sugar Bowl. Starr worked hard to absorb all that he could from Parilli. He later recalled that one of the most important lessons he learned was "huddle demeanor." Starr said that Parilli "taught me how important it was to be the boss in the huddle and to communicate absolute confidence and focus to your teammates, because they will feed off that."[18]

Pat Riley, the longtime NBA coach, told me about his 1981 decision to leave the broadcast booth and become the head coach of the Lakers. Though he'd had a successful playing career, Pat had no coaching experience at any level. And here he was, about to coach a team of highly talented, strong-willed, temperamental athletes. This was the era of Kareem Abdul-Jabbar, Magic Johnson, and James Worthy, and it was going to take an exceptional leader to ride herd on that bunch.

Well, Pat got off to a good start, but before long he ran into some rough patches as he found his authority being challenged by some of his players. In the process, he began to have some self-doubts.

Finally, after one Monday practice, Lakers majority owner, Jerry Buss, approached Coach Riley and said, "Pat, don't be afraid to coach the team." That's all Buss said. That's all he needed to say. Pat Riley told me, "That's the single best piece of leadership advice I've ever gotten."

I have learned over the years that most people only get one opportunity, one crack at proving themselves as a leader. You may get one shot at being the head coach or the senior pastor or the high school principal or the CEO—and if you don't prove that you can be the boss, that you can coach the team, that you can take charge and do what's right, you'll probably never get another chance. It seems to me that the worst feeling in the world would be to find out, years later as you are sitting by the crackling fireplace and looking back over your life, that *you had that opportunity*—and you *blew* that opportunity by failing to lead boldly. You wanted to take charge—but you also wanted to be popular, you wanted to be liked, you didn't want to upset or offend anyone. So your leadership opportunity passed you by.

I don't want you to be haunted by that memory. I want you to seize your opportunity to lead. Step up! Be bold! Be the boss! Take charge!

The ability to take charge boldly is a learned skill. It doesn't come naturally to everyone. But if you aspire to a leadership role at any level, you must acquire the skill of boldly taking charge. As Jack Welch puts it:

> By nature, some people are consensus builders. Some people long to be loved by everyone.
>
> Those behaviors can really get you in the soup if you are a leader, because no matter where you work or what you do, there are times you have to make hard decisions—let people go, cut funding to a project, or close a plant.
>
> Obviously, tough calls spawn complaints and resistance. Your job is to listen and explain yourself clearly but move forward. Do not dwell or cajole.
>
> You are not a leader to win a popularity contest—you are a leader to lead. Don't run for office. You're already elected.[19]

In recent years, we have seen a move away from traditional organizational hierarchies toward more flat, horizontal, or decentralized organizations—especially in smaller companies or small divisions within larger companies. The rationale for a flatter organizational structure is to empower people, involve more people in the decision-making process, and take advantage of the initiative and creativity of everyone in the organization. I support and applaud that.

But regardless of how flat your organization is, you still need bold, courageous leadership. You need leaders to cast and communicate the vision, and to keep the entire organization focused on that vision. You need a few bold leaders who will set the direction for the organization, and hold people accountable for moving the organization in that direction. J. Willard "Bill" Marriott Jr., chairman and CEO of Marriott International, put it this way:

> Human beings like leadership. Even in these days of fashionably "flat" organizations, employees want to know that someone is firmly in charge and they want to make a decision about whether or not they will follow that vision. I don't mean that person must be simply running the business, developing strategy, and making the big decisions—important as those tasks are. I mean that the leader must be visible at the helm.[20]

A leader must often take a lonely, risky, costly stand for his or her vision, principles, and values. Leaders don't have the luxury of always being popular. In fact, all great leaders have had to suffer being reviled and slandered by many of the very people they seek to serve. This kind of pressure comes with the territory. Gene Klann, a retired army commander and faculty member at the Center for Creative Leadership in North Carolina, explains it this way:

Moral courage means standing up for one's convictions and values while risking criticism, censure, ridicule, or persecution. It can also mean a willingness to risk loss of power, position, possessions, or reputation. It means doing what you believe is right and being willing to take an unpopular position regardless of external or internal pressures. . . .

Moral courage involves taking risks and accepting the fear that goes with potentially losing something very important to present or future security. Yet what will be gained from the act of moral courage will generally not be for self but for the benefit of another individual, the team, the organization, the community, or society in general.[21]

General Colin Powell, in *My American Journey*, expresses this truth very succinctly: "Command is lonely."[22]

SWIM UPSTREAM

From the time of its founding in 1968, the Professional Air Traffic Controllers Organization (PATCO) had engaged in work slowdowns and sick-outs in an attempt to force the FAA to hire more controllers and raise salaries. Though illegal, these tactics were successful in forcing the federal government to the bargaining table during the Nixon, Ford, and Carter years. After Ronald Reagan was inaugurated in 1981, PATCO decided to test the new president. Though PATCO had endorsed Reagan's candidacy and Reagan had endorsed PATCO's struggle for better working conditions, the air traffic controllers union declared a strike on August 3, 1981. That strike was a violation of federal law. PATCO had crossed the line.

President Reagan, citing the Taft-Hartley Act, ordered the controllers back to work. He warned that any strikers who failed to return to work within forty-eight hours would be fired and banned from federal service for life. By August 5, only a tiny minority of the thirteen thousand controllers had returned to work. The strikers had called President Reagan's bluff—only he wasn't bluffing. Reagan took charge, kept his word, and boldly fired 11,345 air traffic controllers.[23]

It's important to note that the ramifications of President Reagan's bold decision extended far beyond our shores. Leaders in world capitals, including the Kremlin, took note of Reagan's decisive action. The new president proved early on that he was a man of his word and a leader who took charge. His decisiveness in the PATCO strike gave him added leverage in arms control negotiations with the Soviets.

A reporter once asked President Reagan to explain his approach to decision-making. Reagan replied:

> In the Cabinet meetings—and some members of the Cabinet who have been members of other Cabinets told me there have never been such meetings—I use a system in which I want to hear what everybody wants to say honestly. I want the decisions made on what is right or wrong, what is good or bad for the people of this country. I encourage all the input I can get. . . .
>
> And when I've heard all that I need to make a decision, I don't take a vote. I make the decision.
>
> Then I expect every one of them, whether their views have carried the day or not, to go forward together in carrying out the policy.[24]

Reagan demonstrated that same tough-minded, take-charge decisiveness in his face-to-face negotiations with Soviet Secretary General Mikhail Gorbachev in Reykjavík, Iceland, in October 1986. The goal of the talks was to produce an arms control agreement on intermediate-range nuclear forces. One of the sticking points in the talks was Gorbachev's insistence that the United States discontinue research and development of the Strategic Defense Initiative, also known as "Star Wars." Reagan was intensely committed to SDI, but his advisers wanted him to compromise with Gorbachev and give up Star Wars. President Reagan took a lonely stand against even his most trusted arms control and State Department advisers. Negotiator Max Kampelman later said, "I do not know of a single adviser to the president who agreed with him" at Reykjavík.[25]

As a result of Reagan's tough stance, the talks collapsed. Reagan and Gorbachev returned to their respective countries without an agreement. But on the flight home from Iceland, one of President Reagan's longtime friends, Charles Wick, told him, "Cheer up, Mr. President. You just won the Cold War."[26] As it turned out, Gorbachev returned to the bargaining table the following year and signed the Intermediate-Range Nuclear Forces Treaty—and Ronald Reagan did not have to give up SDI.

The same leadership principles that govern international affairs also govern the sports world, the academic world, the religious world, and the business world. Leaders must make bold decisions, and they must make those decisions stick. As management expert Peter Drucker once observed, "Whenever you see a successful business, someone once made a courageous decision."[27]

It's important for a leader to gather as much information as possible before making an important decision. That's what committees are for. That's what advisers are for. They exist to channel vital information to the leader so that he or she can make an informed decision. But great leaders often have to reject the advice of their own people. Lee Iacocca put it this way:

> Despite what the textbooks say, most important decisions in corporate life are made by individuals, not by committees. My policy has always been to be democratic all the way to the point of decision. Then I become the ruthless commander. "Okay, I've heard everybody," I

say. "Now here's what we're going to do."

You always need committees, because that's where people share their knowledge and intentions. But when committees replace individuals. . .then productivity begins to decline.[28]

Leaders should listen to committees, but leaders should never abdicate the responsibility of decision making to committees. A committee cannot exercise leadership. The collective mind-set of the committee is cautious and hesitant by nature. Boldness and courage are the province of an individualistic mind and are rarely found in an atmosphere of groupthink. Legendary advertising man David Ogilvy expressed it accurately:

In my experience, committees can criticize, but they cannot create.

"Search the parks in all your cities. You'll find no statues of committees.[29]

Committees have their place, but decision making is the leader's job. After you have gathered as many facts as you need to make a decision, it's time to decide. But how many facts are enough? How do you know for certain that the moment of decision has arrived? Answer: You don't. You *never* know for certain. There's always an element of uncertainty. That's why leaders must be bold.

Dr. William A. Cohen, president of the Institute of Leader Arts, is a West Point grad and a retired major general (USAF Reserve) who flew 174 combat missions in Vietnam. He lived in Israel from 1970 to 1973 and flew in the Yom Kippur War. He warns against the paralysis and indecision that come from waiting to gather all the facts:

You will never have all the facts. That's just the nature of leadership. Almost all of the time, you must make decisions without knowing everything that would help you make a decision.

It is true that the longer you wait, the more facts you will have. Sometimes it is necessary to wait for important facts before making a decision. But you must weigh the gain in information against the negative impact of delay. Elements of the situation can change; an opportunity may be lost; your competition may beat you to the market. Those who follow you will at best be uncomfortable at not having a decision. If you make indecisiveness a habit, they will not want to follow you.

Some leaders tell themselves they are putting off a decision to get more facts. . . . Frequently these leaders are simply afraid to make a decision. Failing to make a decision is also a decision. It is a decision to leave everything to chance or the initiative of others. It is certainly not a sign of a take-charge leader—and usually results in failure.[30]

Great leaders understand the value of bold decision-making and the danger of waiting too long to decide. Leadership is the art of making bold decisions then moving heaven and earth to make sure that decision turns out right. Lee Iacocca put it this way: "I have always found that if I move with 75 percent or more of the facts, I usually never regret it. It's the guys who wait to have everything perfect that drive you crazy."[31]

Leaders decide, initiate, take risks—*and live with the consequences of their decisions.* Those who aren't willing to do so aren't leaders. Thomas J. Watson Jr. was president of IBM from 1952 to 1971, and was also the national president of the Boy Scouts of America in the 1960s. He once said, "I never varied from the managerial rule that the worst possible thing we could do would be to lie dead in the water with any problem. Solve it, solve it quickly, solve it right or wrong."[32]

As someone once said, a leader should be a compass, not a weather vane. When everyone around you is being turned this way and that way by the winds of change and uncertainty, your job is to point true north, toward the realization of your vision. Don't wait to gather every scrap of data before you decide. Take the information you have, check it against your vision and goals, apply your core principles and values. . .and *decide*.

You'll be criticized. Don't worry about your critics. Some people will abandon you. Let them go. The majority will be against you. Have confidence in your own instincts and judgment. As Walmart founder Sam Walton once said, "Swim upstream. Go the other way. Ignore the conventional wisdom. If everybody else is doing it one way, there's a good chance you can find your niche by going in exactly the opposite direction. But be prepared for a lot of folks to wave you down and tell you you're headed the wrong way."[33]

When Willard C. "Bill" Butcher was a young junior executive with Chase Manhattan Bank, he received a word of advice from Marion B. Folsom, who was then treasurer of the Eastman Kodak Company (he later served as secretary of health, education, and welfare under Eisenhower). "Bill," Folsom said, "you're going to find that ninety-five percent of all the decisions you'll ever make in your career could be made as well by a reasonably intelligent high school sophomore. But they'll pay you for the other five percent."[34]

It's true. The 5 percent they pay you for are the gutsy decisions you make from a place of courage and boldness. They're the lonely decisions you make when everyone around you is shouting, "You're wrong! Go the other way!" They're the decisions that defy common sense and conventional wisdom.

Anyone can go with the flow. It takes a leader of excellence to swim upstream.

WHAT IF I MAKE A MISTAKE?

You've probably never heard of Cornelius McGillicuddy Sr.—but if you're a sports fan, you've undoubtedly heard of him by his chosen name, Connie Mack. Born in 1862, died in 1956, Connie Mack managed the Philadelphia Athletics for the club's first fifty years before retiring in 1950 at the age of eighty-seven. Connie Mack's A's were my boyhood idols. I spent many golden hours at Shibe Park watching the A's play.

Connie Mack had a philosophy that he succinctly stated as a metaphor: "You can't grind grain with water that has already gone down the creek." It's an old farmer's metaphor, and it's probably lost on a generation that has never seen grain ground into flour by a waterwheel-powered mill. But it's a great truth for every leader to understand and internalize: Don't dwell on the past. Above all, don't dwell on past mistakes. And once a decision is made, don't be too quick to reverse it.

In fact, I would go so far as to say that a decision, once made, should almost *never* be reversed. If you don't have the confidence to stand firmly behind your decisions, then you'd better acquire some confidence quickly—or get out of leadership. Vacillating, wavering, and second-guessing one's own decisions produces uncertainty and paralysis all the way down the line. A leader who lacks confidence in himself cannot inspire others to believe in him.

A decision should only be changed if the circumstances change dramatically or important new information surfaces. But these scenarios are rare. When a leader vacillates and dithers, it is almost always because he or she lacks a clear vision, a clear sense of direction, a clear set of values and convictions, or simply lacks the boldness and courage to make a decision stick.

James E. Burke worked for Johnson & Johnson for four decades and served as CEO from 1976 to 1989. When he was a young product executive at J & J, Burke developed a line of over-the-counter medicines for children. Unfortunately, the product line turned out to be a huge, expensive flop. As a result, he received a summons from the CEO, General Robert Wood Johnson II (son of the cofounder).

"I assumed I was going to be fired," Burke later recalled.

"But instead, Johnson told me, 'Business is about making decisions, and you don't make decisions without making mistakes. Don't make that mistake again, but please be sure you make others.'"[35]

Those are the words of a great leader—a leader who understands that there should be no shame or stigma to making a mistake. A mistake is usually nothing more than a wrong decision, and wrong decisions can be corrected by right decisions. Wrong decisions frequently have enormous teaching value. No leader is infallible, and every great leader invariably has many wrong decisions to his or her credit. Those who make *no* wrong decisions are probably not making *enough* decisions.

So don't beat yourself up for making mistakes. And don't beat up your followers, subordinates, and support staff for making mistakes, either. In fact, I encourage you to make a point of *praising and rewarding* people who make big mistakes, especially when their mistakes are the result of demonstrating initiative, ingenuity, courage, and decisiveness. Never punish those qualities! Encourage gutsy decision making in yourself and in the people around you.

"America's Mayor," Rudy Giuliani, never wasted time wringing his hands over his decisions once they were made. He explains, "I sometimes endure excruciating periods of doubt and soul-searching, and I always try to play out the results of each alternative. However, once I make the decision, I move forward. Something clicks, and all my energies are applied to ensuring the decision works rather than fretting over whether it was the right one."[36]

Face it—unlike golf, there are no mulligans in leadership. Once you make a decision, you can't get it back. But there are plenty of other decisions to be made and plenty of ways to make something good out of a bad decision. Too many people torture themselves, moaning, "If only I had done this, if only I had done that." Sorry, that ship has sailed—but there's always another ship that can get you to your destination.

DO THE THING YOU FEAR

The word *courage* has a long, fine tradition. It comes from the Old French *corage* by way of the Latin *coraticum*, which in turn derives from *cor*, the Latin word for "heart." For thousands of years, this word, *courage*, has spoken of what is in our hearts, what we are truly made of at the core of our being.

Do you have the heart of a leader? To answer yes, you must have courage in all its different forms. You must have *boldness*, the courage to make risky decisions when all the chips are down. You must have *bravery*, the physical courage to confront danger, pain, privation, hardship, and even death in order to achieve a great goal. You must have *uprightness*, the moral courage to make right choices and take right actions even in the face of opposition, temptation, ridicule, or extreme cost.

Courage is not the absence of fear, but the conquest of fear. As Ralph Waldo Emerson once wrote, "Do the thing you fear, and the death of fear is certain."[37] Heroes and cowards both know fear. The difference is that heroes do the thing they fear, knowing it's the right thing to do. Courage is the willingness to take risks, challenge the status quo, seize opportunities, admit faults, and keep going in spite of past failures. Courage is the will to stand firm for one's values and beliefs instead of taking the easy road of compromise. There can be no leadership excellence without the character trait of courage.

The United States Military Academy at West Point maintains a library of very special books. These books were once owned by General George S. Patton, and many of them have been annotated in the margins, flyleaves, and inside covers by Patton himself. Some of these handwritten notations were penned during his cadet days, while others were written well into his illustrious career. These notes give us a glimpse of the thinking of this great military leader.

One of the books in the Patton collection is a textbook from his cadet days at West Point. It's called *Elements of Strategy*. Turning to the final page, you find this revealing note inscribed in Patton's own hand:

QUALITIES OF A GREAT GENERAL
1. Tactically aggressive (loves a fight)
2. Strength of character
3. Steadiness of purpose
4. Acceptance of responsibility
5. Energy
6. Good health and strength
//signed// George Patton
Cadet
USMA
April 29, 1909[38]

Note that each of these six qualities is a form of boldness or courage. To be "tactically aggressive" is to be boldly competitive and decisive. To possess "strength of character" is to be boldly moral and upright. To have "steadiness of purpose" is to be boldly committed to a cause. To demonstrate "acceptance of responsibility" is to be boldly accountable for one's actions. To have "energy" is to be boldly vigorous and enthusiastic. To have "good health and strength" is to be boldly active in a physical, healthy way.

Many of the other notes Patton left for us in his books are statements of different facets of courage and boldness. For example, on one occasion he wrote in a field notebook, "Success in war depends upon the Golden Rule [of] War: Speed—Simplicity—Boldness." He also wrote, "The 'Fog of war' works both ways. The enemy is as much in the dark as you are. BE BOLD!"[39]

William Shakespeare offers great leadership advice in his play *Julius Caesar*. The speaker is Marcus Junius Brutus—the assassin of Julius Caesar, and perhaps not the best of role models. Yet you cannot argue with his leadership logic:

There is a tide in the affairs of men,
Which, taken at the flood, leads on to fortune;
Omitted, all the voyage of their life

Is bound in shallows and in miseries.
On such a full sea are we now afloat;
And we must take the current when it serves,
Or lose our ventures.[40]

Five hundred years later, the Nike sportswear company distilled Shakespeare's grand thought down to a simple, memorable slogan: "Just do it."

Hall of Fame NBA coach Phil Jackson wrote his own commentary on this concept in his book *Sacred Hoops*: "Above all, trust your gut. This is the first law of leadership. Once you've made your move, you have to stand behind your decision and live with the consequences."[41]

One of the greatest trust-your-gut business leaders of all time is Andy Grove, the semiconductor pioneer, who was born in Hungary and survived the Nazi occupation during World War II. In 1946, when Hungary fell to the Communists, Grove, then twenty years old, escaped and came to America. He obtained an undergraduate degree in chemical engineering at City College of New York in 1960 then earned his PhD at UC Berkeley in 1963. Five years later, he was the COO of Intel—then known as Integrated Electronics Corporation. In 1987, Grove became CEO of Intel. Under his leadership, Intel became the world's largest semiconductor company (based on revenue), growing from $18 billion in 1987 to $197 billion in 1998, the year he retired as CEO. Grove was *Time's* Man of the Year in 1997, and in 2004 the Wharton School of Business named him the "Most Influential Business Person of the Last Twenty-Five Years."

Dr. Noel Tichy, professor of organizational behavior at the University of Michigan, made a careful study of Andy Grove's bold leadership style. In *The Leadership Engine*, Tichy observes:

Every two years, Andy Grove plunks down about $2.5 billion to build a plant to produce a new type of microchip. This is essentially a bet on the future of Intel's new technology. So far, the bets have paid off big for Intel. Is Grove lucky, or a great gambler? Hardly. Grove is a great leader who looks for opportunities to change his company before the market changes ahead of it, and then makes it very clear to people what mountain they are about to climb.[42]

Tichy adds that Andy Grove displays "a leadership quality that I have come to call 'edge': the ability to make tough decisions and the willingness to sacrifice the security of today for the sake of a better future. . . . The people who succeed, the winners, are the ones who have edge."[43]

This quality that Noel Tichy calls "edge" is precisely the same quality I call boldness. Tichy learned the term *edge* from former General Electric CEO Jack Welch. Tichy interviewed Welch on the subject of leadership, and Welch explained his view of bold leadership. "A leader's got to have edge," Welch said. "Without that, nothing else matters. . . . A lot of people have good ideas, and good values, and they can even energize others. But for some reason they are not able to make the tough calls. That is what separates, for me, whether or not someone can lead a business."[44]

Ira Eaker earned his pilot's rating in 1918 and served in the army air corps. He was a float plane pilot with the twenty-two-thousand-mile Pan American Goodwill Flight in 1927. Then he set an endurance record (and pioneered the technology of in-flight refueling) as chief pilot of the army's "Question Mark" airplane in 1929, and piloted the first blind (instruments only) transcontinental flight in 1936. He rose to the rank of general, and at the beginning of World War II, the army sent General Eaker to England to help the British form their bomber command. He was named commander of the Eighth Air Force in 1942 and became the architect of a strategic bombing force that ultimately numbered twenty-four hundred heavy bombers and fifteen hundred fighters.

General Eaker advocated daylight precision bombing of military and industrial targets, but Allied leaders were skeptical. So General Eaker took his case directly to Winston Churchill. The result was a plan in which American B-17s would bomb the Germans by day, and British bombers would strike by night. Though daylight bombing was riskier to pilots and planes, it struck directly at Nazi Germany's ability to wage war—and it reduced civilian casualties. His bold plan reinvigorated the stalled Allied war effort and put the Nazi war juggernaut on the defensive for the first time.

Ira Eaker was no "desk general." He put his life on the line, flying many bombing missions over Europe in his B-17 Flying Fortress, the *Yankee Doodle*. In fact, in August 1942, he flew the first American bombing raid to attack German forces in occupied France. General Eaker was a courageous proponent of a daring strategy—and his bold leadership helped win the war in Europe. As he himself once said, "A bold, vigorous assault has won many a faltering cause."[45]

In 1997 Lady Margaret Thatcher spoke at a luncheon I attended in Orlando. Though she was no longer the prime minister of Great Britain, she projected the unmistakable impression of a great leader. After her talk, she took questions, and one questioner asked her what it takes to be a successful leader.

"There are four steps to becoming a great leader," she replied. "First, *know what matters to you*. Have a set of principles and follow them. Your principles serve as the foundation of your leadership. Second, *speak up!* Be bold and fearless about asserting your principles. Third, *anticipate problems*. Use information, instinct, and intuition to foresee problems and crises before anyone else does. Fourth, *make bold decisions*. Base your decisions on your principles and on the information and insight you have. Meet problems and opportunities head-on; then take bold action."

That fourth step—make bold decisions—is the same advice Prime Minister Thatcher gave to President George H. W. Bush after Saddam Hussein's forces invaded Kuwait in 1990.

When Mr. Bush appeared indecisive in his initial response to Saddam's aggression, Thatcher phoned the White House and told him, "This is no time to go wobbly, George."[46] In other words, make a bold decision and do the right thing. Mr. Bush took the Iron Lady's advice, boldly committed America to the war effort, and liberated the people of Kuwait.

In times of crisis, great leaders act boldly and make the tough decisions. Theodore Hesburgh, former president of Notre Dame University, put it this way: "My basic principle is that you don't make decisions because they are easy; you don't make them because they are cheap; you don't make them because they are popular. You make them because they are right."[47]

What are some practical ways that we, as leaders in our own sphere of leadership influence, can demonstrate boldness? In our teams, our organizations, our companies, our military units, our schools, our churches, we are called upon to display courageous leadership. For us, too, this is no time to go wobbly. We display bold, courageous, decisive leadership whenever we:

- take on audacious challenges, bold visions, and extreme dreams—when we set out to do the impossible.
- dare to put our own careers and reputations on the line for a vision we believe in.
- take a stand for our beliefs and values even when the world is against us.
- accept responsibility for our failures, courageously taking our lumps instead of shifting blame.
- stand and fight when others run away.
- accept criticism without defending ourselves.
- step far outside our comfort zone in order to try something completely new.

If we want to be men and women of leadership excellence, we have to stretch our courage. As an old apostle once wrote to a young leader, "For God did not give us a spirit of timidity, but a spirit of power, of love, and of self-discipline."[48]

A VOICE OTHERS WILL FOLLOW

On September 11, 2001, Todd Beamer, an account manager for Oracle Corporation, boarded United Flight 93 in Newark, New Jersey. The plane took off at 8:00 a.m., bound for San Francisco. About ninety minutes into the flight, hijackers took over the plane. Around that same time, hijackers aboard two other planes carried out suicide missions, crashing into the twin towers of the World Trade Center in lower Manhattan.

At 9:45, Beamer used the in-flight telephone to call GTE supervisor Lisa Jefferson. He told Jefferson that Flight 93 had been hijacked by men armed with knives. Most of the passengers had been herded into the first-class compartment up front, but he and nine other passengers, plus five flight attendants, were in the rear of the plane.

Beamer kept the line open with Jefferson while he plotted with fellow passengers Jeremy Glick, Thomas Burnett Jr., and Mark Bingham to disrupt the hijackers' plans. Burnett made several calls to his wife and learned of the suicide attacks in New York City. It was obvious what the Flight 93 hijackers had in mind. Flight attendant Sandra Bradshaw called her husband, explained the crisis, and told him she was brewing scalding water to use against the hijackers.

Meanwhile, Todd Beamer asked the GTE supervisor to pray with him. Together, Beamer and Lisa Jefferson recited the Twenty-Third Psalm. Then Beamer asked Jefferson to call his family—his wife, Lisa, and his sons, David (age three) and Andrew (age one), and give them his love. Then Lisa Jefferson heard Beamer drop the phone and say to his fellow passengers, "Are you guys ready? Let's roll." Todd Beamer was a leader. He had a voice that others followed.

Minutes later, Jefferson heard the line go dead. Flight 93 crashed in a Pennsylvania field at 9:58 a.m. Authorities believe the hijackers intended to crash the plane into the White

House or the Capitol in Washington DC—and they give credit to a bold, courageous group of passengers and crew members for averting that catastrophe.[49]

While these events were unfolding over Pennsylvania, another hijacked passenger plane, American Airlines Flight 77, crashed into the Pentagon in Arlington County, Virginia. The plane exploded, ripping through the western side of the five-sided structure. The crash and fire killed 184 people (not counting the five hijackers). Fifty-nine of the innocent dead were aboard the plane, and the rest were working in the Pentagon.

One of those who survived was army Lt. Col. Victor Correa. He was knocked onto the floor by the blast, but he picked himself up and helped guide others into the hallway, toward safety. The hall was dark, littered with debris, and rapidly filling with smoke. He could see fires burning at the end of the hall, and smoke was burning his nostrils and lungs. He removed his T-shirt, soaked it in water, and pressed it to his face to filter the air.

Lieutenant Colonel Correa is blessed with a powerful, booming voice. So he shouted—and his words echoed down the hallway. "Listen to me," he said with the voice of authority. "Follow my voice."

All down the hallway, people filed out of their offices. They followed his voice through the darkness and smoke—and he led them to safety.

He went in and out of the building several times, each time finding more people who needed help. Again and again, he said, "Follow my voice," and they followed. Dozens of people are alive today because Lieutenant Colonel Correa spoke in a voice that people followed.

Later he had the opportunity to talk with other survivors of that day—people who worked in other offices of the Pentagon, people he had never met. When he spoke his name, their eyes came alight with recognition, and they said, "*That* was the voice I heard."[50]

They had followed Lieutenant Colonel Correa's voice

through the darkened, smoke-filled corridors. They had followed his voice to life and safety. They had followed the voice of a bold, courageous leader.

Now it's your turn. Be the bold, courageous, confident voice that others follow. Take charge. Be the leader.

7

THE SEVENTH SIDE OF LEADERSHIP:
A SERVING HEART

Mom and Dad were leaders. And they were servants.

In the process of writing this book, my sister Ruthie and I have talked about how our parents, Jim and Ellen Williams, led the fight to improve research, treatment, and facilities for people with mental disabilities. Ruthie reminded me of events and memories I hadn't thought about in years.

After Mom passed away in 2006, Ruthie cleaned out the family home where we had spent our childhood years, and where Mom had lived for seventy years. "I came across a lot of letters and photos," she told me. "And I found a journal Dad kept in 1932."

That was the first I'd heard that Dad kept a journal. In 1932 he would have been twenty-five. Ruthie told me that, in many of the journal entries, Dad wrote about his own father, who was a Presbyterian minister in Greensboro, North Carolina.

"Dad repeatedly wrote about his father's expectations of him," Ruthie said. "He talked about wanting to live his life for the betterment of others. These values were instilled in him by his father. Dad wanted his father to be proud of him and proud of the things he did to serve other people. That was a goal and a quest that was a big part of his life. I wish I had known about that. I was a teenager when Dad died, so I never had a chance to talk to him about his goals and values. But there it was—in his own words, his own handwriting, in his journal. That was a gift."

Serving others—that was the pattern of living my sisters and I saw modeled every day by our father and mother. Our parents expected us to be leaders—not in order to gain power and perks for ourselves, but in order to serve others and make the world a better place. They didn't preach to us or lecture us about serving. They just modeled a serving lifestyle, and my sisters and I absorbed that pattern from them by osmosis.

The seventh side of leadership is serving—and that is the hardest dimension of leadership for many people to grasp. There are many five- and six-sided leaders in the world. They're good at what they do—but they fall just one or two notches short of true leadership excellence. What are they missing? They lack a serving heart.

The other six sides of leadership are nouns: vision, communication, people skills, character, competence, and boldness. But the seventh side of leadership is a verb—an action word *serving*. When a leader serves his or her subordinates, team, stockholders, clients, customers, or fans, that leader is *taking action*.

We have not attained positions of leadership and authority merely for the purpose of dominating our followers and subordinates. We lead people in order to actively *serve* them. Our job is to put on a servant's apron every day—and printed on that apron is the title Servant Leader.

In *Credibility: How Leaders Gain and Lose It, Why People Demand It*, James Kouzes and Barry Posner define leadership as serving others. "Leadership is service," they write. "Leaders exist to serve a purpose for the people who have made it possible for them to lead—their constituents. They are servant leaders. Not self-serving leaders, but other-serving leaders. The relationship of leader and constituent has been turned upside down."[1]

Upside down indeed! The traditional organizational model

is depicted as a pyramid, with the leader at the apex and all the levels of underlings and drones spreading out beneath. The leader is the boss, and everyone beneath exists to serve the leader, the leader's goals, and even the leader's whims. But servant leaders stand the pyramid on its head. Yes, the leader still has authority, he or she is still in command, still takes charge; but the people in the organization no longer exist to serve the leader. The leader exists to serve the people.

A serving attitude is the key to leadership excellence.

LEADERSHIP IS SERVING, AND SERVING IS SACRIFICE

In the late 1990s, George Washington Elementary School in New Orleans was renamed Charles Richard Drew Elementary School. The recognition of Charles Drew was certainly appropriate. Drew was an African-American surgeon and medical researcher who invented important new techniques for storing blood during World War II. His innovations allowed medics and field hospitals to save untold thousands of lives through blood transfusions during the war.

Historian Stephen Ambrose, while acknowledging Drew's enormous contributions, lamented the removal of George Washington's name from the school. When Ambrose talked to student audiences about Washington's leadership greatness, students often objected, "But Washington was a slaveholder!" Ambrose replied that, of the nine American presidents who owned slaves, only George Washington gave his slaves their freedom. He told his students:

> Listen, he was our leader in the Revolution, to which he pledged his life, his fortune, and his honor. Those were not idle pledges. What do you think would have happened to him had he been captured by the British Army?
>
> I'll tell you. He would have been brought to London, tried, found guilty of treason, ordered executed, and then drawn and quartered. Do

you know what that means? He would have had one arm tied to one horse, the other arm to another horse, one leg to yet another, and the other leg to a fourth. Then the four horses would have been simultaneously whipped and started off at a gallop, one going north, another south, another east and the fourth to the west.

That is what Washington risked to establish your freedom and mine.[2]

George Washington was a serving leader. He served the soldiers he led. He served his countrymen and his nation. Ultimately, he even served his own servants by setting them free. The essence of leadership greatness is serving—and the essence of serving is sacrifice. Tom Osborne, former head football coach (and current athletic director) at the University of Nebraska, put it this way:

When players see the needs of others being as important as their own needs, they begin to reach out to those around them. They attempt to make others better and are primarily concerned with team success. As one player reaches out to another and demonstrates a willingness to sacrifice personal goals for team objectives, the attitude often spreads. The prevailing attitude on a team can be that of self-sacrifice and concern for the team. The reverse is also true, in that selfishness and self-interest breed increased dissension and alienation among team members.[3]

In order to achieve a leadership vision, everyone on the team, everyone in the organization, must be willing and ready at all times to sacrifice. We must be willing to sacrifice comfort, sleep, safety, financial gain, reputation, and individual goals in order to achieve the common good, the common goal, the common vision. There is no serving without a willingness—even an eagerness—to sacrifice. That is the life of a servant leader.

The term *servant leader* was coined by Robert Greenleaf, a retired AT&T executive, in an essay titled "The Servant as Leader." Greenleaf wrote the essay after reading Hermann Hesse's 1932 novel *Journey to the East*. In Hesse's novel, the narrator describes a journey he takes with a group of mystic poets and artists called The League. One of the members is Leo, a servant. He carries luggage and does menial tasks for the others.

At one point, Leo disappears—and his absence throws The League into disarray. Leo, it turns out, was the glue that held the group together; now the members are at odds with one another, bickering and arguing. The members of The League lose their enthusiasm for the journey. Depressed, angry, and filled with distrust, the narrator leaves The League and strikes off on his own.

Why does the disappearance of Leo the servant cause the group to implode? As Greenleaf interprets Hesse's tale, The League could not exist without the quiet, unassuming leadership of a servant leader.

Ten years go by. The narrator encounters a man—and becomes convinced that this man is Leo, the long-lost servant of The League. The narrator follows the man through the streets, coming at last to the hall where members of The League are gathered. The narrator loses the man in the crowd.

The meeting begins and the leader of The League arrives and steps onto the stage dressed in a royal robe trimmed in gold. It's Leo—the long-lost servant.

The servant is the leader, the leader is the servant. This quiet and humble man is also the authoritative, take-charge leader—and he is the magnetic force that holds The League together. His humble, self-effacing, self-sacrificing personality was the catalyst that made all the other personalities of The League blend together in a healthy, functional way. That's what servant leaders do.

Greenleaf concludes that all leaders of greatness and excellence are like Leo. We meet these leaders first as servants, as people who are motivated by a desire to help, love, empower, and serve others. Their leadership authority emerges out of their desire to serve. Greenleaf concludes:

> The servant-leader is servant first. . . . It begins with the natural feeling that one wants to serve, to serve first. Then conscious choice brings one to aspire to lead. That person is sharply different from one who is leader first, perhaps because of the need to assuage an unusual power drive or to acquire material possessions. . . . The leader-first and the servant-first are two extreme types. Between them there are shadings and blends that are part of the infinite variety of human nature.
>
> The difference manifests itself in the care taken by the servant-first to make sure that other people's highest priority needs are being served. The best test, and difficult to administer, is: Do those served grow as persons? Do they, while being served, become healthier, wiser, freer, more autonomous, more likely themselves to become servants? And, what is the effect on the least privileged in society? Will they benefit or at least not be further deprived?[4]

The old top-down, hierarchical leadership model is a relic of ages gone by. Paradoxically, the "new" leadership model for the twenty-first century—the model of servant leadership—is as old as Lao-tzu in ancient China (more than five hundred years before Christ), Chanakya of ancient India (more than three hundred years BC), and Jesus of Nazareth. In the *Arthashastra*, Chanakya writes, "The king [that is, the leader] shall consider as good, not what pleases himself but what pleases his subjects [or followers]."[5] And in the *Tao Teh Ching*, Lao-tzu writes:

> The highest type of ruler is one of whose existence
>   the people are barely aware.
> Next comes one whom they love and praise.
> Next comes one whom they fear.
> Next comes one whom they despise and defy.
> When you are lacking in faith,
> Others will be unfaithful to you.
> The Sage is self-effacing and scanty of words.
> When his task is accomplished and things have
>   been completed,
> All the people say, "We ourselves have achieved it!"[6]

In the New Testament, there is a scene in which Jesus walks with his disciples along the road to Capernaum. As they walk, some of the disciples lag behind him and argue among themselves as to which is the greatest disciple. They think Jesus doesn't hear them, but when they arrive at the home where they are to stay, Jesus turns and asks, "What were you arguing about on the road?" No one dares to speak. So Jesus says, "If anyone wants to be first, he must be the very last, and the servant of all."[7] He later exemplifies those words by washing the feet of his disciples in the upper room.

What's old is new again. The servant-leadership model of the future is also centuries-old wisdom from the past. Even though bosses still boss people around today, many leaders are rediscovering the most ancient, most effective, most powerful leadership model of all: a serving heart. Only leaders who serve should serve as leaders. Leadership is serving, and serving is sacrifice.

EVERYBODY CAN BE GREAT

Bobby Bowden is a prince among leaders—and a servant's servant. Now in his eighties, Bobby coached the Florida State Seminoles football team from 1976 until 2009. In 2006 he was inducted into the College Football Hall of Fame. His final coaching appearance was at the 2010 Gator Bowl, on New Year's Day, with a 33–21 victory over West Virginia, where he had coached from 1966 to 1975.

I recently had a conversation with Bob Antion, a Penn State grad and high school coach whose life was profoundly affected by the servant leadership of Bobby Bowden. "I was just a scrub at Penn State," Bob said, "but I wanted to go into coaching. That wasn't going to happen there, so I went to West Virginia to get a chance. In the fall of 1974, I arrived as a grad assistant in Morgantown [home of the West Virginia University Mountaineers]. Unfortunately, I got there late, and there was no position open for me.

"Coach Bowden told me I could be a dorm counselor at West Virginia until I could become a full-time grad assistant. That was fine with me. I moved into the dorm early, before the other counselors, and started going to fall football practice. Pretty soon the rest of the counselors arrived on campus, and the head counselor invited me to attend a 'welcome back picnic.' I understood the picnic to be an option, not a requirement, and I preferred being at football practice that evening, so I skipped the picnic.

"The next morning, the head counselor informed me that the picnic was mandatory, and I was fired for not attending. I would have to clear out of the dorm. Later that day, I loaned my car to a guy, and he totaled it. So in one day, I lost my job, my place to live, and my car. I was devastated. I'd have to go home a complete failure.

"I called Coach Bowden and told him what had happened. Coach said, 'Meet me after practice, and we'll go over to the First National Bank.' So we went to the bank, and Coach set up an account called Bobby Bowden Enterprises. What was Bobby Bowden Enterprises? It was a business name he came up with on the spot. He wrote me a check for a thousand dollars so I could get a place to stay. He wrote another check to cover my tuition to the master's program at the university. He told me I could eat my meals at the athletes' training table. Then he called the local Ford dealership and bought me a car. And he paid me five hundred dollars a month as the only employee of Bobby Bowden Enterprises.

"I had known that man for less than a week, yet he sacrificed out of his own personal finances to enable me to stay. The 1974 season was a trying time for Coach Bowden. We ended with a 4–7 season and had lots of problems with the team. The fans were angry, and they hung Coach Bowden in effigy from the trees on campus. But Coach hung in there, and the following season, we had a terrific team and went to the Peach Bowl. The year after that, Coach moved on to a long and amazing career at Florida State.

"After Coach left West Virginia, I took a high school coaching job in Blacksville, West Virginia. I was twenty-four years old. I've been coaching ever since—but I don't know how my life would have gone if not for Bobby Bowden's personal sacrifice and service to a grad assistant he didn't even know."

Bobby Bowden was both a leader and a servant throughout his career—and his commitment to serving others never faltered, even when his own heart was breaking. I'll never forget the shock and sadness I felt when I heard that Bobby's former son-in-law, John Madden, and fifteen-year-old grandson, Bowden Madden, were killed in a freeway pileup on Interstate 10 in late 2004. John, who had played football for Bobby at Florida State, had been married to Bobby's youngest daughter, Ginger. The funeral for Bobby's grandson was held the day before Florida State's season opener against the Miami Hurricanes at the Orange Bowl. Many people expected Bobby to skip the game due to his loss.

But on game day, Bobby was on the sideline, looking stoic on the outside but torn up within. He was committed to serving his players, regardless of his personal pain. Bobby's son Jeff, the Seminoles' offensive coordinator, told reporters, "Dad doesn't show his emotions to a heavy degree, but it has been difficult for both of us to concentrate at times."[8]

Seminoles linebacker Buster Davis said that Coach Bowden was focused on serving his players in spite of his own loss. "We know what [Coach Bowden] must have been going through," Davis said, "but he never showed his emotions. . . . We really got the sense that he didn't want us thinking about what he was going through."[9]

Those were the emotions Bobby took into the game—a tough, low-scoring, defense-dominated game. Bobby Bowden's Seminoles wanted desperately to win the game for their coach after losing to Miami in their previous five encounters.

Late in the fourth quarter, the Seminoles led 10–3. With 3:58 remaining, Florida State attempted a 34-yard field goal—but Miami blocked it, got the ball back, and drove eighty yards in five plays to tie the game at ten. Then Miami scored another touchdown in overtime—another tough loss for Bobby Bowden's Seminoles.

As Bobby trudged toward the tunnel, rowdy Miami fans taunted him, but Bobby didn't appear to hear them. He went to the press room to face reporters, and he explained the loss quite simply: "We had our chance to put them away, and we didn't. They had a chance to put us away, and they did." One reporter asked Coach the unspoken question on everyone's mind: Wasn't it hard to coach in the aftermath of his personal loss?

"It wasn't hard to be here coaching this game," Bobby replied. "But it was hard for my mind not to be somewhere else."[10]

Tampa Tribune columnist Joe Henderson noticed Bobby standing up after the press conference, muttering to no one in particular, "It's awful. Just awful." Henderson knew that the old coach wasn't talking about football.

Henderson went outside and gathered quotes for his column from the Seminole players. Then he heard, "Hey, Joe!" Henderson turned and saw Coach Bowden toss something to him. Henderson caught it—the Florida State cap Bobby had worn during the game. "Give that to your grandson," Bobby said. Then he turned and boarded the bus.[11]

Bobby Bowden is a servant to his family, to his players,

to the fans, and even to the members of the media and their families. He sets aside his own hurts and he sacrifices his own emotional needs in order to serve others. That's why this servant will always be remembered as a great leader.

Florida financier Jimmy Hewitt—the man who convinced me to come to Orlando to start a new NBA franchise—once told me about a conversation he had with Bobby Bowden when Bobby was still coaching the Seminoles. Bobby was then in his late seventies (he retired at eighty). He easily could have retired years earlier as one of the winningest coaches in college football history. Why, then, did he keep going?

He stayed in the game because he wanted to continue influencing young lives. "You can't take a trophy to heaven," he told Jimmy Hewitt. "And you can't influence young people from an easy chair. I don't have any interest in becoming a *former* coach." That's a servant leader talking.

The truly great leaders are always role models and teachers of servanthood. They are continually conscious of their influence on others, and they never pass up an opportunity to teach lessons of servanthood to those they serve.

Another great servant leader in the sports world is Coach Mike Krzyzewski of Duke University. In a profile of Coach K, *Investor's Business Daily* tells the story of a time during a basketball practice when a student assistant handed a cup of water to the coach. To borrow a football metaphor, Coach K fumbled the exchange. The cup fell and splashed water on the hardwood floor. The student assistant ran to the towel cart and returned, towel in hand, ready to wipe up the spill.

"Here, I'll take that," Coach K said. Then he turned and addressed his players, "When you are the CEO of your own company, I want you to remember that you should still clean up your own mess."

Then he got down on his knees and mopped up the floor.[12]

Coach K doesn't just teach basketball. He teaches leadership and servanthood. He teaches lessons that his players will take far beyond the locker room and into the boardrooms, conference rooms, newsrooms, and classrooms of the future. C. William Pollard, former CEO of ServiceMaster, expresses the mind-set of Coach Mike Krzyzewski and all great leaders when he writes, "A servant leader's results will be measured beyond the workplace, and the story will be told in the changed lives of others. There is no scarcity of feet to wash. The towels and the water are available. The limitation, if there is one, is our ability to get on our hands and knees and be prepared to do what we ask others to do."[13]

The late Carl Rieser, former writer and editor for *Business-Week*, *Fortune*, and the Committee for Economic Development, found the truth of servant-leadership beautifully expressed in the symbolism of American sign language.

> I have been told that sign language has the uncanny ability to cut through to the real meaning of the word, and I believe it. In sign language, the sign for servant is this: hands out in front with palms up and moving back and forth between the signer and the signee. In this case, the sign takes us back to powerful implications that [the word] servant seems to have had four millennia ago. . . .
>
> This simple gesture says some very powerful things about trusting, being open, offering help, caring, and being willing to be vulnerable. It has a strong sense of mutuality; it connects us.
>
> The gesture evokes what I call the servant within, who is there to help and to serve both you and me. Not just you or me. Us. I have come to see this archetypal servant within as the key to my relationship with myself, with other humans, and perhaps with creation. I have even made this gesture a part of my own daily devotional life because it catches this thought so beautifully.[14]

Dr. Martin Luther King, Jr. was a servant leader who

preached what he practiced and practiced what he preached. A collection of his speeches, *A Knock at Midnight*, includes a transcript of his sermon "The Drum Major Instinct" (complete with all the "amens" from the audience). In that sermon, Dr. King said (and the congregation responded):

> Everybody can be great, *(Everybody)* because everybody can serve. *(Amen)* You don't have to have a college degree to serve. *(All right)* You don't have to make your subject and your verb agree to serve. You don't have to know about Plato and Aristotle to serve. You don't have to know Einstein's theory of relativity to serve. You don't have to know the second theory of thermodynamics in physics to serve. *(Amen)* You only need a heart full of grace, *(Yes, sir. Amen)* a soul generated by love. *(Yes)* And you can be that servant.[15]

Everybody can be that servant. I can be that servant—and so can you. And by serving, you can be a great leader.

A SERVANT IS NEVER FRUSTRATED

Michael Bergdahl is an author and speaker who once worked directly with Walmart founder Sam Walton at the company's Bentonville, Arkansas, headquarters. Walton gave Bergdahl the nickname "Bird Dawg." In his book *What I Learned from Sam Walton*, Bergdahl writes of his former boss:

> He was the kind of person who would never ask anyone else to do anything he personally wasn't willing to do. At Wal-Mart they called it walking the talk. He preached his servant-leadership concept, which he believed was the most important attribute of great leaders. To be a true servant-leader requires that you

be a servant first, by serving the people who report to you, and a leader second with the respect that you gained by serving first. Servant-leadership comes from the heart and requires that the leader sincerely care about people.[16]

According to Bergdahl, servant leadership is truly the source of Walt-Mart's amazing success and unique corporate culture.

Having been an insider at Wal-Mart, I had a unique opportunity to see the value of servant leadership firsthand. Sam talked about it all the time. . . . In his own leadership, he modeled the behaviors he expected everyone else to adopt in their personal leadership. . . .

Servant leadership is a top-down cultural concept. It has to be embraced and brought to life at the highest levels. Until and unless a company is willing to flip the traditional organizational pyramid, making the people who really do the work the most important in the organization, servant-leadership philosophies can't be implemented.[17]

Now, let's think about what that really means. Everyone in the organization, from top to bottom and side to side, must become a genuine servant. A lot of bosses *talk* about serving, but it's merely a pose—a servanthood act.

As leaders, we need to experience a radical conversion of our thinking. We have to dump the traditional "I'm the boss" model of leadership and the old "What's in it for me" way of doing business. We have to stand the old organizational pyramid on its head. The CEO must truly aspire to be the least and lowliest servant in the organization. Everyone in the company who wants to become a leader must set aside the traditional ambitions for power and perks and corner offices and executive washroom keys, and must aspire to join the fellowship of the towel and basin. Leaders have to start washing the feet of subordinates instead of bossing subordinates around.

Some people reading these words are undoubtedly thinking, *Can't I get the same results by* impersonating *a servant? I could use a lot of servanthood jargon and con my subordinates and my customers into thinking I really care. Once I'm able to fake sincerity, I should have it made!* Well, if you think you can get real results with fake servanthood, good luck with that. But I'm telling you right now, it'll never work.

Michael Bergdahl observed that the reason Sam Walton's servant-leadership model worked so well was that everyone *knew* he was the real deal. When Sam visited Walmart stores, the company's employees didn't hesitate to walk right up and talk to him like an old friend. His down-to-earth manner, Bergdahl observed, attracted people "like steel to a magnet."[18]

Servant leadership was not an act for Sam Walton. He exemplified and personified servant leadership right up to the end of his life.

Bergdahl recalls seeing Sam Walton lying on his back in a hospital bed, receiving intravnous chemotherapy treatments—but the hospital bed was *not* in a hospital; it was in Sam's office. Sam wanted to keep working, keep serving his people, even while he was receiving anticancer treatments. The story of Sam Walton's unceasing servanthood to his company and to his people has become part of the lore, legend, and culture of Walmart.[19] That tradition of serving remains central to Walmart to this day.

As Sam himself once said, "Let's spoil those wonderful customers. Let's appreciate them every day on every visit and tell them so. The key to our success, though, must be that we all truly embrace the philosophy of being servant leaders, both with our customers and each other."[20]

One way C. William Pollard practiced servant leadership as CEO of ServiceMaster was by making himself available to his employees at all times. Pollard writes:

As leaders act on their belief in people, they listen and learn. They work at making themselves available. Their door is always open. They are out and about, talking and listening to people at all levels of the organization. They should always be willing to do whatever they ask of others. This is a simple yet profound test of the servant leader. . . .

We have designed our executive offices as a reminder of this principle of listening, learning, and serving. Nobody works behind closed doors. Glass is everywhere, confirming our desire to have an open office and open minds. No executive office captures an outside window. The view to the outside is available to all working in the office.[21]

During Pollard's leadership of the company, ServiceMaster was selected by *Fortune* magazine as the number one service company among the Fortune 500. It's fitting that a company whose only product is service should be built around a philosophy of serving the customer—and serving one another in the organization.

In early 2010, I flew to Cincinnati for a speaking engagement. A driver named Bob Ward met me at the airport and took me to my hotel. After my stay, Bob also picked me up and drove me back to the airport. Over the years, I've made a habit of asking my drivers one question: "Who was the most memorable person you've ever had in your limo?"

Without hesitation, Bob said, "That would have to be General Colin Powell. He arrived in a private plane at a small airport near Cincinnati. He got into the car and said, 'Before we go to the hotel, I need to stop at a place called the Sherman House.' I'd never heard of it, so I called my dispatcher for directions. The dispatcher looked it up and said, 'Man, that's in a really bad neighborhood.'

"But the general wanted to go, so we went. When we got there, I discovered that it's a housing facility for homeless veterans. I went in with General Powell, and he spoke for about twenty minutes to the guys who lived there. He showed them a good time, and they had a lot of laughs. At the end of it all, the general thanked them for their service. I could tell it had been quite a while since some of those men had heard one of their countrymen say, 'Thank you.'

"After that, I drove him to his hotel. General Powell was in Cincinnati to give a corporate speech—but I think the way he went out of his way to serve those homeless vets and say 'thank you' was his most important mission."

As Oren Harari notes in *The Leadership Secrets of Colin Powell*, "Through his words—and also through his deeds—Powell makes a strong case that 'the only way to accomplish your mission is through those troops entrusted to your care. . . . At the end of the day. . .it's some soldier who will go up a hill and correct your mistakes and take that hill.'"[22]

One of the most ironic and paradoxical truths of servant-leadership is that if you set your ego and ambitions aside and become a true servant, you can become a great leader. But you have to mean it. You have to have the sincere and humble mind-set of a servant, or it will all just be a meaningless pose. Educator Frank F. Warren, president of Whitworth College during the 1940s and 1950s, put it this way: "If you wish to be a leader, you will be frustrated, for very few people wish to be led. If you aim to be a servant, you will never be frustrated."[23]

LEADERSHIP IS A JOB, NOT A POSITION

In *The Greatest Communicator*, former Reagan pollster Dick Wirthlin writes, "Future presidents must remember what Ronald Reagan never forgot: the presidency. . .belongs to the people. It is an institution far greater than one human being. And that's why Ronald Reagan never took his coat off in the Oval Office—he wasn't in 'his' office. He was a visitor, a temporary steward, and he never let himself or the power he possessed delude him into thinking otherwise."[24]

Reagan's daughter, Patti Davis, wrote a loving tribute called *The Long Goodbye*, which was published soon after her father died. In the book, she tells a story that reveals yet another facet of Ronald Reagan the leader—his serving heart. It's the story of when Ronald Reagan and Mikhail Gorbachev met for a superpower summit in Geneva in 1985.

"It would not be overly dramatic to say that the fate of the world was at stake," Davis writes, "yet [my father] never lost sight of the smaller, human concerns." President Reagan and his wife, Nancy, stayed in a villa on Lake Geneva. The Swiss family who owned the villa had moved out so that President and Mrs. Reagan, along with their security detail, could have the run of the house.

In the bedroom where the Reagans stayed was a fishbowl containing goldfish. The goldfish belonged to the children of the Swiss family, and President Reagan had promised to faithfully feed the goldfish. Even with all the weighty concerns of strategic arms limitation and jailed Soviet dissidents and the many other issues that Mr. Reagan and Mr. Gorbachev discussed, the American president kept his promise and fed the goldfish.

One evening Reagan entered the bedroom and found one of the goldfish floating. He had one of his staffers put the dead fish in a box, take it to a pet store in the city, and find a suitable replacement. The staffer returned with two goldfish, which President Reagan placed in the bowl. Then the president wrote a note to the children, apologizing for the loss of the other goldfish and explaining that he had replaced the dead fish with two brand-new goldfish. That is a leader with a genuine serving heart.[25]

Michael Reagan reminds us that his father used to read and answer his own mail, sometimes sent money out of his own bank account to people who were in need, was the first president to honor heroes during the State of the Union address, was the first president to salute the marine honor guard as he exited the Marine One helicopter, and never disembarked from Air Force One without thanking his flight crew.

President Reagan always spent Thanksgiving holidays with his family at his Santa Barbara ranch, yet he spent every Christmas at the White House. Why did he do that? Simply because he wanted to be a servant to his Secret Service agents. He was grateful to them for protecting him with their lives, so he believed they should spend Christmas Day at home with their families. By remaining in the White House over Christmas, he gave his security detail time off.

Michael Reagan tells a beautiful story that occurred when his father was in the late stages of Alzheimer's and could no longer speak or recognize people. Even so, the gracious serving heart that had always characterized President Reagan still seemed to define him in the final throes of his illness.

Michael recalls visiting his father at the Reagan home in Bel Air. Entering his father's room, Michael saw a Secret Service agent standing at the former president's bedside, spoon-feeding him. The agent started to back away so that Michael could step closer, but the former president reached out, grasped the agent's arm, and kissed his hand. It was his way of saying "thank you." Michael saw gratitude in his father's eyes—and there were tears in his own eyes.[26]

Don't you want to live your life in such a way that, even if a terrible disease like Alzheimer's steals everything from you—your memories, the power of speech, the ability to recognize your loved ones—*something* of who you once were will still remain? And don't you want that *something* to be your kindness, your love, your gratitude, your serving heart?

Michael Reagan shares another story about his father, from 1976, when Reagan was running against incumbent President Gerald Ford. Then–Governor Reagan had just addressed a "Reagan for President" rally in North Carolina when a woman approached his aide, Dana Rohrabacher. The woman had brought a group of blind children to the rally and asked if Governor Reagan could greet them.

Rohrabacher conveyed the woman's request to another

staffer, and Governor Reagan overheard the conversation. "Bring the kids over to the bus," Reagan said, "and I'll talk to them. But look, fellas, don't let the press find out. I don't want anyone to think I'm exploiting blind children for my campaign."

So Reagan's staff brought the children to the bus. There were half a dozen kids, ages ten through twelve. Reagan chatted with the kids for a while and then asked, "Would you children like to touch my face?"

Now, it takes a serving heart to understand that, in order to "see" him, the children would have to touch his face. So he invited them to do so—and they did.

"I thought to myself," Rohrabacher later told Michael Reagan, "'What politician in this country wouldn't give millions to have his picture on the cover of *Time* or *Newsweek* with all these little hands stretched out to touch him?'" But Ronald Reagan wouldn't even think of using the children for his own political gain. As a servant leader, he was there to serve *them*.[27]

As both governor and president, Ronald Reagan seemed to intuitively understand what Max De Pree explains in *Leadership Jazz*:

> Leadership is a job, not a position. The people who work with you are not your people; you are theirs. Leadership is good work because leaders feel a strong need to express their potential and because they wish to serve the needs of others. This is the essence of becoming a "servant leader."
>
> Good leaders know that moving up in the hierarchy does not magically confer upon them competence. They know that being elected president, for instance, gives them the opportunity to become president. Leaders also know that their real security lies in their personal capabilities, not in their power or position.[28]

De Pree is right. Leadership is a job—and the leader's job description is serving. Another great leader who clearly understands servant leadership is former Indianapolis Colts head coach Tony Dungy. Asked to explain his role as coach, he replied that he was there to "be a role model and serve my team." As much as he wants to teach them about football, he says, "I also want to help them be good people, do well in the community and do well after football. . . . Therefore, I am hopefully serving them as individuals, serving their families, and also serving them by giving everything I have to make them the best players they can be."[29]

HOW TO BECOME A SERVANT

Here are some tips I have acquired along the way that have helped me to become a more effective servant leader:

Servant-Leadership Tip No. 1: Relinquish the Right to Control. A servant, by definition, is someone who has no control. Servants serve; they don't control anything.

Herb Kelleher, cofounder of Southwest Airlines, is a great proponent of servant leadership. During the years when he was active at Southwest, he often walked down the aisles of his planes along with the flight attendants, serving drinks and handing out peanuts. On the ground, he was frequently seen helping baggage handlers move luggage on and off the planes. As CEO, he encouraged his people to be servants and to do whatever it took to solve problems and serve the needs of their customers. Kelleher once said:

> A financial analyst once asked me if I was afraid of losing control of our organization. I told him I've never had any control and I never wanted it. If you create an environment where the people truly participate, you don't need control. They know what needs to be done, and they do it. And the more that people will devote to your

cause on a voluntary basis, a willing basis, the fewer hierarchies and control mechanisms you need. We're not looking for blind obedience. We're looking for people, who on their own initiative, want to be doing what they're doing because they consider it to be a worthy objective. I have always believed that the best leader is the best server. And if you're a servant, by definition, you're not controlling.[30]

At this point, you may be thinking, *Hold it right there! What about Rule 13?* If you remember Rule 13 from the previous chapter, give yourself some extra credit. Rule 13, of course, is Norman Schwarzkopf's tenet: "When placed in command, take charge." And Rule 14 is "Do what's right." How can we be in charge yet have no control?

For you as a leader, there are things you should be in charge of and things you should not want to control. You should take charge of setting the vision for the organization. You should take charge of communicating that vision. You should take charge of organizing the effort to achieve that vision. You should take charge of holding people accountable for working toward that vision.

But you should not try to control people or micromanage their activities. You'll get much more out of people if you give them the freedom to use their own initiative, their own imagination, their own creativity to solve problems and advance the organization to its goals. Yes, people will make mistakes—and they will learn from those mistakes and become even more valuable to your organization.

Let me give you an excellent example of what can go wrong when leaders try to have too much control. In April 2011, parts of Alabama, Mississippi, Georgia, and several other states were hit by an outbreak of devastating tornadoes. More than 350 people were killed and thousands of structures, including schools, were damaged or destroyed.

The Federal Emergency Management Agency (FEMA) stepped in and offered to build hardened tornado shelters for many schools in the area to protect kids in the event of future tornadoes. FEMA paid 75 percent of the cost, and local agencies and school districts paid the rest. These structures are able to house six hundred or more people and can withstand winds of up to 250 mph. They represent the state of the art in emergency shelters. At five hundred thousand dollars per unit, they are not cheap.

The problem is that FEMA is a government agency that operates under tight bureaucratic controls. According to FEMA regulations, these incredibly strong, hardened, reinforced structures are classified as "temporary"—even though they are about as temporary as the Rock of Gibraltar. The reason they are classed as temporary is that they were built to protect children while their school buildings were being repaired. In order to keep the shelters permanently, schools must purchase the structures outright from FEMA. Otherwise FEMA will give the schools *more* taxpayer money to bulldoze the shelters and haul away the debris. Federal rules don't allow FEMA to do the sensible thing and let the schools have the shelters. The next time a tornado passes through these areas, thousands of kids will have no safe place to go because the federal government turned their shelter into rubble and hauled it away.[31]

Now, that is sheer insanity. These rules make no sense to you or me, but they make perfect sense to a government bureaucrat, because that bureaucrat can go to the FEMA book of red tape and find rules to cover every situation. This kind of rampant stupidity takes place on a daily basis wherever bureaucratic control is substituted in place of genuine servant leadership.

What if the federal government were to replace bureaucratic control with servant leadership? What if we empowered people in the government to actually make commonsense decisions that would serve people instead of tearing down perfectly good emergency shelters? Some would say, "But if we empower people to make decisions, they might waste taxpayer money." You mean (*ahem!*), as opposed to the way things are now?

If you try to control all the actions of the people in your organization, either through a book of rules or by physically breathing down their necks, this is the result you will get: people will be afraid to think for themselves, afraid to use their common sense and initiative, and afraid to act as servants. Instead, they will do only what they are told to do or what some rulebook says, for fear of making a mistake and getting yelled at. You'll get an organization that behaves stupidly because no one dares to be a servant.

As a servant leader, your goal is to surrender control and empower people to do great things for you and your organization. A fine example of an organization that surrenders control and empowers its people is the Ritz-Carlton hotel chain. I've had the privilege of speaking at Ritz-Carlton corporate events, and I'm fascinated by their corporate culture. The Ritz-Carlton philosophy is expressed in this simple statement: "Ladies and gentlemen serving ladies and gentlemen."

Robert Cooper and Ayman Sawaf, in their book *Executive EQ*, write that the Ritz-Carlton chain "actively promotes trust as the core of its organizational culture. Every Ritz-Carlton employee, including junior bellhops, can spend up to two thousand dollars on the spot to fix any guest's problem. No questions asked."[32] As a leader, would you trust the people in your organization with two thousand dollars' worth of discretion? If not, why not? Didn't you hire great people? Imagine the goodwill and customer loyalty you would acquire if everyone in your organization became totally focused on serving your customers, solving their problems, and meeting their needs—*and if they had the authority to take the necessary action right on the spot.*

The Ritz-Carlton corporate culture is based on twelve service values, which include the following statements:

> I am empowered to create unique, memorable, and personal experiences for our guests. .... I continuously seek opportunities to innovate and improve The Ritz-Carlton experience. ... I own and immediately resolve guest problems .... I create a work environment of teamwork and lateral service so that the needs of our guests and [my fellow employees] are met.[33]

Understand, Ritz-Carlton employees not only have *permission* to instantly resolve problems and create memorable experiences for their guests, but they have been emphatically *commanded* to do so by Ritz Carlton's take-charge leadership. Now, perhaps you can see how a leader can take charge of a team or organization yet relinquish control. It's a balancing act but one that every genuine servant leader understands.

People want their work to have meaning—and your willingness to cede control enables them to feel that they are trusted members of the team, that their work is significant, and that they are contributing value to the customer's experience. When you give people a vision to reach for, and you empower them to use their own initiative and creativity along the way, you tap into a reservoir of energy and resources you can scarcely imagine.

Servant-Leadership Tip No. 2: Learn to See Servanthood as an End, Not a Means to an End. I've seen people use a pretense of servanthood as just another way of manipulating and controlling people. The leader does a favor for a subordinate under the guise of serving, but it's actually a form of arm-twisting: "I served you; now you owe me."

Servanthood is not a means to an end. It's an end in itself. Don't serve other people in order to get something in return. Serve for the sake of serving. Serve expecting nothing in return. Even if no one follows your lead, even if no one thanks you, even if no one responds to your role model of servant leadership, keep serving. Keep meeting people's needs.

The Albanian nun we remember as Mother Teresa was once a young teacher at a Catholic high school in an upper-middle-class part of Calcutta. When she went into the streets of the city, she saw hopeless victims of leprosy. She felt God calling her to live her life as a servant among India's lepers. Over the years, her Missionaries of Charity medical outreach helped thousands and thousands of leprosy sufferers.

During a visit to New York City to address the United Nations, Mother Teresa visited Sing Sing Prison and met four prisoners with AIDS. These AIDS sufferers reminded her of the lepers of Calcutta. She left the prison and went to the office of Mayor Ed Koch and asked his help in creating a treatment facility for AIDS patients. She planned to start with the four prisoners from Sing Sing.

Mayor Koch called Governor Mario Cuomo and put Mother Teresa on the phone. She said, "Would you release those four prisoners to me? I'd like them to be the first four in the AIDS center."

"We have forty-three AIDS cases in the state prison system," Cuomo replied. "I'll release them all to you."

"I'd like to start with four," Mother Teresa replied. "Let me tell you about the building I have in mind—and I'm going to give you the honor of paying for it."

"Okay," said Cuomo, approving a huge expenditure with a single word.

Mother Teresa turned to Mayor Koch. "I need to have all the permits for the center cleared by Wednesday. Can you do it?"

Mayor Koch replied, "As long as you don't make me scrub the floors." And Mother Teresa had her AIDS facility—just like that.[34] Mother Teresa might have been a mere ninety-eight-pound servant to lepers and AIDS patients, but she didn't let governors or mayors or bureaucratic red tape stand in her way. She served for the sake of serving, and her servant leadership gave her all the force and momentum of a charging rhino.

Servant-Leadership Tip No. 3: Let People See You Serve. Bosses like to be seen in "bossy" settings—the corner office, the board room, the country club. They like to be seen doing "bossy" stuff—giving orders, making demands, intimidating underlings, being served. Servants, however, are found in places a boss wouldn't be caught dead. Though servants may certainly be found in the corner office, the board room, or the country club, they are perfectly at ease in humble surroundings doing humble acts of serving. You'll find servant leaders taking out trash, scrubbing toilets, setting up chairs, serving in soup kitchens, listening to people's problems, and doing whatever is required.

Dr. Charles Swindoll is a pastor and chancellor of Dallas Theological Seminary. When Swindoll was a first-year student at Dallas in 1959, he studied Greek under Dr. Bert Siegle—and he found his life subtly influenced by this soft-spoken academician. "I did not know what it was that made such an impact on us as we sat in Dr. Siegle's classroom," Swindoll recalls, "but at times it was as though we had been lifted into the heavenlies."[35]

A year or two after taking that class, Swindoll was saddened to hear that the old professor had passed away. Swindoll attended the funeral, and only then did he learn the full extent of Dr. Siegle's serving heart. The professor had taught at Dallas Seminary since the Depression Era. In the hard times of the 1930s, the seminary often was unable to meet its payroll. So Dr. Siegle and some of his fellow professors sacrificed, often working without pay so that the school would survive through hard times.

Dr. Siegle believed in the mission of the school and the influence it had. So, in addition to his teaching responsibilities, he became a janitor. He emptied wastebaskets in classrooms and dormitories. He hauled trash and served on the maintenance crew. He cleaned toilets and laid tile in the restrooms. Dr. Siegle was a leader because he was a servant.

"When I heard that," Dr. Swindoll concluded, "I realized

what it was about the man that had endeared him to us: His heart of humility had won our respect."[36] It's hard to imagine a more perfect example of a servant leader than Dr. Bert Siegle.

Hockey defenseman Glen Wesley of the Carolina Hurricanes spent nearly two decades in the NHL without winning a championship. Then, in June 2006, the Hurricanes defeated the Edmonton Oilers in the Stanley Cup Finals—and Glen Wesley finally got to hold the coveted championship trophy. Each member of the team got to keep the Cup for a day. For his day, Wesley chose to take the Cup to Camp Lejeune, a marine corps base near Jacksonville, North Carolina. He wanted to use the trophy to serve marines at the Wounded Warrior Barracks there—and he wanted his three children to see him serving. So he loaded his entire family in the car, along with the Cup.

When Wesley walked into the barracks with his family behind him and the Stanley Cup held high above his head, the injured marines shouted and applauded. They got to place their hands on the 114-year-old Cup, which has been touched by hundreds of NHL stars over the decades. Wesley spoke to the marines, thanking them for their service in Afghanistan and Iraq. In turn, the marines asked him questions, such as, "Do you still have all your teeth?" Wesley showed a video with highlights from the championship game and stood with the marines for photographs.[37]

Glen Wesley was a servant leader to those warriors—and to his children. His kids will never forget the example of service he set that day. His example challenges you and me. Set an example of leading by serving. Exemplify servant leadership to others.

Find some windows that need washing. Find some trash that needs hauling. Find some people who need your help. Shovel a sidewalk. Tutor a child. Let someone go ahead of you in the checkout line. Be a servant—and let people see you serve.

Servant-Leadership Tip No. 4: Get Your Shoulders Dirty. Gil McGregor, a former NBA forward, has been a broadcaster for the Charlotte and New Orleans Hornets for more than two decades. I learned a principle from Gil that he calls the "Dirty Shoulders Principle." Gil says, "You can tell a guy with a serving attitude by looking at his shoulders. If his shoulders are dirty, he's a real servant."

Why dirty shoulders? Because servants get their shoulders dirty when they lift others up and let them stand tall on their shoulders. A genuine servant doesn't care who gets the credit and the glory. Servants just want to lift people up. A servant leader thinks *we*, not *me*.

In the old hierarchical leadership model, the boss says, "My people serve me to make me successful." But the servant leader says, "I serve my people to make them successful. I lift people up on my shoulders. When they succeed, their success becomes our success."

While we are busy getting our shoulders dirty, we must remember that we are where we are because of the dirty shoulders of those who went before us. NBA legend Kareem Abdul-Jabbar has written a book called *On the Shoulders of Giants*, in which he writes:

> Sir Isaac Newton, one of history's most significant scientists, put his own world-changing accomplishments in a modest perspective when he wrote, "If I have seen further [than other men], it is by standing upon the shoulders of giants." Now, because I stand seven feet two inches, most people probably think I can see just fine without standing on anyone's shoulders.
>
> They'd be wrong.
>
> My height is a matter of genetics. Can't take any credit there. But who I am, how I see the world, and what impact I want to have on others in my community—that all comes from my heart and brain. And what my heart feels and my brain thinks have been shaped by the many

> "giants" in my life. . . . My father taught me to have passion for jazz and basketball, and my mother taught me to have compassion for others. And, because I've always had a keen interest in history, I've had the additional advantage of a whole range of giants from the past. Their thoughts, their accomplishments, and even their mistakes have helped me choose the paths I've walked in my life.[38]

You may never be able to pay back all the giants whose shoulders have been scuffed and dirtied by your shoes throughout your lifetime. At the time, you may not have even realized they were lifting you onto their shoulders. Only by looking back do you see how your life has been shaped by people who invested in you, mentored you, and taught you by their example. You can never pay them back, and they probably wouldn't want you to. They'd just say, "The best way to pay me back is to pay it forward. Lift up other people, let them stand on your shoulders. Serve them as I served you. Invest in their lives as I have invested in yours. Just be a servant leader, and that will be enough."

Servant-Leadership Tip No. 5: Focus on Influence. "Leadership is influence—nothing more, nothing less," writes John Maxwell.[39] Servant leaders are focused on their role as influencers. Servant leaders run every decision through the filter of their influence, asking themselves, "How will my decision affect the people who look up to me? How will my decision affect my reputation? Will it be consistent with the values I preach—or will this decision expose me as a fraud and a hypocrite?" If leadership is influence, then we must continually be aware of the impact our words and actions have on the people around us.

I'm reminded of the words of my late friend Hall of Fame baseball manager Sparky Anderson, who said:

Athletes who say they ain't role models for our youth are dumber than Bozo. They don't deserve a dime of their millions. They are totally missing the boat. God gave them all this special ability, and then they take the money and snub their noses at the kids or anybody who happens to be in their way. They've got to understand that they have the chance to be a leader. They can teach our young people by the way they live their lives.

Whether they like it or not, every athlete is a role model. So is every adult. Our children look up to us. Every day, we get the chance to influence more young lives than we can ever imagine. Sometimes, it just takes a smile or a pat on the shoulder. Maybe all it takes is a couple of minutes to listen to a youngster's problems. I believe that if an athlete does something dumb, like getting hooked on drugs or alcohol, he should then be penalized double. That's the price for abusing the precious gift they've been given.[40]

As people of influence, we must be aware that other people are watching us at all times. The people who look up to us notice when we cut ethical corners, fudge on our expense accounts, and take liberties with the traffic laws. We are continually influencing the people around us—for better or worse. Since leaders live their lives in a goldfish bowl anyway, let's take advantage of all the scrutiny we receive and use it to have a positive influence on others.

Florence Griffith-Joyner (also known as Flo-Jo) was a track and field athlete who set world records in the 100 and 200 meter events. She won three gold medals and a silver at the 1988 Seoul Olympics. The world was shocked in September 1998 when Flo-Jo died in her sleep. Her life was ended far too soon by a previously undiagnosed brain abnormality that led to a massive seizure and cardiac arrest.

I first met Flo-Jo in 1995 at an awards dinner in Washington DC. We sat together at the head table, and she told me about growing up poor in South Central Los Angeles. At age eight, she met boxing champ Sugar Ray Robinson. Florence told me, "Sugar Ray looked me in the eye and said, 'It doesn't matter where you come from, what your color is, or the odds against you. All that matters is that you have a dream, that you believe you can achieve it, and you commit yourself to that dream. It *can* happen—and it *will* happen.' Right then and there, I was sold. At age eight, I was all fired up about what my future could be."

I was amazed and challenged by Flo-Jo's story. Sugar Ray Robinson used his influence wisely, and his words had a huge impact on a little girl's life. The future belongs to the next generation, and their lives will be shaped by our influence. Few things in this world are more important than the words we speak and the example we set for our kids and the young people all around us. Leadership is influence, and servant leaders always live to influence the next generation.

Servant-Leadership Tip No. 6: When People Fail You, Dispense Forgiveness and Grace. Servant leaders believe in the power of forgiveness. The act of forgiving another human being is an expression of servantlike humility. It's a way of saying, "My relationship with you is far more important to me than the fact that you disappointed or hurt me. You're not perfect, but neither am I. We all need forgiveness from time to time, so I choose to forgive you."

Forgiveness is the key to getting the best performance from the people in your organization. In 1981, when I was general manager of the Philadelphia 76ers, we had a new owner, Harold Katz, who ran the team with a lot of energy and emotion. He was always looking for ways to improve attendance at the games. One time I approached him with an idea for a God and Country Night promotion, and Mr. Katz endorsed the plan. The event was huge, a complete sellout.

The following day, Mr. Katz said to me, "Brilliant promotion, Pat! I'm as proud of you as if you were my own son."

Wow! His praise really revved me up! So I began cooking up more promotional ideas. Weeks later I came up with a promotion that totally fizzled. In fact, it not only failed to draw the fans, I think it might have scared them off! The next morning, Mr. Katz called me into his office, and there were flames shooting out of his ears. He really let me have it, telling me what a lame-brained idea that promotion was. I felt like he had squished me into the carpet with the sole of his shoe. He concluded with the words, "I'm taking this out of your paycheck!"

No, he didn't actually dock my pay, but I knew he wanted to. From then on, I really hesitated to take creative risks. Every time I brainstormed promotional ideas, I heard the voice of Mr. Katz shouting, "I'm taking this out of your paycheck!" I went from taking exciting risks to merely playing it safe. Looking back, I'm sure that Mr. Katz would have gotten a lot more bang for that paycheck if he had shown me a bit of forgiveness for that one bad promotion. I've always tried to remember that lesson whenever people have disappointed me. I have tried to be a leader who forgives.

Ben Lichtenwalner is the founder of ModernServant-Leader.com and senior manager of e-commerce at Whirlpool Corporation. While in Italy on a transatlantic business trip, Ben struck up a conversation with a pair of British businessmen who were lodging at the same bed-and-breakfast. As they sat in front of the fireplace, the two Britons explained that they had been engaged in some tough negotiations. The older man of the pair was the leader, and he demonstrated a reserved demeanor and came across as very patient, calm, and reasonable. The younger man was the subordinate, and he was more intense and volatile.

As they talked, the two businessmen explained that only the older man, the leader, had gone to the negotiation session—the younger man, being more hotheaded, stayed away lest he completely upset the negotiations.

"You would have destroyed [the negotiations]!" the leader told his subordinate.

And the subordinate readily agreed, adding, "I would not have been a good fit in that trip."

The business trip had been successful because these two men had worked out a balanced relationship. They knew when it was best to apply the calm restraint of the leader, when to apply the impetuous intensity of the subordinate, and when it was best for both of them to work together. The more senior gentleman explained how their relationship worked: "I'm not perfect and he's not perfect. We both have weaknesses. However, he forgives bits of me and I forgive bits of him, because together, we work."[41]

Now, that is a great statement of the power of forgiveness as it operates in an atmosphere of servant leadership. We all have weaknesses, and when we forgive those weaknesses in each other—when I forgive bits of you and you forgive bits of me—we are able to mesh our personalities into a team that can achieve far more than we are able to imagine.

At the end of every summer, my good friend Jay Strack and I have dinner together with our wives. Jay is the founder of Student Leadership University, and every year I enjoy hearing him tell about taking hundreds of students to places like China, Israel, and Europe. His goal is to instill in these young people the principles of leadership excellence.

In August 2011, while this book was being written, Jay and I sat down together, and he told me, "We just completed a fascinating leadership event in Washington DC. We had two hundred students there, and our guest speaker was Timothy Goeglein, who used to work in the Bush White House. Tim has just finished writing a book called *The Man in the Middle*, and he absolutely lays his soul bare."

Jay proceeded to tell me a truly amazing story about servant leadership—a story about Tim's boss, President George W. Bush. After Jay finished the story, I said, "Jay, I have to have Timothy Goeglein on my radio show to tell his story."

So I got a copy of *The Man in the Middle* and read it. Tim's story is riveting, a must-read. Days after reading the book, I had Tim Goeglein as a guest on my show. He had spent nearly eight years in the Bush White House as deputy director of the office of public liaison, serving as a deputy to Karl Rove. Tim had been part of the Bush team going back to 2000. He had worked for then–Governor Bush's primary campaigns in Iowa, New Hampshire, and Florida. I said, "Describe for me the George W. Bush you've come to know."

"He's a man of deep integrity," Tim replied, "a man who says what he means and means what he says, and a man who, at the end of the day, cannot be understood apart from his Christian faith. . . . George W. Bush is a rare politician. He's the same in private as he is in public."

"Tim," I said, "how hard was it to write that opening chapter in your book?"

"It was both one of the most difficult things I've ever done," he replied, "and one of the most liberating things I've ever done. I had a remarkable tenure in the White House that was among the most wonderful experiences of my life. . . .

"But unfortunately, with no excuses and only myself to blame, I was becoming a prideful person. I have a dear friend, who—speaking of a completely different president in a different era—said, 'It's a rather sobering, riveting thing when you see that you are speaking to the leader of the free world and he's taking notes.' That shows how easily a person can become prideful. . . .

"While I was working in the White House, I was also writing a column for my hometown newspaper. It wasn't a political column. It was about all the other things I love and enjoy in life. And I'm sorry to have to confess that I began plagiarizing those columns.

"One morning, I came back from breakfast with a friend at the Hay-Adams Hotel. Arriving at my office in the Eisenhower Building, next to the White House, I opened my e-mail, and there in front of me was an e-mail from a reporter, asking if it was true that I had plagiarized a recent column in my hometown newspaper.

"I fell to my knees and I said, 'God, help me.' I knew that my life as I had known it was over. I wrote back and told the reporter that it was true.

"I had embarrassed the president. I had embarrassed my colleagues. I had embarrassed my wife and children and all the people, over a long lifetime, who had invested so much in me. I confessed it and I resigned that afternoon. . . .

"In the political classes, if you embarrass the president, there is a kind of divorce that takes place. And I knew I would be cut off—only that's not what happened. The president's chief of staff, Josh Bolten, told me that 'the Boss' (meaning the president) wanted to see me. I went to the Oval Office, and I expected I was about to receive my woodshed moment. I knew I deserved everything I was about to get. I entered the Oval Office, closed the door, and turned to the president. I said 'Mr. President, I owe you—' and I was about to make my heartfelt apology.

"But before I could finish, he said, 'Tim, I forgive you.'

"I said, 'But Mr. President, I owe you—'

"And he interrupted me again and said, 'Tim, I've known grace and mercy in my own life, and I am offering it to you now. You are forgiven.'

"I said, 'But Mr. President, you should have taken me by the lapels and tossed me into Pennsylvania Avenue. I've embarrassed you—and after all you have given to me and my family.'

"'Tim, you're forgiven,' he said again. 'Now, we can spend the next few minutes together talking about all this—or we can spend the next few minutes here talking about the last eight years.'

"Then President Bush did something extraordinary. He asked me to sit in the chair of honor below the portrait of George Washington, in front of the fireplace—the place where dignitaries sit. And we had a good talk. Then we prayed together and we embraced. And I thought, 'This is the last I will ever see of George W. Bush.' Only it wasn't.

"As I was leaving, President Bush asked me to bring my wife and my sons to the Oval Office in the next few days so he could tell them what a great father and husband I am. This is the leader of the free world, the most powerful man on this planet. I was an inconsequential aide. Yet his magnanimity and his sense of forbearance and forgiveness were gigantic.

"And sure enough, a few days later, my wife and sons came with me to the Oval Office. The president embraced them, gave them gifts, and we had a wonderful time together. And subsequently we were invited back to the White House a few more times. In fact, we were on hand at Andrews Air Force Base when President and Mrs. Bush left Washington and departed for Texas. And I have been in touch with President Bush since that time.

"George W. Bush extended to me the greatest mercy and forgiveness I ever could have experienced, and I am everlastingly grateful. . . . I learned the hard way that greatness and true leadership are rooted in a sense of servanthood. . . . Great leadership is, first of all, service to others."

I was amazed as Timothy Goeglein spoke those last few words. He had just summed up the very essence of these pages. Leadership is servanthood. Great leadership is—first, last, and always—service to others. And one of the most powerful ways great leaders serve is by forgiving.

So be a servant leader. Relinquish the right to control. Learn to see servanthood as an end, not a means to an end. Let people see you serving. As you lead and serve, make sure you get your shoulders dirty. Always be conscious of your influence on others. And when people fail you (as they certainly will), freely dispense forgiveness and grace.

The leader who serves will never fail—and will never be forgotten.

EPILOGUE
A Leader Who Has It All

In the summer of 2010, I hired Tommy Ford, a longtime member of the University of Alabama athletic program, to help me write a book called *Bear Bryant on Leadership*. In addition to being a fine writer and collaborator, Tommy connected me with scores and scores of people who had known Bear Bryant so that I could interview them and collect stories and insights about the legendary coach of the Crimson Tide.

Tommy told me, "One guy you've just got to talk to is John Croyle. He played for Coach Bryant back in the day and had a vision of a ranch for disadvantaged and abandoned children. He has an incredible story to tell you. Here's his number."

I tracked down John Croyle by phone and asked him my standard interview questions: "How well did you know Coach Bryant? What made him a great leader? What did you learn about leadership from him? Do you have a story about Bear Bryant that captures his leadership qualities?" Well, John Croyle had quite a story to tell me.

"I played defensive end at Alabama for three years, 1971 through 1973," he said. "During my three seasons there, we had a 32–4 record, won the Southeastern Conference championship three times, and won the national championship in 1973. Coach Bryant always told the team, 'You players come first. You're my top priority.' A lot of coaches say that, but Coach Bryant meant it and lived it.

"While I was in college I had a vision—actually more of a calling. I spent summers working at a children's ranch in Lumberton, Mississippi. I started as a boys' counselor, and by my third summer there, they made me director of the ranch. That was my senior year in college. I realized that God had given me a passion to help kids who were abandoned or neglected."

John later told me about a life-changing experience he had during his first summer at the Lumberton ranch. He was nineteen, and one of the boys he counseled had come straight from the mean streets of New Orleans. The boy's mom was a prostitute, and she had him working as an "employee" in her "business," taking care of her money while she was "working." John befriended the boy and talked to him about life, values, relationships, and right and wrong. The boy listened without saying much, and at the end of the summer, he returned to the streets of New Orleans.

The following summer, the boy came back to the ranch and said he'd been thinking about all the things John had said the previous summer. That's how John Croyle knew he had gotten through to this young man—and that's how he learned he had a gift for working with troubled kids.

John Croyle could have had a great career in the NFL—but he just didn't have the desire to play pro football. Sacking a quarterback is fun, he told me, but it doesn't compare to the thrill of making a difference in the life of a child. So John Croyle began to dream big dreams. He envisioned opening a ranch for neglected children—not just a summer camp, but a year-round home for kids who had no real home. It was quite a vision—the kind I call an "extreme dream." It would take a lot of money and hard work to make it happen—and John Croyle was a twenty-one-year-old college student with very little money to his name.

One day during his senior year, John went to Coach Bryant's office to lay out his vision and ask for Coach's advice. While the two men were in the inner office talking, the coach's secretary knocked and opened the door. She said, "I have Vice President Agnew, Bob Hope, and Roone Arledge of ABC Sports all on hold. What should I do?"

Coach Bryant said, "Tell them to keep holding. I'm in a

meeting with John Croyle." Then he turned to John and said, "Now, tell me more about this ranch idea."

As John Croyle told me that story, he said, "That was a moment that changed my life. Coach had always told us that his players came first, and I never doubted he meant it. But man, when he put our meeting ahead of those important guys—that really showed me that Coach walked the talk. His message to me was, 'Go build the ranch. Follow your dreams.' He knew I was built to do this."

In fact, Coach Bryant gave John Croyle the first check for his ranch, a very substantial amount of money. (He ultimately contributed more than seventy thousand dollars of his own money and coaxed other wealthy benefactors to donate even more.) Coach Bryant also gave John valuable advice on how to communicate his vision and promote his dream.

In late January 1973, while many of John's Crimson Tide teammates were preparing for the NFL draft, John was trying to close a deal on a 120-acre plot of land. Problem: John needed to raise fifty thousand dollars in cash within forty-eight hours, and he had only five thousand dollars in his bank account. He approached a Birmingham oral surgeon, a big Alabama fan, and the man readily pledged fifteen thousand dollars. When John's teammate, offensive lineman John Hannah, was drafted by the New England Patriots, he donated his thirty thousand dollar signing bonus to John's cause—and John had the land he needed.

So in 1974, John founded the Big Oak Boys' Ranch near Gadsden, Alabama. It's a working ranch, and the kids live in comfortable residential homes, eight kids to a house—no dormitories. Each house is led by a husband-and-wife team—real parental figures in a genuine family atmosphere. "The family unit is fundamental to everything we do at the ranch," John told me. Kids range in age from six to eighteen—and as the children grow older in the program, they become caring older siblings to the younger kids. His philosophy is that every child can be a winner if given a chance.

Initially, John saw Big Oak Ranch as a program for boys only, because he knew little about helping troubled girls. But after the boys' ranch had been running for a decade or so, he encountered a twelve-year-old girl named "Shelley." She had been physically and sexually abused by her father—and Shelley's mother, instead of protecting her, had actually held Shelley down while the father abused her.

John went to court and pleaded with the judge to let Shelley live at the Boys' Ranch. But because the ranch didn't have facilities specifically designed for girls, the judge refused John's request and returned Shelley to her parents' home. John told the court that the girl would be dead in six months, but the judge would not alter his decision. Three months later, Shelley's father killed her.

"When I learned of Shelley's death," John said, "my stomach knotted so tightly I could barely breathe. I made a promise to God that when the time was right, we would build a home for girls. In the fall of 1988, we opened Big Oak Girls' Ranch."[1]

Today Big Oak Boys' Ranch consists of 143 park-like acres with nine residential homes, a gymnasium, a swimming pool, and an equine center. Big Oak Girls' Ranch is a completely separate facility located on 325 acres, with eight residential homes, gym, pool, and equine center. Kids from both ranches are educated at a school owned by Big Oak Ranch, and many children from the surrounding community also attend there.

As John was telling me the story of how Big Oak Ranch came to be, I thought back over the joys and challenges I've had as a father of nineteen children (four by birth, fourteen by international adoption, and one by remarriage), and I asked John, "How many boys and girls have you helped raise at the ranch?"

"Pat," he said in his rich Alabama drawl, "I'm 'Daddy' to more than eighteen hundred boys and girls. I've been there for their graduations, I've been there for their weddings, and I've been there when their children were born. I've told them,

'No matter what happens in your life, you can always come to me, and you can always count on me.'"

Right then, as I was listening to John Croyle over the phone, something happened that almost never happens to me: I choked up and started to weep. Now, I'm not a weepy guy. I don't wear my emotions on my sleeve. I honestly can't remember the last time I puddled up like that. But as John Croyle told me in his humble, unaffected way about his influence on those eighteen hundred young lives, it really hit me hard.

John said, "Pat, you need to come up here, meet the kids, and see what we're doing." I told him I would.

I wasn't able to get to Alabama right away, but in July 2011, about a year after that conversation, I spoke at the Gridiron Men's Conference in Tuscaloosa, along with Pat Summerall, Heisman-winner Danny Wuerffel, and—wouldn't you know it?— John Croyle. Tommy Ford was there, too, and after John Croyle got up and spoke about Big Oak Ranch, Tommy said to me, "Tell you what—after we finish on Saturday morning, let's all drive up to the ranch. You can take a look at the whole operation."

So I drove up to the ranch along with John, Tommy, and some other men. We spent three hours taking the grand tour of the Girls' Ranch. The setting is lush and green, with rolling hills and pasturelands. The kids start each day with devotions and then do chores. They raise cattle, hogs, chickens, vegetables, and hay. There are lakes for fishing, horses to ride, a softball field, and a gym with a basketball court. The kids play team sports, learn the value of hard work, and are rewarded with an allowance.

John told me about an upcoming trip to the beach in Florida for all the kids at the ranch. As he talked about how much popcorn the kids would consume on that trip, I could see that John was just a big sixty-year-old kid (though he's trim, athletic, and looks like he's in his forties). John was looking forward to the beach trip every bit as much as those kids were.

During our tour, John showed me a wall covered with pictures of the children who had lived at the Boys' Ranch and the Girls' Ranch over the years. John knew every one of their names, where they are living, and what they are doing today. It's amazing to realize that all of those lives had been transformed by the vision of a twenty-one-year-old college student.

When it was time for us to leave Big Oak Ranch, it happened again. I went to John, thanked him for the tour, gave him a big hug—and then I felt those same emotions I had felt when I interviewed him over the phone. Now, I was *determined* not to let it happen again—but it *did* happen again. There I was, hanging onto this six-foot-six former Alabama defensive end, and I was choked with tears.

In all my seventy-one years, I have never had a leader touch the inner fiber of my being like John Croyle did. He really got to me, once by phone and once in person. And here I go crying *again* as I write this closing part of the book! What is it about this man that tugs my emotions and makes me cry? Is it the impact he's had on all those young lives? Is it the big caring heart that John Croyle wears on his sleeve? I think it's all of that and more.

I believe that whenever you encounter a genuine seven-sided leader like John Croyle, you'd better brace yourself for impact. A real seven-sided leader will rock you at a very deep level—and mark your life forever. Leaders like John never let go of you. The example they set and the impression they make will put a choke hold on your life. John is one of best examples I've ever met of a complete, seven-side leader.

THE FIRST SIDE OF LEADERSHIP: VISION

John Croyle's leadership journey began, as all such journeys do, with a vision. He discovered a vision for his life when he was still in college, counseling young people in a Mississippi summer ranch program. As this vision took shape, he saw exactly what this ranch for abandoned and neglected children would look like. He saw the fishing lakes, the beautiful homes, the green landscape, the baseball field, and the horse corral—

he saw it all in his mind long before it became a reality. Most importantly, he saw the faces of those kids who would receive a chance to overcome the abuse and neglect of the past.

From the time that vision gripped him, there wasn't anything else John Croyle wanted to do with his life, not even a lucrative, exciting career in pro football. John told me, "This is my life. I was never tempted to do anything else; I never flirted with anything else. This ranch is who I am and what I do."

THE SECOND SIDE OF LEADERSHIP: COMMUNICATION

Once the vision took over his life, John had to communicate his vision all over the state of Alabama. He's blessed with a deep, resonant southern voice, and when you hear him speak, you stop in your tracks and listen. John has been communicating his vision for almost four decades, using his voice to paint word pictures that have inspired thousands of people to support the mission of Big Oak Ranch. He carries his message to corporate board rooms and churches and conference grounds. He shares the message in TV and radio interviews. He tells anyone who'll listen story after story of children whose lives have been changed by the ranch.

Again and again, when John Croyle speaks, something happens inside of those who listen. They may not get all choked up like I do, but don't bet against it. They are touched and moved to give to this great work. This is not manipulation—it's inspiration. It takes a great leader to inspire people to get involved, and John Croyle is one of the most inspirational leaders I've ever met.

THE THIRD SIDE OF LEADERSHIP: PEOPLE SKILLS

The greatest people skill of all is love—unconditional, *agape* love. I've never met a leader who loves people more than John Croyle. He loves his kids, and he also loves grown-ups. You hear the love in his voice when he speaks of Coach Bryant. And you feel the love radiating from him when you meet him in person.

He shows his love for everyone he leads by being visible

and available, by listening to these kids and their problems, by empowering these kids to believe in themselves. But above all else, he showers unconditional love on these children. All the love they never received from their parents, John Croyle pours into their lives. And you can see his love for them reflected in the way they love him back.

Can you imagine what it's like to have eighteen hundred children call you Daddy?

THE FOURTH SIDE OF LEADERSHIP: CHARACTER

Big Oak Ranch is built on a foundation of trust in one man's character. If John Croyle were not a man of sterling character, the entire program would have collapsed long ago like a house of cards. If there had been one crack in his character, one lapse in his integrity, one whiff of scandal, one hint of financial or personal indiscretion, this grand vision could have gone up in smoke.

Imagine the disappointment and disillusionment in the hearts of all those kids if John Croyle—their Daddy, their hero and role model—had allowed his integrity to crumble. All those people who depended on him and patterned their lives after his. A moral failure on his part would not only have destroyed his life's work—it would have damaged vulnerable lives. Thank God, John Croyle is a man who guards his integrity well.

Big Oak Ranch has been entrusted with all of these kids because John Croyle is a man of trustworthy character. He is able to recruit couples to serve as houseparents because he's a man of trustworthy character. He attracts media attention and funding for his program because of his trustworthy character. Big Oak Ranch exists and thrives and continues to heal lives because John Croyle is a leader of character.

THE FIFTH SIDE OF LEADERSHIP: COMPETENCE

A competent leader is good at what he does. John Croyle is good at setting goals and achieving them, good at solving problems, good at team building, good at speaking and motivating and selling his vision, good at administration, good at running a large youth program that is also a working ranch. Above all, he's good at listening to kids, finding out where they hurt, and saying the exact words they need to hear in order to grow and heal.

How did John Croyle become a competent leader? He paid his dues. He learned the ropes. During his summers away from college, he worked at a children's ranch in Lumberton, Mississippi. He started as a boys' counselor, and then he worked on the maintenance crew, and by his third summer, he was directing the whole shebang! Obviously, John Croyle learns quickly—and he has taken what he learned from three summers at the ranch in Mississippi, and he invested that competency and knowledge in building Big Oak Ranch in Alabama. If not for the outstanding competence of this seven-sided leader, the Boys' Ranch and Girls' Ranch would not be here today.

THE SIXTH SIDE OF LEADERSHIP: BOLDNESS

Is John Croyle bold? You'd better believe it! All six feet six inches of John Croyle is bold, including his big, bold voice. He's a take-charge leader. He has firm, no-nonsense rules, and he enforces them. Discipline at the Ranch is loving and reasonable yet firm. There is no messing around. All the kids at Big Oak Ranch live by John Croyle's rules.

Above all, John Croyle never hesitates to take big, bold risks to achieve his vision. How many twenty-one-year-olds do you know who have attempted an undertaking on this scale? While still in college, John Croyle dreamed a big dream and made a bold decision—and eighteen hundred kids have been the beneficiaries of his bold leadership.

THE SEVENTH SIDE OF LEADERSHIP: A SERVING HEART

What more needs to be said about the serving heart of John Croyle, except to talk about just a few of the kids he has rescued?

In the winter of 1974, when the Big Oak Ranch was still being built and only one house had been completed, John Croyle took in five abused boys. From that day on, there was never a shortage of kids who needed saving.

During the first year of the ranch's operation, railroad workers found a boy who had been living in a boxcar for weeks, and they brought him to John Croyle.

Another boy was found wandering near a highway by state troopers. He said his only relative was his pregnant, eighteen-year-old sister, and she had thrown him out of the house. The troopers brought him to John.

A boy came to John who had been living in a barn, huddling under cardboard boxes because he had no blankets to keep him warm.

Another boy came to John with burns on his body because his mother had dipped him in hot grease.

One boy (if you can believe this) was even dumped on John Croyle's doorstep by parents who quickly drove off—in their Mercedes.[2]

Those are just a few of the hundreds of kids whose lives have been affected by John Croyle. Does this man have a serving heart? You tell me.

John and his lovely wife, Tee, have raised two children of their own. Daughter Reagan is married to John David Phillips, a former Alabama quarterback, and she is a servant leader to the girls at the Girls' Ranch. John's son, Brodie, who also quarterbacked at Alabama, has played in the NFL with the Kansas City Chiefs and the Arizona Cardinals. So John has taught the principles of leadership to his own two children.

There are many arenas of leadership, and John Croyle lives out the seven sides of leadership excellence in the arena of reaching kids and changing lives. He's a leader who has it all.

Seven-sided leadership is just as crucial to leadership excellence in the political arena, the business arena, the religious arena, the academic arena, or any other field of endeavor. You may not be called to rescue young lives as John

Croyle is, but I promise you this: whatever you are called to do as a leader, if you have all seven sides of leadership locked in place, there is no vision too big, no dream beyond your grasp, no bold and audacious goal you can't achieve.

Great leaders shape the future. Build these seven principles of leadership excellence into your life—just as John Croyle has done—and there are no limits to the exciting life you can lead or the amazing feats you can accomplish.

NOTES

Introduction: They Just Led
  1. Peggy Noonan, "Once upon a Time in America," *Wall Street Journal*, October 1, 2011, http://online.wsj.com/article/declarations.html.

1. The First Side of Leadership: *Vision*
  1. Oren Harari, *The Leadership Secrets of Colin Powell* (New York: McGraw-Hill, 2002), 126.
  2. Steve Forbes and John Prevas, *Power Ambition Glory: The Stunning Parallels between Great Leaders of the Ancient World and Today and the Lessons You Can Learn* (New York: Random House, 2009), 5.
  3. Paul Jansen, "Why Good Pilots Make Great CEOs," Merawan.com, May 2011, http://www.merawan.com/musings-why-good-pilots-make-great-ceos.
  4. John C. Maxwell, *The 21 Indispensable Qualities of a Leader* (Nashville: Thomas Nelson, 2006), 150.
  5. Mark Eppler, *The Wright Way: 7 Problem-Solving Principles from the Wright Brothers That Can Make Your Business Soar* (New York: AMACOM, 2004), 89.
  6. Annette Moser-Wellman, *The Five Faces of Genius: Creative Thinking Styles to Succeed at Work* (New York: Penguin, 2001), 192.
  7. John W. Drakeford, *The Awesome Power of Positive Attention* (Nashville: B&H, 1991), 74.
  8. Andy Stanley, *Visioneering: God's Blueprint for Developing and Maintaining Personal Vision* (New York: Random House, 1999), 9–10.
  9. Carmine Gallo, *The Presentation Secrets of Steve Jobs: How to Be Insanely Great in Front of Any Audience* (New York: McGraw-Hill, 2010), 32–33.
  10. Steve Lohr, "Without Its Master of Design, Apple Will Face Many Challenges," *New York Times*, August 24, 2011, http://www.nytimes.com/2011/08/25/technology/without-its-master-of-design-apple-will-face-challenges.html.
  11. Jon Swartz, "Silicon Valley Ruminates over Loss of Leader," *USA Today*, August 23, 2011, http://www.azcentral.com/business/articles/2011/08/25/20110825silicon-valley-steve-jobs.html.
  12. Marco R. della Cava, "Apple Changed the Way We Play," *USA Today*, August 26, 2011, http://www.istockanalyst.com/business/news/5380823/apple-changed-the-way-we-play.
  13. Gallo, *Presentation Secrets of Steve Jobs*, 34.
  14. Richard Branson, "Richard Branson on the Power of Your People," Entrepreneur.com, January 4, 2011, http://www.entrepreneur.com/article/217810.
  15. John C. Maxwell, *Put Your Dream to the Test: 10 Questions to Help You See It and Seize It* (Nashville: Thomas Nelson, 2011), 71.
  16. Ayn Rand, *The Fountainhead* (New York: Signet, 1952), 678.
  17. President John F. Kennedy, May 25, 1961, "President Kennedy and the Moon Decision," Smithsonian National Air and Space Museum, July 1999, http://www.nasm.si.edu/exhibitions/attm/md.3.html.
  18. President John F. Kennedy, "Remarks at the Dedication of the Aerospace Medical Health Center," San Antonio, Texas, November 21, 1963, http://www.jfklibrary.org/Research/Ready-Reference/JFK-Speeches/Remarks-at-the-Dedication-of-the-Aerospace-Medical-Health-Center-November-21-1963.aspx.

19. Michael Reagan, *The New Reagan Revolution* (New York: St. Martin's Press, 2011), 236.
20. Ibid., 229.
21. Ibid., 59–60.
22. Michael Reagan, *The City on a Hill* (Nashville: Thomas Nelson, 1997), 212, 214.
23. Dinesh D'Souza, *Ronald Reagan: How an Ordinary Man Became an Extraordinary Leader* (New York: Simon & Schuster, 1997), 28.
24. Reagan, *New Reagan Revolution*, 29.
25. Robert Ajemian, "Where Is the Real George Bush?" *Time*, January 26, 1987, http://www.time.com/time/magazine/article/0,9171,963342-2,00.html.
26. Martin J. Medhurst, *The Rhetorical Presidency of George H. W. Bush* (College Station: Texas A&M University Press, 2006), 34.
27. Harry C. Stonecipher, "The Power of a Vision," Fifth Annual Companywide Energy Resources, Conservation and Recycling Conference, Seattle, Washington, June 1, 1998, http://www.boeing.com/news/speeches/1998/stonecipher060198.html.
28. David Rosen, "John Adams' Vision of July 4th in Future Generations," Selling Tomorrows, July 4, 2009, http://sellingtomorrows.typepad.com/home/2009/07/john-adams-vision-of-july-4th-in-future-generations-.html.
29. Gene N. Landrum, *Profiles of Power & Success: Fourteen Geniuses Who Broke the Rules* (New York: Prometheus, 1996), 352.
30. Stephen C. Harper, "Visionary Leadership: Preparing Today for Tomorrow's Tomorrow," *Industrial Management*, March–April, 1991, http://findarticles.com/p/articles/mi_hb3081/is_n2_v33/ai_n28600923.
31. Chris Brady and Orrin Woodward, *Launching a Leadership Revolution: Mastering the Five Levels of Influence* (New York: Hachette, 2005), 76.
32. Angela Reynolds, "How Successful People Think—Explore Possibility Thinking," ChristianBusinessBooks.com, March 18, 2011, http://blog.christianbusinessbooks.com/blog/christian-leadership-books-2; some dialogue has been paraphrased.
33. Aaron Popp, "Geosynchronous Orbitals," Uni.edu, http://www.uni.edu/ihsmun/resources/GUIDES/Orbitals.htm; Molly K. Macauley, "Allocation of Orbit and Spectrum Resources for Regional Communication: What's at Stake?" Rff.org, December 1997, http://www.rff.org/documents/RFF-DP-98-10.pdf.
34. Robert Slater, *Jack Welch and the GE Way: Management Insights and Leadership Secrets of the Legendary CEO* (New York: McGraw-Hill, 1999), 139.
35. Warren Bennis, *On Becoming a Leader* (New York: Basic Books, 2009), 128.
36. Peter M. Senge, *The Fifth Discipline: The Art and Practice of the Learning Organization* (New York: Random House, 2006), 192.
37. Interview with John C. Maxwell and Ron F. McManus, "Turning Vision into Reality," *Enrichment Journal*, http://enrichmentjournal.ag.org/200001/020_turning_vision.cfm.
38. Gregory K. Morris, *In Pursuit of Leadership* (Lakeland, FL: Leadership Dynamics, 2006), 156.
39. John W. Gardner, *On Leadership* (New York: Free Press, 1990), 195.
40. Ibid.
41. *Business 2.0*, vol. 2, 2001, p. 57, http://www.google.com/search?hl=en&biw=1128&bih=789&q=%22Everybody%20at%20Intuit%20has%20two%20jobs%22&um=1&ie=UTF8&tbo=u&tbm=bks&source=og&sa=N&tab=wp.

2. The Second Side of Leadership: *Communication*

1. Dale Carnegie, *How to Win Friends and Influence People* (New York: Pocket Books, 1975), 5.
2. Dave Kraft, *Leaders Who Last* (Wheaton, IL: Crossway, 2010), 123.
3. Daniel Harkavy with Steve Halliday, *Becoming a Coaching Leader: The Proven Strategy for Building a Team of Champions* (Nashville: Thomas Nelson, 2007), 78–79.
4. David A. Lax and James K. Sebenius, *3-D Negotiation: Powerful Tools to Change the Game*

in Your Most Important Deals (Boston: Harvard Business Press, 2006), 75, author's paraphrase.

5. Peggy Noonan, "2001: A Bush Odyssey," *Wall Street Journal*, January 4, 2002, http://www.peggynoonan.com/article.php?article=130.

6. From an address to Pentagon officials, Washington, DC, August 5, 2004; BBC, "President Gaffes in Terror Speech," BBC.com, August 6, 2004, http://news.bbc.co.uk/2/hi/americas/3541706.stm.

7. From a campaign speech in Poplar Bluff, Missouri, September 6, 2004. Transcribed from embedded YouTube video at http://www.youtube.com/watch?v=OF48IghIN7c&feature=player_embedded.

8. From a town hall meeting on Social Security in Greece, New York, May 24, 2005; "President Participates in Social Security Conversation in New York," May 24, 2005, http://georgewbush-whitehouse.archives.gov/news/releases/2005/05/20050524-3.html.

9. From a White House address urging the reauthorization of the No Child Left Behind Act, September 26, 2007; Reuters, "'Childrens Do Learn,' Bush Tells Kids," Reuters.com, September 26, 2007, http://www.reuters.com/article/2007/09/26/us-bush-grammar-idUSN2623880720070926.

10. BBC, "President Gaffes in Terror Speech."

11. Scott Hennen with Jim Denney, *Grass Roots: A Commonsense Action Agenda for America* (New York: Threshold/Simon & Schuster, 2011), 169–70.

12. John F. Kennedy, "United States Citizen," April 9, 1963, The Churchill Centre and Museum at the Churchill War Rooms, London, WinstonChurchill.org, http://www.winstonchurchill.org/learn/speeches/speeches-of-winston-churchill/125-united-states-citizen.

13. Jon Gruden with Vic Carucci, *Do You Love Football?! Winning with Heart, Passion, and Not Much Sleep* (New York: HarperCollins, 2003), 89.

14. Thomas Dexter Lynch and Peter L. Cruise, *Handbook of Organization Theory and Management: The Philosophical Approach* (Boca Raton, FL: Taylor & Francis, 2006), 596.

15. Eugene C. Gerhardt, *Quote It Completely! World Reference Guide to More Than 5500 Memorable Quotations from Law and Literature* (Buffalo, NY: William S. Hein, 1998), 1104.

16. Terry L. Paulson, *The Optimism Advantage: 50 Simple Truths to Transform Your Attitudes and Actions into Results* (Hoboken, NJ: Wiley, 2010), 10.

17. Kati Marton, *Hidden Power: Presidential Marriages That Shaped Our History* (New York: Random House), 256.

18. Jimmy Carter, "Crisis of Confidence," The White House, July 15, 1979, The Carter Center, http://www.cartercenter.org/news/editorials_speeches/crisis_of_confidence.html.

19. Warren Bennis, *On Becoming a Leader* (New York: Basic Books, 2009), 254.

20. Harry S. Truman, *Mr. Citizen* (New York: Geis Associates, 1960), 132.

21. Rich DeVos, *Hope from My Heart: 10 Lessons for Life* (Nashville: Thomas Nelson, 2000), 44.

22. Donald T. Phillips, *Martin Luther King, Jr., on Leadership: Inspiration & Wisdom for Challenging Times* (New York: Warner Books, 2001), 289–90.

23. Dennis N. T. Perkins, with Margaret P. Holtman, Paul R. Kessler, and Catherine McCarthy, *Leading at the Edge: Leadership Lessons from the Extraordinary Saga of Shackleton's Antarctic Expedition* (New York: American Management Associates, 2000), 61.

24. Ibid., 1–151; Alfred Lansing, *Endurance: Shackleton's Incredible Voyage* (New York: Carroll & Graf, 2002), 1–262; Sir Ernest Shackleton, *South! The Story of Shackleton's Last Expedition 1914–1917*, full text retrieved at http://www.gutenberg.org/files/5199/5199-h/5199-h.htm.

25. Philip Yancey, *Reaching for the Invisible God: What Can We Expect to Find?* (Grand Rapids: Zondervan, 2000), 95.

26. Robert F. Kennedy, "On the Death of Martin Luther King," Indianapolis, Indiana, April

4, 1968, The History Place: Great Speeches Collection, http://www.historyplace.com/speeches/rfk-mlk.htm.

27. Phil Jackson with Michael Arkush, *The Last Season: A Team in Search of Its Soul* (New York: Penguin, 2004), 137.

28. Phil Jackson, *Sacred Hoops: Spiritual Lessons of a Hardwood Warrior* (New York: Hyperion, 1995), 154.

29. Ibid., 122.

30. Ibid., 53.

31. Ibid., 53–54.

32. Ibid., 163.

33. Bill Russell with Alan Hilburg and David Falkner, *Russell's Rules: 11 Lessons on Leadership from the Twentieth Century's Greatest Winner* (New York: Penguin, 2001), 192.

34. Stewart Levine, *Getting to Resolution: Turning Conflict into Collaboration* (San Francisco: Berrett-Koehler, 2009), 85.

35. Philip Yancey, *The Jesus I Never Knew* (Grand Rapids: Zondervan, 2008), 94–95.

36. Matthew 13:34.

37. Diana McLain Smith, *Divide or Conquer: How Great Teams Turn Conflict Into Strength* (New York: Penguin, 2008), 217.

38. Christopher Witt with Dale Fetherling, *Real Leaders Don't Do PowerPoint: How To Sell Yourself And Your Ideas* (New York: Crown, 2009), 110.

39. Doris Kearns Goodwin, *Team of Rivals: The Political Genius of Abraham Lincoln* (New York: Simon & Schuster, 2005), 50.

40. Ibid., 8, 150.

41. John Steinbeck, *East of Eden* (New York: Penguin, 2002), 268.

42. Scott S. Smith, "Dell on . . . the World according to Michael Dell," *Entrepreneur*, April 1999, http://www.entrepreneur.com/magazine/entrepreneur/1999/april/17492.html.

43. Michela Rimondini, *Communication in Cognitive Behavioral Therapy* (New York: Springer, 2011), 111.

44. Jack Ramsay, *Dr. Jack's Leadership Lessons Learned from a Lifetime in Basketball* (Hoboken, NJ: Wiley, 2004), 80.

45. Ibid., 80–81.

46. 1 Corinthians 14:8.

47. Alan Axelrod, *Patton on Leadership: Strategic Lessons for Corporate Warfare* (Paramus, NJ: Prentice Hall, 1999), 43.

48. Charles P. Garcia, *Leadership Lessons of the White House Fellows: Learn How to Inspire Others, Achieve Greatness, and Find Success in Any Organization* (New York: McGraw-Hill, 2009), 109–10.

3. The Third Side of Leadership: *People Skills*

1. Eddie Robinson with Richard Lapchick, *Never Before, Never Again: The Stirring Autobiography of Eddie Robinson, the Winningest Coach in the History of College Football* (New York: St. Martin's Press, 1999), 114.

2. Chuck Cannon, "Robinson Funeral Fills Arena," University of Louisiana System, *Today's News*, April 13, 2007, http://www.louisianau.com/news_results4.php?Inst_id=12.

3. Ibid.

4. Ibid.

5. Rick Reilly, "For Crying Out Loud!" *Sports Illustrated*, September 21, 1999, http://sportsillustrated.cnn.com/inside_game/magazine/life_of_reilly/news/1999/09/21/lifeofreilly/.

6. James M. Kouzes and Barry Z. Posner, *The Truth about Leadership: The No-Fads, Heart-of-the-Matter Facts You Need to Know* (San Francisco: Jossey-Bass, 2010), 137–38.

7. Mark Maske, "Gruden Delivers Goods," *Washington Post*, January 18, 2003, http://www.

capecodonline.com/apps/pbcs.dll/article?AID=/20030118/SPORTS/301189974.

8. Vince Lombardi, Jr., *What It Takes to Be #1: Vince Lombardi on Leadership* (New York: McGraw-Hill, 2001), 91.

9. Lee Iacocca with William Novak, *Iacocca* (New York: Bantam Dell, 2007), 60–61.

10. Lorin Woolfe, *The Bible on Leadership: From Moses to Matthew—Management Lessons for Contemporary Leaders* (New York: AMACOM, 2002), 67.

11. Ray Marano, "Culture Club," Smart Business Pittsburgh, April 29, 2003, http://www.sbnonline.com/2003/04/culture-club-how-medrad-breeds-a-high-performance-employee-culture/.

12. Chris Brady and Orrin Woodward, *Launching a Leadership Revolution: Mastering the Five Levels of Business* (New York: Hachette, 2005), 6.

13. Neil Cavuto, "Truett Cathy, Founder of Chick-fil-A," *Your World with Neil Cavuto*, November 12, 2002, http://www.foxnews.com/on-air/your-world-cavuto/2002/11/12/truett-cathy-founder-chick-fil.

14. Lee G. Bolman and Terrence E. Deal, *The Wizard and the Warrior: Leading with Passion and Power* (San Francisco: Jossey-Bass, 2006), 224.

15. NBT Interview, "Senate President Thomas V. Mike Miller," *New Bay Times*, January 15–21, 1998, http://bayweekly.com/old-site/year98/lead6_2.html.

16. Red Auerbach with John Feinstein, *Let Me Tell You a Story: A Lifetime in the Game* (New York: Little, Brown, 2004), 28.

17. John Wooden interview, "Basketball's Coaching Legend: The Wizard of Westwood," Academy of Achievement, http://www.achievement.org/autodoc/page/woo0int-4.

18. National Trust for Historic Preservation, "The Civil War Setting," President Lincoln's Cottage at the Soldier's Home, 2009, http://www.lincolncottage.org/about/civilwar.htm.

19. Brad Gilbert, *I've Got Your Back: Coaching Top Performers from Center Court to the Corner Office* (New York: Penguin, 2004), 7.

20. Mike Allen and Robin Wright, "Bush Surprises Troops in Iraq," *Washington Post*, November 28, 2003, A01; Mike Allen, "Inside Bush's Top-Secret Trip," *Washington Post*, November 28, 2003, A47.

21. John J. Pitney Jr., *The Art of Political Warfare* (Norman: University of Oklahoma Press, 2001), 58.

22. Bo Schembechler with John U. Bacon, *Bo's Lasting Lessons: The Legendary Coach Teaches the Timeless Lessons of Leadership* (New York: Hachette, 2007), 182–183.

23. John Salka with Barret Neville, *First In, Last Out: Leadership Lessons from the New York Fire Department* (New York: Penguin, 2005), 85.

24. Oren Harari, *The Leadership Secrets of Colin Powell* (New York: McGraw-Hill, 2003), 12.

25. Evan S. Connell, *Son of the Morning Star: Custer and the Little Bighorn* (New York: HarperPerennial, 1997), 257.

26. Orin Grant Libby, *The Arikara Narrative of Custer's Campaign and the Battle of the Little Bighorn* (Norman: University of Oklahoma Press, 1998), 91–92.

27. Thomas Powers, "How the Battle of Little Bighorn Was Won," *Smithsonian*, November 2010, http://www.smithsonianmag.com/history-archaeology/How-the-Battle-of-Little-Bighorn-Was-Won.html?c=y&page=8.

28. Jon Gruden with Vic Carucci, *Do You Love Football?! Winning with Heart, Passion, and Not Much Sleep* (New York: HarperCollins, 2003), 67–68.

29. H. Norman Schwarzkopf with Peter Petre, *It Doesn't Take a Hero: The Autobiography of General Norman Schwarzkopf* (New York: Bantam, 1992) 185–87.

30. Stuart Crainer, *Big Shots: Business the Jack Welch Way* (Oxford: Capstone, 2002), 107.

31. Michael Armstrong, *How to Be an Even Better Manager: A Complete A–Z of Proven Techniques and Essential Skills*, 7th ed. (London: Kogan Page, 2008), 55.

32. Ibid., 56.

33. Crainer, *Big Shots*, 107.

34. Detroit News, *They Earned Their Stripes: The Detroit Tigers' All-Time Team* (Champaign, IL: Sports Publishing, 2001), 28.

35. Bob LaMonte with Robert L. Shook, *Winning the NFL Way: Leadership Lessons from Football's Top Head Coaches* (New York: HarperCollins, 2004), 77.

36. Ibid., 77–78.

37. Peter Krass, ed., *The Book of Business Wisdom: Classic Writings by the Legends of Commerce and Industry* (Hoboken, NJ: Wiley, 1997), 227.

38. Richard Wirthlin with Wynton C. Hall, *The Greatest Communicator: What Ronald Reagan Taught Me about Politics, Leadership, and Life* (Hoboken, NJ: Wiley, 2004), 1–2.

4. The Fourth Side of Leadership: *Character*

1. Jack Canfield, Mark Victor Hansen, and Pat Williams, *Chicken Soup for the Soul: Inside Basketball—101 Great Hoop Stories from Players, Coaches, and Fans* (Cos Cob, CT: Chicken Soup for the Soul, 2009), 126.

2. Bill Walsh with Steve Jamison and Craig Walsh, *The Score Takes Care of Itself: My Philosophy of Leadership* (New York: Portfolio, 2010), Kindle ed., unnumbered pages.

3. Josephson Institute of Ethics, "Quotes to Inspire: Character," 2011, http://josephsoninstitute. org/quotes/quotations.php?q=Character.

4. Wendy Solomon, "'Integrity' Often Questioned in '05," *Los Angeles Times*, December 25, 2005, http://articles.latimes.com/2005/dec/25/nation/na-language25.

5. Pat Williams, "Integrity Is King," *Charisma*, December 2009, http://www.charismamag. com/index.php/charisma-channels/men/25493-integrity-is-king. *Optimize* magazine ceased publication in July 2007.

6. John Wooden with Steve Jamison, *The Essential Wooden: A Lifetime of Lessons on Leaders and Leadership* (New York: McGraw-Hill, 2007), 179.

7. Patrick S. Renz, *Project Governance: Implementing Corporate Governance and Business Ethics in Nonprofit Organizations* (New York: Springer, 2007), 113.

8. Billy Graham, *Just As I Am* (New York: HarperCollins, 1997), 127–28.

9. Ibid., 128–29.

10. Marcia Ford and Angie Kiesling, *Checklist for Life for Leaders: Timeless Wisdom & Foolproof Strategies for Making the Most of Life's Challenges & Opportunities* (Nashville: Thomas Nelson, 2004), 61.

11. Encyclopedia of World Biography: Notable Biographies, Sh-Z, "Patricia Head Summitt Biography," http://www.notablebiographies.com/news/Sh–Z/Summitt-Patricia-Head.html.

12. Al Browning, *I Remember Paul "Bear" Bryant* (Nashville: Cumberland House, 2001), xxii.

13. John C. Maxwell, *Leadership Gold: Lessons Learned from a Lifetime of Leading* (Nashville: Thomas Nelson, 2008), 17.

14. Robert Debs Heinl Jr., *Dictionary of Military and Naval Quotations* (Annapolis: Naval Institute Press, 1966), 59.

15. Bill George, *True North: Discover Your Authentic Leadership* (San Francisco: Jossey-Bass, 2007), xxxiii; italics in the original.

16. Swen Nater, "Two Styles of Discipline," Coach Swen's Blog, January 19, 2010, http://blog. coachswen.com/2010/01/19/two-styles-of-discipline.aspx?ref=rss.

17. Vince Lombardi Jr., *What It Takes to Be #1: Vince Lombardi on Leadership* (New York: McGraw-Hill, 2001), 116.

18. Alan Loy McGinnis, *The Friendship Factor: How to Get Closer to the People You Care For* (Minneapolis: Augsburg, 2004), 38.

19. Brent Zwerneman, *Game of My Life: 25 Stories of Aggies Football* (Champaign, IL: Sports Publishing, 2003), 47–49.

20. Julie Sloane and Tom Monaghan, "Tom Monaghan Domino's Pizza: The Pioneering Pizza-Delivery Chain I Started Almost Didn't Make It Out of the Oven," *Fortune Small Business*, September 1, 2003, http://money.cnn.com/magazines/fsb/fsb_

archive/2003/09/01/350799/.

21. Mike Krzyzewski with Donald T. Phillips, *Leading with the Heart: Coach K's Successful Strategies for Basketball, Business, and Life* (New York: Warner Books, 2000), 40–42.

22. Winston S. Churchill, "The Price of Greatness Is Responsibility," speech given at Harvard University, September 6, 1943, The Churchill Centre and Museum at the Churchill War Rooms, London, WinstonChurchill.org, http://www.winstonchurchill.org/learn/speeches/speeches-of-winston-churchill/118-the-price-of-greatness.

5. The Fifth Side of Leadership: *Competence*

1. Robert Slater, *The Wal-Mart Decade: How a New Generation of Leaders Turned Sam Walton's Legacy into the World's #1 Company* (New York: Portfolio, 2003), 4, 7.

2. Warren Bennis and Joan Goldsmith, *Learning to Lead: A Workbook on Becoming a Leader* (New York: Basic Books, 2010), 2.

3. Leonard Ravenhill, "Prayer," Ravenhill.org, http://www.ravenhill.org/prayer.htm.

4. Colin L. Powell with Joseph E. Persico, *My American Journey* (New York: Ballantine, 1996), 50.

5. Jennifer Dixon, "Neil Cavuto Deals with MS," WebMD the Magazine, February 02, 2007, http://www is.webmd.com/multiple-sclerosis/features/neil_cavuto_deals_with_ms.

6. Neil Cavuto, "Why 'Your Money or Your Life'?," FoxNews.com, April 25, 2010, http://www.foxnews.com/story/0,2933,169915,00.html.

7. Neil Cavuto, "Common Sense," *Your World with Neil Cavuto*, Fox News Channel, September 1, 2011, transcribed by the author from the broadcast.

8. David DuPree, "Coaching Class Is in Session," *USA Today*, June 13, 2001, http://www.usatoday.com/sports/nba/01playoffs/finals/2001-06-13-cover-coaches.htm.

9. James C. Humes, *Speak Like Churchill, Stand Like Lincoln: 21 Powerful Secrets and History's Greatest Speakers* (Roseville, CA: Prima, 2002), ix.

10. Larry King with Bill Gilbert, *How to Talk to Anyone, Anytime, Anywhere: The Secrets of Good Communication* (New York: Three Rivers Press, 1994) 109–11.

11. John Wooden with Steve Jamison, *The Wisdom of Wooden: My Century On and Off the Court* (New York: McGraw-Hill, 2010), unnumbered pages.

12. Chris Brady and Orrin Woodward, *Launching a Leadership Revolution: Mastering the Five Levels of Influence* (New York: Hachette, 2005), 120.

13. Oxford College, "Leadership Certificate Program," Emory University/Oxford College, http://oxford.emory.edu/life/student-involvement-leadership/leadership-programs/Leadership_Certificate_Program.dot.

14. Harry S. Truman, *Strictly Personal and Confidential: The Letters Harry Truman Never Mailed*, ed. Monte M. Poen (Columbia: University of Missouri Press, 1999), 139.

15. Vincent Fortanasce, *The Anti-Alzheimer's Prescription: The Science-Proven Plan to Start at Any Age* (New York: Gotham, 2008), 54.

16. Pat Williams, *The Pursuit: Wisdom for the Adventure of Your Life* (Ventura, CA: Regal Books, 2008), 185.

17. Ibid.

18. Kareem Abdul-Jabbar, "Appreciating the Wisdom of Wooden," *New York Times*, December 10, 2000, http://tv.nytimes.com/2000/12/10/sports/10JABB.html?printpage=yes.

19. Vince Lombardi Jr., *The Lombardi Rules: 26 Lessons from Vince Lombardi—The World's Greatest Coach* (New York: McGraw-Hill, 2002), 53–54.

20. Antonia Felix, *Condi: The Condoleezza Rice Story* (New York: Newmarket Press, 2005), 120–21.

21. Ibid., 121.

22. Noel M. Tichy and Eli B. Cohen, *The Leadership Engine: How Winning Companies Build Leaders at Every Level* (New York: HarperCollins, 2002), 71.

23. Mike Krzyzewski, "Quotes," CoachK.com, September 2006, http://coachk.com/coach-k-media/quotes/.

24. Video Clip: "The Miracle of the Huddle," viewed and transcribed at http://billcurry.net/video06.html.

25. Swen Nater, "Say It without Saying It," Coach Swen, January 2, 2011, http://blog.coachswen.com/2011/01/02/say-it-without-saying-it.aspx.

26. Adapted from Pat Williams with Jim Denney, *Extreme Dreams Depend on Teams* (New York: Hachette, 2009), 283.

27. Lan Liu, *Conversations on Leadership: Wisdom from Global Management Gurus* (San Francisco: Jossey-Bass, 2010), 100.

28. José Luis Romero, "Team Building Quotes," Leader Newsletter, http://www.skills2lead.com/team-building-quotes.html.

29. Patrick Lencioni, *The Five Dysfunctions of a Team: A Leadership Fable* (San Francisco: Jossey-Bass, 2002), vii.

30. Tom Osborne, *Beyond the Final Score: There's More to Life Than the Game* (Ventura, CA: Regal, 2009), 158–59.

31. Phil Jackson with Michael Arkush, *The Last Season: A Team in Search of Its Soul* (New York: Penguin, 2004), 1.

32. Tommy R. Franks with Malcolm McConnell, *American Soldier* (New York: HarperCollins, 2004), 140–42.

33. Rudy Socha and Carolyn Darrow, *Above and Beyond: Former Marines Conquer the Civilian World* (Paducah, KY: Turner, 2003), 68.

34. John Wooden with Steve Jamison, *The Essential Wooden: A Lifetime of Lessons on Leaders and Leadership* (New York: McGraw-Hill, 2007), 65–66.

35. James M. Kouzes and Barry Z. Posner, *The Truth about Leadership: The No-Fads, Heart-of-the-Matter Facts You Need to Know* (San Francisco: Jossey-Bass, 2010), xxiii.

36. Gregory K. Morris, *In Pursuit of Leadership: Principles and Practices from the Life of Moses* (Lakeland, FL: Press, 2006), 179.

37. David Harris, *The Genius: How Bill Walsh Reinvented Football and Created an NFL Dynasty* (New York: Random House, 2008), 91.

38. Roger Highfield and Paul Carter, *The Private Lives of Albert Einstein* (New York: St. Martin's, 1993), 234.

39. Wooden, *The Essential Wooden*, 121.

40. John Wooden with Steve Jamison, *Wooden on Leadership* (New York: McGraw-Hill Professional, 2005), 131–34.

41. John Hareas, "Inspired by Holzman, Jackson Arrives in Springfield," NBA.com, September 7, 2007, http://www.nba.com/news/jackson_070907.html; Ken Peters—Associated Press, "Lakers Think 'Happy Thoughts,'" *Augusta Chronicle* (Georgia), June 8, 2002, http://chat.augustachronicle.com/stories/2002/06/08/nba_343040.shtml.

42. John A. Barnes, *John F. Kennedy on Leadership: The Lessons and Legacy of a President* (New York: AMACOM, 2005), 51.

43. Peter Collier and David Horowitz, *The Kennedys: An American Drama* (San Francisco: Encounter Books, 2002), 125.

44. Walt Frazier with Dan Markowitz, *The Game within the Game* (New York: Hyperion, 2006), 16–17.

45. Mark K. Updegrove, *Baptism by Fire: Eight Presidents Who Took Office in Times of Crisis* (New York: St. Martin's, 2008), 206.

46. Ibid., 207.

47. Winston Churchill, "Their Finest Hour," June 18, 1940, The Churchill Centre and Museum at the Churchill War Rooms, London, WinstonChurchill.org, http://www.winstonchurchill.org/learn/speeches/speeches-of-winston-churchill/122-their-finest-hour.

48. Brian Tracy, *How the Best Leaders Lead: Proven Secrets to Getting the Most Out of Yourself and Others* (New York: AMACOM, 2010), 19–20.

49. David McCullough, "The Course of Human Events," 2003 Jefferson Lecturer in the

Humanities, David McCullough Lecture, National Endowment for the Humanities, May 15, 2003, http://www.neh.gov/whoweare/mccullough/about.html.

50. Roberta Page, "Truman's School Years," *Independence Examiner*, Truman Centennial Edition, May 1984, Harry S. Truman Library & Museum, http://www.trumanlibrary.org/whistlestop/schlyears.htm.

51. Harry S. Truman, *Mr. Citizen* (New York: Geis Associates, 1960), 262.

52. Ibid., 265.

53. Kurt Senske, *Executive Values: A Christian Approach to Organizational Leadership* (Minneapolis: Augsburg Fortress, 2003), 88.

54. Henry Blackaby, Richard Blackaby, *Called to Be God's Leader: How God Prepares His Servants for Spiritual Leadership* (Nashville: Thomas Nelson, 2004), 37.

55. Noel M. Tichy and Warren G. Bennis, *Judgment: How Winning Leaders Make Great Calls* (New York: Portfolio, 2007), 4.

56. Thom Loverro, *Hail Victory: An Oral History of the Washington Redskins* (Hoboken, NJ: Wiley, 2006), 85.

57. Vince Lombardi Jr., *What It Takes to Be #1: Vince Lombardi on Leadership* (New York: McGraw-Hill, 2001), 56.

58. Willy Stern and Elias Levenson, "Secrets of the Survivors," *BusinessWeek,* October 9, 1995, http://www.businessweek.com/archives/1995/b344582.arc.htm.

59. John R. Wooden with Steve Jamison, *Wooden: A Lifetime of Observations and Reflections On and Off the Court* (New York: McGraw-Hill, 1997), 191.

60. John C. Maxwell, *The 21 Indispensable Qualities of a Leader: Becoming the Person Others Will Want to Follow* (Nashville: Thomas Nelson, 1999), 30.

61. Warren Bennis, *On Becoming a Leader* (New York: Perseus Books, 1994), 131, 133.

6. The Sixth Side of Leadership: *Boldness*

1. Gergen, in Warren G. Bennis and Robert J. Thomas, *Geeks and Geezers: How Era, Values, and Defining Moments Shape Leaders* (Boston: Harvard Business School Publishing, 2002), xxiii.

2. Jonathan Daniels, *The Man of Independence* (Columbia: University of Missouri Press, 1998), 95–97.

3. David Gergen, foreword in Bennis and Thomas, *Geeks and Geezers*, xxiv.

4. David McCullough, *Truman* (New York: Simon & Schuster, 1992), 436.

5. Ibid., 430.

6. David M. Kennedy and Thomas A. Bailey, *The American Spirit: US History as Seen by Contemporaries*, vol. 2 (Boston: Wadsworth, 2010), 425.

7. Harry S. Truman, *Mr. Citizen* (New York: Geis Associates, 1960), 263.

8. Alan Axelrod, *Profiles in Audacity: Great Decisions and How They Were Made* (New York: Sterling, 2006), 42.

9. Ibid., 42–43.

10. Richard Goldstein, "Gerard Zinser, Last Surviving PT-109 Crewman, Dies at 82," *New York Times*, August 29, 2001, http://www.nytimes.com/2001/08/29/obituaries/29ZINS.html.

11. Thomas Maier, *The Kennedys: America's Emerald Kings* (New York, Basic Books, 2003), 170.

12. James Carville and Paul Begala, *Buck Up, Suck Up—and Come Back When You Foul Up: 12 Winning Secrets from the War Room* (New York: Simon & Schuster, 2002), 64.

13. Brian Lamb, "C-SPAN Booknotes, "Gen. Norman Schwarzkopf: It Doesn't Take a Hero," November 22, 1992, http://www.booknotes.org/FullPage.aspx?SID=35014-1.

14. H. Norman Schwarzkopf with Peter Petre, *It Doesn't Take a Hero: The Autobiography of General Norman Schwarzkopf* (New York: Bantam, 1992), 198.

15. Ibid.

16. J&J Foods, "Operation Shaving Cream," JandJFoods.com, 2011, http://www.jandjfoods.

com/operation-shaving-cream.

17. H. Norman Schwarzkopf, "Visionary Commander, Unwavering Leader," Academy of Achievement interview conducted June 26, 1992, Las Vegas, Nevada, http://www.achievement.org/autodoc/page/sch0int-3.

18. Keith Dunnavant, *Bart Starr and the Rise of the National Football League* (New York: St. Martin's, 2011), 31.

19. Jack Welch and Suzy Welch, *Winning* (New York: HarperCollins, 2005), 72.

20. James J. Schiro, *Memos to the President: Management Advice from the Nation's Top CEOs* (Hoboken, NJ: Wiley, 2004), 105.

21. Gene Klann, *Building Character: Strengthening the Heart of Good Leadership* (San Francisco: Jossey-Bass, 2007), 22–23.

22. Colin L. Powell with Joseph E. Persico, *My American Journey* (New York: Ballantine, 1996), 308.

23. Margot Morrell, *Reagan's Journey: Lessons from a Remarkable Career* (New York: Threshold/Simon & Schuster, 2011), Kindle ed., unnumbered pages.

24. Michael Reagan, *The New Reagan Revolution* (New York: St. Martin's, 2011), 61.

25. Ibid.

26. Ibid., 5.

27. Pilar Jericó, *No Fear: In Business and In Life* (New York: Palgrave Macmillan, 2009), 95.

28. Lee Iacocca with William Novak, *Iacocca* (New York: Bantam Dell, 2007), 55–56.

29. David Ogilvy, *Ogilvy on Advertising* (New York: Vintage, 1985), 20.

30. William A. Cohen, *Heroic Leadership: Leading with Integrity and Honor* (San Francisco: Jossey-Bass, 2010), 215.

31. John Cook, Leslie Ann Gibson, *The Book of Positive Quotations* (Minneapolis: Fairview, 2007), 412.

32. Thomas J. Watson, Jr., "The Question of Organization," in *The Book of Business Wisdom: Classic Writings by the Legends of Commerce and Industry*, ed. Peter Krass (Hoboken, NJ: Wiley, 1997), 216.

33. Sam Walton with John Huey, *Made in America: My Story* (New York: Doubleday, 1992), 249.

34. John C. Maxwell, *Developing the Leaders around You* (Nashville: Thomas Nelson, 1995), 30.

35. Dana Telford and Adrian Robert Gostick, *Integrity Works: Strategies for Becoming a Trusted, Respected and Admired Leader* (Layton, UT: Gibbs Smith, 2005), 47.

36. Rudolph Giuliani with Ken Kurson, *Leadership* (New York: Miramax, 2007), 141.

37. Brian Tracy, *The Art of Closing the Sale: The Key to Making More Money Faster in the World of Professional Selling* (Nashville: Thomas Nelson, 2007), 58.

38. Carlo D'Este, *Patton: A Genius for War* (New York: HarperCollins, 1995), 105–6.

39. Ibid., 306.

40. William Shakespeare, *Julius Caesar*, Act IV, Scene III, *The Complete Works of William Shakespeare*, http://www.shakespeare-literature.com/Julius_Caesar/13.html.

41. Phil Jackson, *Sacred Hoops: Spiritual Lessons of a Hardwood Warrior* (New York: Hyperion, 1995), 73.

42. Noel M. Tichy and Eli B. Cohen, *The Leadership Engine: How Winning Companies Build Leaders at Every Level* (New York: HarperCollins, 2002), 190.

43. Ibid., 190–91.

44. Ibid., 191.

45. William A. Cohen, *The Wisdom of the Generals: From Adversity to Success, and From Fear to Victory—How to Triumph in Business and in Life* (New York: Prentice Hall, 2001), 18.

46. Presidential Library of George Bush, Sr., "Bush Library," Margaret Thatcher Foundation, http://www.margaretthatcher.org/archive/us-bush.asp.

47. William D. Hitt, *Ethics and Leadership: Putting Theory into Practice* (Columbus, OH: Battelle, 1990), 129.

48. 2 Timothy 1:7.

49. Jim McKinnon, "The Phone Line from Flight 93 Was Still Open When a GTE Operator Heard Todd Beamer Say: 'Are You Guys Ready? Let's Roll,'" *Pittsburgh Post-Gazette*, September 16, 2001, http://www.post-gazette.com/headlines/20010916phonecallnat3p3.asp.

50. Associated Press, "Pentagon 'Heroes' Knew What to Do," AP, September 17, 2001, http://www.military.com/Content/MoreContent/?file=IM_heroes_091701.

7. The Seventh Side of Leadership: *A Serving Heart*

1. James Kouzes and Barry Posner, *Credibility: How Leaders Gain and Lose It, Why People Demand It* (San Francisco: Jossey-Bass, 2011), 39.

2. Stephen E. Ambrose, "Flawed Founders," *Smithsonian*, November 2002, http://www.smithsonianmag.com/history-archaeology/Flawed_Founders.html.

3. Tom Osborne, *Faith in the Game: Lessons on Football, Work, and Life* (Colorado Springs: Waterbrook, 1999), 125.

4. Robert K. Greenleaf, "The Servant as Leader," 1970, quoted in "What Is Servant Leadership?" Greenleaf Center for Servant Leadership, http://www.greenleaf.org/whatissl/.

5. Jack King, "The Foundation of 'Greatness,'" Walnut Ridge Consulting, May 14, 2011, http://www.walnutridgeconsulting.com/?p=613.

6. Lao Tzu, *Tao Teh Ching*, trans. John C. H. Wu (Boston: Shambhala, 1961), 25.

7. Mark 9:33, 35.

8. Hubert Mizell, "Football Takes Backseat for Bowden Family," *St. Petersburg Times*, September 9, 2004, http://www.sptimes.com/2004/09/09/Columns/Football_takes_backse.shtml.

9. Joe Henderson, "It Was Hard for My Mind Not to Be Somewhere Else," Tampa Bay Online, September 12, 2004, retrieved at http://sports.tbo.com/sports/MGBH9J7G0ZD.html.

10. Ibid.

11. Various sources, "Other Views: Excerpts from Florida, National Columnists on Bobby Bowden's Retirement," TCPalm.com, December 2, 2009, http://www.tcpalm.com/news/2009/dec/02/other-views-excerpts-from-florida-national-on/.

12. Curt Schleier, "Mike Krzyzewski Wins by Valuing Teamwork Strategy for Success," *Investor's Business Daily*, April 11, 2002, http://www.accessmylibrary.com/article-1G1-106002907/mike-krzyzewski-wins-valuing.html.

13. C. William Pollard, "The Leader Who Serves," in *The Leader of the Future*, ed. Frances Hesselbein, Marshall Goldsmith, Richard Beckhard (San Francisco: Jossey-Bass, 1996), 248.

14. Carl Rieser, "Claiming Servant-Leadership as Your Heritage," in *Reflections on Leadership: How Robert K. Greenleaf's Theory of Servant-Leadership Influenced Today's Top Management Thinkers*, ed. Larry C. Spears (Hoboken, NJ: Wiley, 1995), 49–50.

15. Martin Luther King Jr., *A Knock at Midnight: Inspiration from the Great Sermons of Reverend Martin Luther King, Jr.*, ed. Clayborne Carson and Peter Holloran (New York: Warner Books, 1998), 182.

16. Michael Bergdahl, *What I Learned from Sam Walton: How to Compete and Thrive in a Wal-Mart World* (Hoboken, NJ: Wiley, 2004), 78.

17. Ibid., 50.

18. Ibid., 71.

19. Ibid.

20. Julie M. Fenster, *In the Words of Great Business Leaders* (Hoboken, NJ: Wiley, 2000), 91.

21. C. William Pollard with Carlos H. Cantu, *The Soul of the Firm* (New York: HarperBusiness, 1996), 131.

22. Oren Harari, *The Leadership Secrets of Colin Powell* (New York: McGraw-Hill, 2002), 139.

23. Lance H. K. Secretan, *Inspire! What Great Leaders Do* (Hoboken, NJ: Wiley, 2004), 136.

24. Richard Wirthlin with Wynton C. Hall, *The Greatest Communicator: What Ronald Reagan Taught Me about Politics, Leadership, and Life* (Hoboken, NJ: Wiley, 2004), 213.

25. Patti Davis, *The Long Goodbye* (New York: Knopf, 2004), Kindle ed., unnumbered pages.

26. Michael Reagan, *The New Reagan Revolution* (New York: St. Martin's, 2011), 295–96.

27. Ibid., 324–25.
28. Max De Pree, *Leadership Jazz: The Essential Elements of a Great Leader* (New York: Doubleday, 1992), 169–70.
29. Jill Ewert, "InVALUEable: Indianapolis Colts' Head Coach Tony Dungy Breaks Down FCA's Core Values," Sharing The Victory, August/September 2007, http://www.sharingthevictory.com/vsItemDisplay.lsp?method=display&objectid=67821149-65D6-4D97-9FEBAD590F783CCC.
30. Dov Seidman, *How: Why How Do We Do Anything Means Everything—In Business (And In Life)* (Hoboken, NJ: Wiley, 2007), 247.
31. John Roberts, "Rules Stymie Conversion of Temporary FEMA Shelters into Permanent School Structures," FoxNews.com, September 14, 2011, http://www.foxnews.com/politics/2011/09/14/rules-stymie-conversion-temporary-fema-shelters-into-permanent-school/; Robin DeMonia, "Alabama Schools Complain They Will Lose New Tornado Shelters," *Birmingham News*, September 3, 2011, http://blog.al.com/spotnews/2011/09/alabama_schools_complain_they.html.
32. Robert K. Cooper and Ayman Sawaf, *Executive EQ: Emotional Intelligence in Leadership and Organizations* (New York: Perigee, 1998), 87.
33. Mark DeCocinis, "The Portman Ritz-Carlton: Setting Up Our Ladies and Gentlemen for Success," 9, http://media.ft.com/cms/5aa22940-74a7-11db-bc76-0000779e2340.pdf.
34. Dale Carnegie and Associates, *The Leader in You: How to Win Friends, Influence People, and Succeed in a Changing World* (New York: Pocket Books, 1993), 23–24; some dialogue paraphrased by the author.
35. Charles R. Swindoll, *Elijah: A Man of Heroism and Humility* (Nashville: Thomas Nelson, 2000), 48.
36. Ibid.
37. Tracee L. Jackson, "Wounded Warriors Welcome Hockey's Greatest Prize," *Camp Lejeune Globe*, December 21, 2006, http://www.camplejeuneglobe.com/sports/base/article_2052421d-b0f2-5eb2-92c4-a1155a6bdfb2.html.
38. Kareem Abdul-Jabbar with Raymond Obstfeld, *On the Shoulders of Giants: My Journey through the Harlem Renaissance* (New York: Simon & Schuster, 2007), 2.
39. John C. Maxwell, *The 21 Most Powerful Minutes in a Leader's Day: Revitalize Your Spirit and Empower Your Leadership* (Nashville: Thomas Nelson, 2000), 17.
40. Pat Williams and Jay Strack, *The Three Success Secrets of Shamgar* (Deerfield Beach, FL: Faith Communications, 2004), 108–9.
41. Ben Lichtenwalner, "Foregiveness for Balance," ModernServantLeader.com, March 8, 2010, http://modernservantleader.com/other/foregiveness-for-balance/.

Epilogue: A Leader Who Has It All
1. John Croyle with Ken Abraham, *Bringing Out the Winner in Your Child* (Nashville: Cumberland House, 1996), 17.
2. Tom Cushman, "A True Alabama Hero," Moody Political Forum, December 22, 2002, http://moodypolitics.tripod.com/moodypoliticalforum/id65.html.

ACKNOWLEDGMENTS

With deep appreciation I acknowledge the support and guidance of the following people who helped make this book possible:

Special thanks to Dan DeVos, Rich DeVos, and Alex Martins of the Orlando Magic.

Hats off to my associate Andrew Herdliska; my proofreader, Ken Hussar; and my ace typist, Fran Thomas.

Thanks also to my writing partner, Jim Denney, for his superb contributions in shaping this manuscript.

My thanks to the entire Advantage|ForbesBooks team—including Adam Witty and George Stevens—for their vision, professionalism, and skill in helping me to shape this message for publication.

And, finally, special thanks and appreciation go to my wife, Ruth, and to my wonderful and supportive family. They are truly the backbone of my life.

CONTACT THE AUTHOR

You can contact Pat Williams at:
Pat Williams
Orlando Magic
8701 Maitland Summit Boulevard
Orlando, FL 32810
Phone: 407-916-2401
pwilliams@orlandomagic.com

Visit Pat Williams's online at:
www.PatWilliams.com
Facebook.com/OrlandoMagicPatWilliams
@OrlandoMagicPat

For Pat Williams speaking or media inquiries, please contact Andrew Herdliska at 407-916-2401 or aherdliska@orlandomagic.com.

We would love to hear from you. Please send your comments about this book to Pat Williams via any of the above channels listed. Thank you.

ABOUT THE AUTHORS

Pat Williams is a motivational speaker, author of over 100 books, and senior vice president of the NBA's Orlando Magic. He and his wife, Ruth, are parents of 19 children, including 14 adopted from four nations. An Army veteran, former minor league baseball player, and host of three radio programs, Pat also teaches Sunday school in his Orlando church. He has also completed 58 marathons in the past 16 years.

Jim Denney has co-written scores of books with many authors, including NFL legends Reggie White and Bob Griese, supermodel Kim Alexis, and radio host Michael Reagan. He's also the author of the Timebenders science-fantasy series for young readers. Jim lives in California.

Printed in the USA
CPSIA information can be obtained
at www.ICGtesting.com
JSHW012020140824
68134JS00033B/2784